WHY I AM A
MENNONITE

WHY I AM A MENNONITE

Essays on Mennonite Identity

Edited by
Harry Loewen

HERALD PRESS
Kitchener, Ontario
Scottdale, Pennsylvania

Canadian Cataloguing in Publication Data

Main entry under title:
Why I am a Mennonite

ISBN 0-8361-3463-X

1. Mennonites - Ethnic identity.   2. Mennonites -
Biography.   I. Loewen, Harry, 1930-   -4

BX8141.W48 1988   305.6'87'022   C87-095335-4

WHY I AM A MENNONITE
Copyright ©1988 by Herald Press, Kitchener, Ont. N2G 4M5
   Published simultaneously in the United States by Herald Press,
   Scottdale, Pa. 15683. All rights reserved.
Library of Congress Catalog Card Number: 87-62522
International Standard Book Number: 0-8361-3463-X
Printed in the United States of America
Design by Paula M. Johnson/Cover art by Gwen Stamm
95 94 93 92 91 90 89 88 10 9 8 7 6 5 4 3 2 1

*To my students and colleagues
with whom I have discussed
questions of Mennonite identity
for many years*

The editor and publisher are grateful to the following organizations and individuals for their generous financial contributions toward the publication costs of this book:

C. C. DeFehr and Sons Distributors Ltd., Winnipeg, Canada
A. C. DeFehr and Sons Distributors Ltd., Winnipeg, Canada
B. B. Fast and Sons Distributors Ltd., Winnipeg, Canada
William and Erna DeFehr, Winnipeg, Canada
P. W. Enns Family Foundation Inc., Winkler, Manitoba, Canada
John Friesen, Winnipeg, Canada
John Schroeder, Assiniboine Travel Service Ltd., Winnipeg, Canada
Katie Funk Wiebe, Hillsboro, Kansas, USA
Ted Friesen, D. W. Friesen Printers, Altona, Manitoba, Canada
Carol A. N. Martin, Elkhart, Indiana
David K. Friesen, D. W. Friesen Printers, Altona, Manitoba, Canada
DeFehr Foundation Inc., Winnipeg, Manitoba, Canada
C. P. Loewen Enterprises Ltd., Steinbach, Manitoba, Canada
Cornelius and Tamira Martens, Winnipeg, Manitoba, Canada
Gertrude Loewen, Winnipeg, Manitoba, Canada

Preface and Acknowledgments

The beginning of this book goes back to the summer of 1985 when I found myself doing work in Germany again. In a bookstore in Mannheim I came across a book edited by Professor Walter Jens of Tübingen, entitled *Warum ich Christ bin* (1982). As I read the twenty-four stories about what it means to be a Christian, the thought came to me that a similar book could be compiled on why one is a Mennonite. I was convinced that a collection of essays on this subject was needed at this time and that it would be of interest to readers—certainly to Mennonite readers—who struggle with the questions of who and what they are in today's society.

Compiling a list of possible contributors of essays was no easy task. I wished to include men and women from all walks of life who would represent Mennonites in Canada, the United States, and Europe and who could speak to issues that Mennonites face in the Western world. (The voices in this collection come mainly from the North-European and South-German-Swiss Mennonite traditions and those persons who joined them in North America. Mennonites in the two-thirds-world have their own story to tell. It is to be hoped that their story will be told in the not too distant future.) Those who were eventually chosen—and I apologize to all those who for reasons of space could not be included—were sent a letter inviting them to become part of this writing project. The response to my "call for papers" was most encouraging. With few exceptions, the persons I wrote or spoke to not only accepted the writing assignment but also expressed enthusiasm for the proposed book.

The authors in this collection were given complete freedom to write their autobiographical essays as they saw fit. Some chose simply to tell their stories of why they became or remained Mennonite. Others chose to reflect on or argue about what it means to them to be a Mennonite. Whatever the approach or form, it was hoped that each submission would be an honest attempt, however controversial, to answer in some way the question implied in the title of this book.

I am most grateful to the many writers who were willing to share—

often in agony—their thoughts and feelings within these pages. Many expressed to me by letter or telephone how difficult it was for them to come to terms with themselves and their tradition. Several told me that they had never written anything as difficult as their personal story. One writer told me that she literally wept into the typewriter as she was writing about her father and mother and what they had meant to her.

I am also greatly indebted to my colleagues and friends Professors Victor Doerksen, George Epp, and Al Reimer, who read many of the submissions and offered helpful suggestions with regard to style and format. The pieces by Johannes Harder and Hans-Jürgen Goertz which had been written in German were translated into English by Victor Doerksen. Several persons and organizations in Canada contributed financially toward the publication of this book. And Herald Press, especially its general book editor, Paul M. Schrock, saw this book efficiently and professionally through the publication process. To all my heartfelt thanks!

—Harry Loewen

Table of Contents

Introduction

Several decades ago Harold S. Bender and his colleagues in Goshen, Indiana, developed what became known as "the recovery of the Anabaptist vision." It was a most necessary and successful attempt to reconstruct the historical events surrounding the origin of the Anabaptist movement and to encourage present-day Mennonites to appropriate the Christian vision which had animated the Swiss Brethren and other peaceful Anabaptists. More recently it has become evident, however, that the Anabaptist vision of Reformation time may not have been as focused and unified as we were led to believe. There were in fact several Anabaptist origins and visions—not only those of the Swiss Brethren—and a great variety of beliefs and practices among the early Anabaptists and Mennonites.

This variety among original Anabaptism is reflected in the many different Mennonite communities and individuals today. Moreover, if in the past centuries there was at least a semblance of theological and ethical uniformity among Mennonites, there is today among Mennonite people a marked tendency, even movement, toward pluralism in religious faith and conduct. It is thus not surprising that the question of Mennonite identity has become a burning issue among Mennonites and non-Mennonites everywhere.

The title of this book, *Why I Am a Mennonite,* may be misleading in that it implies that the answers given by the many respondents are simple and straightforward. It may thus come as a surprise to some readers to find that both the questions and the answers are not only complex but also at times confusing. In reading some of the autobiographical essays, the reader will wonder whether the authors are Mennonite at all. It may not be difficult to recognize the traditional or conservative Mennonites among some of the authors, but when others speak of Mennonites in nonreligious terms and tell us that they are nonpracticing or not churchgoing Mennonites, readers will no doubt find it difficult to accept them as Mennonites.

Yet with all the diversity among Mennonites today—a diversity reflected within the pages of this book—this collection of essays seeks to address the complex issue of Mennonite identity or simply what it means to be a Mennonite. As will become apparent, there is no one clear, discernible Mennonite identity. If in the past adherence to a traditional church-related group called Mennonite was an unmistakable sign of being Mennonite, this is no longer necessarily true. For example, there are many persons who still belong to a Mennonite church, yet who are no longer Mennonite in their faith and practice, feeling greater affinity to evangelicals or some other Protestant denomination than to Mennonites. Conversely, there are persons who may find it difficult to identify with a Mennonite church or community, yet in their hearts and way of life are Mennonite to the core.

This book then encourages readers to reflect upon what it means to be a Mennonite in the modern world. It will no doubt be found that there are as many Mennonite identities or labels as there are individuals thinking seriously about this issue. This multiplicity may not be so much a reflection on the splintering nature of Mennonitism (the so-called Anabaptist sickness) or the erosion of Mennonite beliefs and values, as the result of the complex world in which Mennonites live. In the past when Mennonites existed in more or less closed communities, a unified faith and ethical behavior were possible, even desirable. Today, however, Mennonites reflect the wide range and complexity of urban and rural existence within a society which is becoming more fragmented with each passing year.

Does this then mean, it might be asked, that we can no longer identify Mennonite characteristics, beliefs, and practices with some degree of precision? While this question is not easily answered, there are, according to the writers of this book, certain characteristics which identify an individual or group as Mennonite. For some writers in this collection the accidents of birth and family background are important Mennonite distinguishing marks. They feel that one is born a Mennonite, the way one is born a German or Spaniard. For some being Mennonite means identifying with the faith and life of the early Anabaptists and joining a church that goes under the name Mennonite. For still others being Mennonite means applying the gospel, as understood by Mennonites, to new situations and times which are entirely different from those of the distant past.

And there are the creative writers who explore their Mennonite background in fiction and poetry. While some of them may no longer belong to the Mennonite church, their artistic sensibilities were formed by their early Mennonite experiences. The theologians in this collection tell us that their thinking and views were informed by their faith in earlier years and their training in Mennonite institutions. Then there are the converts to Mennonitism, who may be the "purest" Anabaptist-Mennonites of all, having decided, for whatever reason, to join a Mennonite church. Finally, there are persons who live on the "fringes of Mennonitism," as it were, yet who identify with at least some aspects of Mennonite peoplehood.

However different or varied the emphases, categories, and definitions of the authors in this book, there is one thing they all seem to have in common: they either think of themselves as being Mennonite or they are in some way, however distantly, related to the Mennonite people. They are not Catholic, Lutheran, Baptist, Jewish, Hindu, Muslim, or whatever—they are Mennonite. Some may not be accepted by some readers as Mennonites and some may certainly not be Mennonite in the traditional sense or according to orthodox Mennonite belief and practice. Nevertheless, all authors in this book see themselves as being or as having been Mennonite, however they understand that label.

This mosaic of Mennonitism is not only historically grounded but holds a promise for the present and future. As already mentioned, the early Mennonites were diverse and variegated individuals and groups. There were the peaceful and quietistic Anabaptists and Mennonites who relied on the Spirit of God in their work and lives. There were the spiritualistic and mystical radical reformers who cared little for church organization, institutions, and clerical authority. There were the social Anabaptist reformers who not only sympathized with the "common man" but also sought to implement their ideals of justice and equality in the real world. There were the intellectuals and rationalists who speculated about the divine mysteries and were considered heretical by mainline reformers as well as by their own groups. And there were those free spirits who did not recognize any spiritual or temporal authority except their own and the spirits which seemed to move them.

In this multiplicity of Anabaptist-Mennonite radicalism, there was at least one overriding concern which united the various individuals and groups. In their understanding of the gospel and the Christian life they opposed the old structures and institutions of their time and sought to apply the Christian message to issues of justice, tolerance, concerns for the spiritual and material well-being of people, and freedom to live according to the dictates of their conscience. Some were pacifists; some were not. Some lived in closed communities; some lived in or owned private households. Some lived and worked as craftspeople in towns and cities; some made their living as tenants and farmers. Whatever their views or occupations, most Anabaptist-Mennonites were misunderstood by society, often hated, discriminated against, and sometimes persecuted, exiled, and even executed.

If present-day Mennonitism reflects the multiplicity of sixteenth-century Anabaptist radicalism, it might not be amiss to ask whether the common concerns of the early radical reformers are also evident among the modern Mennonites. According to the authors of this collection, the question might be answered in the affirmative. All of them wrestle with the question of who they are, what their place in society is, and how they can contribute to the world in a meaningful way as Mennonites. Whether they are theologians, historians, writers, businesspersons, farmers, professors, or ministers of the church—all of them seek to make the world around them a better place to live in, or to put it in religious terms, to contribute to the building of the kingdom of God. And, after all, is this not the most significant legacy the Anabaptists and early Mennonites have bequeathed to their spiritual heirs?

It may be objected, as some writers in this collection do, that when all is said and done, being Mennonite is not ethnicity, culture, tradition, and not even activity toward some positive goal, but primarily a matter of faith in God and redemption in Christ. There are some writers in this book who make a good case for this faith-only Mennonitism, believing that all else is irrelevant and that only an evangelical Christian faith will attract non-Mennonites to their churches. This view holds sway among a great number of Mennonites today. There are many other writers, however, who recognize that a religious faith cannot be detached from society, culture, history, and tradition—not even from ethnic peoplehood. According to them, Mennonites, like the Jewish people, have developed traditions and institutions which have helped them to survive as a people and enabled them to contribute values and skills which have come from their rich and unique heritage.

Some Christians from the evangelical wing of the church who are not as tradition-bound and historically conscious as Mennonites are, have expressed time and again their appreciation, even envy, for the historical-cultural content of the Mennonite faith. Even some of the ethnic characteristics of Mennonites—as displayed in food, clothes, and certain religious practices—are not viewed by them negatively but as part of a people who are unique and who seek to contribute their understanding of the gospel and way of life to the church at large and to society. Many Mennonites, however, are embarrassed by their historical tradition and Mennonite label. They wish to shed their ethnic garb and join mainstream Evangelicalism and society. The many "community" churches and "fellowships" from which the Mennonite name has been removed indicate that some groups, even their leaders, do not wish to identify with Mennonites.

The debate concerning Mennonite faith and culture will continue and no doubt intensify as Mennonites everywhere wrestle with the question of who and what they are. Those who insist that there ought to be a strict separation between faith and what they consider to be ethno-culture, do not seem to realize that it is *faith* which forms the basis of a religious peoplehood. The Jewish people may serve as an example here. According to Genesis 12, God called Abraham to follow him into a country that he would show him and promised to make of Abraham a great nation. As Abraham and his descendants obeyed God and sought to follow him through time and space, they became a people. It was their faith (theology) and their history which shaped them into a separate peoplehood.

Similarly the Anabaptists of the sixteenth century developed from their initial understanding of the gospel and the Christian life (different from both Catholics and Protestants) into an Anabaptist-Mennonite peoplehood. Their faith was one of the major reasons for their ostracism by society, and their suffering, persecution, and exile. Wherever they were tolerated and allowed to settle (in the Palatinate, Moravia, North Germany, Poland, Prussia, Russia, Pennsylvania, Canada, and Latin America), they practiced their faith and lived their life in isolation from the rest of society. Having inherited their faith and culture, they became more cohesive as a group, developed their own language (Low German, Pennsylvania German) and thus became the Mennonites we know today.

Mennonite church-communities in Asia and Africa are also developing their own distinct traditions. They will not—and cannot be expected to—become European or North American Mennonites. They must and will continue to integrate their faith and Christian life with the ethno-culture of their own traditions. The French-Canadian Mennonites, for example, are not expected to learn Low German or Pennsylvania German, or to adopt the customs of the older Mennonite groups, in order to be full-fledged Mennonites. They will be French-Canadian Mennonites, maintaining and developing their particular tradition. The significance of the Mennonite-Christian faith is that it can and must become incarnational (that is, become human and living) wherever persons seek to believe and live according to the first- and sixteenth-century radical believers.

The late Johannes Harder of Germany used to say that to deny one's history and tradition was to deny the God of one's fathers and mothers who led and sustained his people for centuries. To be antihistorical is thus to be godless, to be cut off from one's people and God's ways with them. In the Old Testament God always challenged his people to remember their beginnings and the principles and ideals which had given rise to their faith community. Outsiders like Ruth, for example, who wished to join Israel were willing to embrace God's people, their tradition, and their God. The "new converts" did not demand that Israel deny her background and peoplehood. They recognized that God's leading through history had made the Jewish people what they were.

Mennonites are part of the New Testament community and covenant, but here too God's people are asked to be faithful to the traditions which they have inherited and the ways along which they have been led (2 Timothy 1:5-12; 1 Peter 2:9-10). Moreover, the historical-biblical insights and principles of peace, love, justice, tolerance, community building, and peoplehood are an essential part of the Mennonite tradition, not found with such an emphasis elsewhere. Nearly all writers in this book attest to the fact that one or more of these historic principles either attracted them to the Mennonite faith or induced them to remain with the Mennonite people.

While faith and life, including traditions and culture, belong together, most writers in this collection believe that Mennonites ought to be on guard against an ethnocentrism which has plagued some Mennonite groups throughout history. Purely ethno-cultural traits, according to them, have little place in the church service or in attempts to make "outsiders" feel at home among Mennonites. Ethnocentrism, wherever it exists, should give way to an emphasis on Mennonite theological and ethical distinctives, including such things as attempts at conflict resolutions, raising war and peace concerns, applying the Christian message to human needs, witnessing to governments and society at large, and stressing freedom from material and secular aspects of life. While some of the contributors are critical of certain aspects of modern Mennonite life, most of them agree that historically Mennonites were known as people who sought to live according to the demands of the gospel.

To live by and proclaim the gospel of love, peace, and freedom has been the essence of Mennonite-Christian peoplehood for more than four and a half centuries. For these New Testament principles Mennonites were willing to suffer and move from place to place in search of a home. As soon as they believed they had found a haven of rest, they were again forced to pull up stakes and move on, as if to be reminded that the world was not to be their permanent home. Their message of freedom and liberation was thus enforced and backed by their freedom from the world. It thus seems appropriate that this collection of essays ends with a reminder to modern Mennonites— who are tempted to feel at home in today's society—that the mission of the Anabaptist-Mennonite church is to proclaim and practice liberation from the many shackles of the world's institutions and systems.

The many essays in this collection, written either by persons who have been Mennonites for a long time or by "new converts" to the Mennonite faith and life, are in a sense a celebration of Mennonite peoplehood and an expression of gratitude for God's gracious leading of his people. The voices in this book may be varied, sometimes contradictory, and certainly individualistic. However, these independent melodies are combined in a polyphony whose harmony will be recognized and appreciated by those who feel themselves to be part of the wider Mennonite community.

—Harry Loewen
University of Winnipeg
August 1987

1

Flowing Like a River

Lois Barrett

Lois Barrett was born in Oklahoma and grew up in the home of a Christian Church (Disciples of Christ) minister. She first became acquainted with the General Conference Mennonite Church as a voluntary service worker in Wichita, Kansas, in 1969-70. Since she became a Mennonite in 1971, she has continued her interest in mission and service, having published a book on home missions: The Vision and the Reality. *Lois lives in Wichita with her husband, Thomas Mierau, and their children.*

I did not grow up Mennonite. It would be easy to write only about how I freely chose to become a Mennonite, as if I had set about to look at all the possible church traditions with which I could identify myself and then chose the Mennonite church. But that is not exactly true. I am a Mennonite partly by choice and partly by Providence. I suspect even those who grew up Mennonite could say the same.

Until I was a sophomore at the University of Oklahoma, I had never met a Mennonite. In second-year German class, I met three: a young man whom I started dating, a middle-aged pastor's wife who had started back to school, and the professor himself. The professor was actually an ex-Mennonite, who had left Russia during the Revolution, who had made his way to Canada, where he at least had oatmeal to eat, and whose only current connection with Mennonites was his love of the Low German language. Occasionally, he wrote a Low German article or poem for *Der Bote*. He told wonderful stories, but he was not my introduction to the Mennonite church.

The pastor's wife was friendly and invited the Mennonite young man and me to her Mennonite Brethren church. It was a new church, meeting in their converted garage, where twenty people sat on folding chairs in neat rows facing an ancient pulpit that had seen a lot of use somewhere else. They sang English gospel songs written in the 1890s about the second coming and "Gott ist die Liebe," and they had funny names. I was not particularly interested in visiting again.

If it hadn't been for the young man and the Vietnam War, I might never have given Mennonites another chance. The young man himself did not actually know much about Mennonites. His father's job had required him to move frequently, usually to towns where there was no Mennonite church. He had gone to visit his grandparents during the summers and had been baptized in a Mennonite church there. But most of his actual church experience had been in Baptist churches.

He knew, however, that Mennonites did not believe in fighting in wars. When the time of his graduation from college drew closer (and thus his probable induction into the U.S. army, then fighting in Vietnam), he decided to register as a conscientious objector. Through the General Conference Mennonite offices, he made the connection with a Mennonite pastor in nearby Oklahoma City who helped him fill out the forms necessary for conscientious-objector status. In the process, that pastor helped him back into the Mennonite church.

I had never heard of conscientious objectors to war, but I realized that I was becoming one, also. Until I was nineteen or twenty, I had been unquestioningly patriotic. But that was before I found out what was happening in Vietnam. I helped my psychology professor conduct a survey on attitudes toward the war and discovered, with him, that the more facts that students knew about the war, the more they were opposed to it. I started joining demonstrations at the university against the war in Vietnam, not because I knew that all war was wrong, but because I was sure that this war was wrong.

After graduation I followed my boyfriend into Mennonite voluntary service in Wichita. There I found a Mennonite church that was unapologetically against the war. In the church in which I had grown up, to be against war or to take a strong stand on social justice issues meant to be a minority in the church. Here, the majority was against war—not just the Vietnam War, but all war. I read *The Mennonite* with interest. I went to a church-sponsored conference on war taxes. I found a theological basis for what I had started to feel about war. I had a chance to put some of my social concerns into action in my voluntary service assignments.

I married the young man and joined the Mennonite church. Choice or Providence? Both, I think.

Two things attracted me to the Mennonite church fifteen years ago. The first was the peace theology. Mennonites were for peace in a different way than were the mainline Protestant churches. The mainline Protestant churches were for peace because of a general feeling that God wanted us to love everybody and the political sense that it was wrong to support a dictatorship in Vietnam. But there also seemed to be a sense that, if the political situation in Vietnam had been clearer, if our government had been supporting good guys, it might have been all right to be at war.

Mennonites were for peace because they read the Bible. Being a peacemaker was part of following Jesus. They took the Sermon on the Mount seriously. They talked about loving enemies. They related peacemaking to the center of the gospel—the cross. When Jesus was arrested, he told Peter to put up his sword. Jesus was willing to die rather than use violence to defend himself. Mennonites were willing to talk about peace and act for peace even when it was not politically advantageous. Mennonites gave me a theology of peace.

The second thing that attracted me to Mennonites was their sense of community. Mennonites expected something to be going on in church besides having a number of individuals support each other's private worship of God. Relationships within the church were not just a nice by-product of coming to church, but important in themselves. They talked about discernment together, church discipline, sharing.

The year I joined a Mennonite church, I also joined a Mennonite intentional community with some other families who had decided to stretch out the experience of the first-century church in Jerusalem to the twentieth-century in Wichita. We had high ideals. We shared our income. We shared a house. We learned to decide and argue and laugh together. We learned to give up some of our individualism. We learned some things about how to be a community, and we learned that we could not always create community by human efforts.

I have to admit that sometimes the Mennonite sense of community was exclusive, rather than inclusive. In those early years of being a Mennonite, I was working as associate editor of *The Mennonite* at General Conference offices in Newton, Kansas. As I traveled around the continent to various Mennonite conferences, I met many people who did not know how to talk to me, once they found they did not know any of my relatives. One woman at a conference told me, upon learning that my husband had grown up Mennonite and I had not, "That's all right, honey. We have a lot of mixed marriages in our congregation, too, and those are fine people."

I have struggled to keep my composure when people asked me if "Barrett," my maiden name, was a Mennonite name. I have kindly told them, "It is now."

The people whose Mennonite identity is connected with *zwieback* and shoofly pie keep reminding me how varied is Mennonite community. It is people who call themselves Mennonite because that is their cultural background, but never attend a Mennonite church. It is people whose biological heritage is Mennonite, but whose theological heritage is fundamentalist or evangelical or liberal. It is people who find their spiritual ancestors in the sixteenth-century Anabaptists. It is people who find in Mennonites a community that keeps pushing the boundaries on what it means to be faithful to the gospel of Christ. It is people who embody a part of a radical perspective on the gospel, and from that perspective, bring to birth a new ethnicity, a new sense of peoplehood not based on genealogy.

To become a Mennonite is to step into a flowing river, with many currents—many ways of being part of the river. By choice and by Providence I stepped into that river and became a part of it. But I have put my boat into one current of that river, without wanting to be drawn into all of the currents.

I do not hesitate to identify myself as a Mennonite. But I have to admit that I would not feel at home in every Mennonite church in North America. What I am saying by being Mennonite is that I have placed myself into a stream of history and theology which has power to help me understand the gospel in its most compelling way. No matter how some Mennonites may have misinterpreted that stream (from my perspective), this river is the one that will lead me where God wants me to go.

I remain a Mennonite for the same reasons for which I became a Mennonite: peace and community. However, I have developed these two ideas beyond what I knew as a young voluntary service worker.

I still believe deeply that peace is God's way. I still believe that all war is wrong, and that violence destroys the community which God means for human beings around the world to have with each other.

Now I see that peace is not just another article in the confession of faith, but a whole way of living. Peace is not just another commandment, but is essential to the gospel. On the one hand, peace is a way of relating to other people which aims for the wholeness and healing of the other person, and wholeness and healing of the community. Peace is a way to be in contact with those with whom we disagree without trying to hurt each other.

But peace is more than just another word for love. Peace means a radical trust in God. If I trust in God and God's way of doing things, then I put away all other gods. I no longer trust in being the biggest to get my way. I no longer trust in the military to protect me. I no longer trust in money to provide me with all I need. If I really trust in God alone, I do not need violence to ensure my security. God is my security, and I need to reject all idols that pretend to provide security. I trust that even if evil kills me, God will bring the eventual victory within history or at the end of history, because my God is the same God who raised Jesus from the dead after evil killed him.

I am still a Mennonite because the Mennonite community is working on peace issues and trying to reconnect peace with the center of the gospel. Mennonites are continuing to teach me about peace, and I am invited to be part of the process of reformulating a peace theology that goes beyond avoiding conflict and war. Mennonite peace theology is flowing like a river—developing, changing, becoming clearer. I am happy to put my boat into that stream.

And I am still a Mennonite not only because I believe in the community-nature of the church, but because I have become part of the community. I no longer feel like an outsider in the Mennonite church. I have built relationships with Mennonites in local circles, in conference circles, and in inter-Mennonite circles. Mennonite community is not a river running only by high cliffs. Every so often there is a boat ramp so new folks can put their boats on the river (although we need to build more boat ramps that are not so hard to find).

As a member and, now, minister in Mennonite Church of the Servant in Wichita, Kansas, I have had the opportunity to help create a form of Mennonite community in our congregation. We have valued the sense of community of rural Mennonites. But in an urban area, we need to redefine community for our setting. Our congregation is made up of four house churches: face-to-face churches that meet in homes to worship, pray, share, study, play, decide, and discern. We have learned new ways of being the church—new because they are different from the rural churches from which many of our members have come, but not so new because we can read in the New Testament of the experience of the first-century house churches.

Mennonite community does not look the same everywhere. It is expressed in different ways in Mountain Lake, Minnesota, and Wichita, Kansas. It is sometimes difficult to allow people of a variety of ethnic backgrounds to flow together into a new ethnicity—a new peoplehood. In spite of that, I am glad to be part of a Mennonite community that takes the church seriously. I have pushed off from shore into one Mennonite stream of what it means to be the church. I want to be part of a church that values relationships within the church, that holds each other accountable, that not only worships together, but decides together. The shape of Mennonite community is changing, and I am glad to be part of that change.

All this does not mean that I don't value other Christian traditions. I still like participating in the Lord's Supper weekly, as does the Christian Church (Disciples of Christ), the tradition in which I grew up. I wish Mennonites were less solemn about the Lord's Supper and more celebrative. I admire the combination of spirituality and concern for social justice that I see in post-Vatican-II Catholics. I appreciate the Quaker teaching on the living Christ, the Christ within. I am learning from charismatics about prayer and inner healing.

But I am not going around with a checklist comparing various denominations to see whether any of them get a higher rating than Mennonites. Partly by choice, partly by Providence, I am a Mennonite. I have become part of the Mennonite community. Mennonites are now my people. Whether I can affirm every part of the tradition is not important when talking about being part of a community, a set of relationships. Being Mennonite is committing myself to being in dialogue with this group of people, whether or not we agree on every point.

Yes, I have chosen to be a Mennonite. In fact, I choose it again every year when our congregation has a recovenanting service. But yes, I'm also here by Providence. God has drawn me to Mennonites. God has used Mennonites to open up for me new ways of thinking about the gospel and living out the gospel. I believe that God will keep using Mennonites for my spiritual growth, and that God will keep using me in the work that God wants Mennonites to do.

The Mennonite river is still flowing, and I am still afloat on it.

2

how i got saved

di brandt

*Di Brandt is a poet, teacher, editor and critic. She grew up in Rein-
land, a Mennonite village in southern Manitoba. She currently
lives in Winnipeg, Manitoba. Her first book of poetry,* questions i
asked my mother *was published by Turnstone Press in 1987.*

i grew up in Reinland which everyone knew was the heart of southern Manitoba & the world not the worldly world out there full of complacency & sin but the Mennonite world the real world of flower gardens & apple trees & green villages with names like Blumenort & Rosengart & Schönwiese both gentle & proud   there were three scary things in Reinland from which we needed saving Rosie & i farm dogs huge hungry beasts guarding driveways on the way home from school a daily terror Oola Jiesbrajcht with his streaming white hair & wide toothless grin the ancient of days who scared even the dogs with his stick   my mother warned us to stay in the house when he came around on his monthly rampage because he molested young girls molested them how we wanted to know she would never say & i could never envision him so much as touching anyone so he stayed a mystery muttering to himself & swinging his stick at the village dogs the third scary thing was hell a constant underlying threat a concept running through everything undermining our sense of what was real hell was connected not so much with the devil he was considered slightly frivolous not exactly fictional but hardly incarnate   sin in Reinland was much subtler than that with its small daily temptations toward anger & evasion   hell was related rather to God whose stern face looked down at us all around in the forbidding features of the village fathers the heads of families pillars of the church   obedience that was the great task the terrible requirement to keep us out of hell & in the father's good graces but it wasn't so easy to accomplish it was easy enough to keep out of the way of official sins the big ones like debauchery & fornication they kept their distance in any case well beyond the flowery hedge that separated us from the world one would have had to actively seek them out a kind of social suicide unless you

were never coming back   it was also easy to do as they said most of
the time there were hardly ever alternatives you had to be pretty
dumb to ask for Priejl time & again much easier to agree with them &
be over & done   the real stickler was attitude doing the right thing
was not enough you had to want to do it without resentment or illwill
obedience according to God & the Reinland fathers required complete surrender of the will a formidable art even for the chastened
wives our humble mothers   the choice we knew lay every moment
entirely with us *choose ye this day whom ye will serve* though the
responsibility for their children's obedience to be fair lay equally
heavily on both the mothers whose job it was to train & instruct us in
the faith & the fathers home after a heavy day's work in the fields
who enforced it whatever way they could   the more articulate ones
called on reason & the authority of their male presence the less intellectually inclined used bare hands sometimes leather belts   the
real trick was to break the will at an early age say nine months or a
year any occasion would do sitting still at the table say or not dropping one's spoon on the floor the only time i ever saw my mother
openly contradict my father was over an incident of this sort he got
unusually carried away with his disciplining at dinnertime & she
made him stop undoing years of exemplary behavior with a single
sharp word   after that it was merely a matter of reinforcing the impression of the father's total power with occasional reminders & *voilà*
you were on your way to heaven & God   when i was three we
started going to Sunday school which was both scary & nice   we got
to wear new shoes & carry red flowered vinyl purses with pennies to
put in the collection for China but you had to walk past the furnace
room with its rumbling monster to get to the washroom & the toilets
looked bottomless   i dropped a penny in by accident once i was so
nervous i hoped God wouldn't notice when he counted the collection
after dismissal   we sang songs like *Gott ist die Liebe & Jesus liebt
mich ganz gewiss* & got little cards with Bible verses *Lobet den Herrn
& Seid dankbar alle Tage* printed in Gothic script & bordered with
lilacs & white roses   Sunday school apart from the toilets gave me a
warm glowy feeling about God & the world i could lift up mine eyes
whenever i liked to the Pembina hills a thin blue haze in the west &
know they were the place from whence cometh my help i mean it was
incredible to be personally loved & cared for by the Lord who made

heaven & earth to be able to call on him anytime & know he would help guide & keep you from harm it was like being cradled in your mother's arms or being led by an angel across a treacherous bridge like the children in the picture on my grandma's bedroom wall who would have drowned in the river otherwise we used to steal in sometimes & wonder at their saving & steal out again quickly before the stuffed grey owl in the corner could fix us with its yellow stare   once when i was eight or so we saw a film about the end of the world the entire village gathered on straight wooden benches in the Reinland school we saw old men with boils on their faces strange turmoil in the streets the worst thing by far was missing persons a family all nicely dressed was sitting in church waiting for the father to join them but he never came he had been whisked off into clouds   the entire congregation sat in pews becoming restless but the minister never showed slowly everyone realized the Rapture had happened though their loved ones had been taken they were left behind to live out empty & meaningless lives in the godless millennium   the film reduced most of us village children to tears some to hysterics i had nightmares about this frightening vision for years even now certain cloud formations particularly the kind which creates strong vertical yellow lines out of the suns rays in the late afternoon strike a chill in my heart about the Second Coming & my mind begins racing over all my outstanding sins   my parents i should say disapproved of the film & its emotional effect they preferred a sober approach to morality & salvation but it was hard for them to make a solid counterargument since every scene was based literally on some verse in the Bible   so we were all left uneasy & disturbed   when i was ten we ran into another version of the saving game Rosie & i in the form of summer camp   you had to memorize fifty Bible verses in order to qualify a number for which we were extremely grateful only ten years earlier we were told it was as high as two hundred or more   the big attraction was swimming something we never had a chance to do on the farm my mother bought us new bathing suits at Winkler Co-op for the occasion an unusual extravagance   for one hour a day in the muddy yellow waters of the Assiniboine we would gladly have memorized another seventy verses the only catch was if you forgot any of them you had to miss swimming to relearn them so you might as well not have come   it never happened to me thank

God but many of my comrades i regret to say fell miserably under this stern decree   there were a number of new angles to the problem of our reluctant children's souls at camp   one was the Talk with the counselor this caught me by complete surprise i was sitting at the blue picnic table under the trees one afternoon with my counselor Miss Krahn i had just finished reciting the entire lot of verses from Abraham & Isaac to *In the beginning was the Word* feeling relieved & not a little proud when she asked me quite suddenly was i a Christian yes i answered quickly startled at the question & when did you become one she asked   i don't know i said i can't remember   but you're sure you're saved she said doubtfully pencil poised above my card   God they're keeping a file on us i thought & i don't have a date   from that day for many years i worried about the problem of my conversion which came to a head every summer at Bible camp some years i felt miserable & dark despair about my inevitable damnation other years i cited some uplifting religious experience or another & thus located my salvation temporarily on the calendar i'm wondering now if it was a cumulative file & whether they did graphs on the fluctuation of our spirits from one year to the next every summer i wanted desperately to say no i'm not saved to see what they'd do to me how they'd snare me 'n make me a Christian but i never quite trusted them to meet the demand of the moment they would see me slipping into hell i thought & they wouldn't be strong enough to pull me out so i let it pass   the second form of soul torment was communal in nature every night before lights out the dozen or so girls in our cabin participated in a circle prayer with the counselor   this was agony for me you were supposed to say something casually when the Spirit moved   most of the girls seemed to have no trouble with this even the most rambunctious ones with the short shorts & the off-color jokes in the daytime could recompose themselves seemingly without effort & rattle off thank yous & pleases without so much as a quaver in their voices   it always took me to the end of the week to get up the nerve to say anything at all the problem was finding something lighthearted enough to pray about in public with eternal condemnation weighing on my soul   inevitably by the time i found the courage to clear my throat & compose my lips the counselor would whip through the closing benediction without her customary pause having given up on me days ago   i never knew

which was worse the dreaded minute or so during which a dozen girls
willed me to pray or its abrupt disappearance when i was finally ready
the third occasion for spiritual anguish happened on Saturday night
closing night at the wiener roast in the woods there was a lot of laughing & horsing around during supper a boy from Reinland made a bet
with somebody & ate a dozen hotdogs without getting sick but we
all knew this was mere prelude to the real event of the evening
Testimony time   it is hard to imagine now the tremendous pressure
there was to get up & declare one's eternal loyalties in the reddish
light of the campfire i can still see the redhot sparks issuing from the
flames & disappearing in the night sky still hear the rustling of leaves
behind us in the growing dark still feel the ice spreading in my
stomach as one after another of my friends got up & recited the one
Bible verse which assured them a permanent place in heaven how i
ached to do the same & couldn't   every summer we went back there
to Assiniboine Mennonite Mission Camp to the horseflies & the
poison ivy & the river & the woods we went freely without much encouragement from our parents to wrestle with our soul's destinies &
immerse our bodies in the Assiniboine River which held such
promises for our parched prairie limbs & never disappointed us with
its secret delights   Danny Orlis & his gang played another part in
my saving these were evangelical fictional counterparts to the Hardy
boys we weren't allowed to borrow books from the public library but
we eagerly devoured each Danny Orlis story in the form of weekly in-
stallments on the radio & later through the Good News Book Club i
think now what fascinated me most about Angle Inlet & Iron Mountain & the adventures that went on there was their proximity to the
world of fictionmaking   every week we knew a committee sat down
to decree the fate of Danny & his friends & Bernard Palmer the
author retired to his study to write another chapter of their lives   it
was like God & the angels looking down at the world & shaping
human destiny or the Pentagon meeting to decide the fate of nations
the morning Roxie Orlis died Rosie & i wept at the radio in the
corner of the kitchen my mother looking over at us in alarm but i
remember also thinking they only invented that they sat in the committee room & decided to make her die for being beautiful &
selfwilled just to make us cry   what i liked most was the writing itself
words the intricate spelling out of adventure upon adventure i still

remember with pleasure phrases like *beads of sweat glistened on his forehead   his breath came in great rasps   he half grinned*   i practiced that in the mirror   i thought i would like to be a writer someday & capture people's imaginations with words though the possibility seemed as far away then as my elusive saving   one story began with a girl on a ranch looking after her horse watching the sunset & feeling this great empty ache of loneliness in her chest   that's me i thought excited i've finally found a story about me   the girl's adventures on the ranch were complicated & dangerous but they were not the main point in the final chapter she found Jesus as her personal Saviour & the ache inside her went away   a friend of mine tells me he used to read these same stories & skip the conversion bits they were so predictable   for me they were as inevitable as Testimony time at camp & each time as terrible a betrayal i must have tried a hundred variations of the conversion formula & none of them worked the ache would not go away & life went on the next day   there were no neat endings or new beginnings to bind up the ragged silhouettes of our lives despite all the promises there was no salvation in Reinland from the mundane intensity of growing up its daily wounding   meanwhile my father & i carried on monumental arguments about everything under the sun but especially about Truth & God & the nature of faith one of his favorite topics was why we are Mennonites the major tenets for him were nonresistance & not taking the oath nonresistance was much bigger than not taking up arms though he liked telling stories of CO camp during the war   it extended for my father to refusing all semblances of uniform & rank he strongly disapproved of our 4H uniforms though he couldn't exactly forbid them since my mother was a leader & we were engaged after all in useful activities like sewing   i heckled him mercilessly about his pacifism what if someone was killing your children would you stand by & watch you pay taxes don't you you're still a Canadian you're part of the national defense program even if you don't pull the trigger   i battered my head against his contradictions his incredible faith the priesthood of believers the equality of all men before God & the subordination of all women adult baptism with its assumption of the innocence of children & the extreme humiliation of learning obedience i chafed & squirmed under his gentle voice his iron will   his other passion was language   not taking the oath meant a strict adherence to truth telling he took this literally you were not allowed to say for example the milkpail was so heavy yesterday it just killed me   was there a murder he would ask   you must say always & only exactly what you mean   he was offended by irony & ambiguity he was offended by fiction of any kind though he admired Shakespeare whom he remembered from school & of course the Bible which he read to us every morning at breakfast   he was a terrible reader it was the only book he ever read he was much better at talking & arguing so i fought him with words we fought passionately & hard my father & i all those long years until i left home   with the words of the Bible my father's words coursing through my head & my mother's soft humming   i thought then i could get away from Reinland & its decrees by walking out into the world by transgressing its hedges   every friend i made every book i read was for me a displacement a dispossession each in its way a terrible losing   i didn't know then i carried Reinland with me didn't know it lay patiently waiting to leap out & growl & tear at my innards when i wasn't looking   i was living in Toronto a thousand miles from home when my mother's car was smashed by a drunk man in a truck near Altona he was killed instantly & so was a young girl a 4Her in my mother's car my sister's pelvis was broken in four places the other girls had broken hips thighs   coming home to this i had forgotten how God uses fate in southern Manitoba to bring people to their knees makes them repent their life's follies with traffic accidents   i wasn't ready for another great saving Reinland caught me off guard with its green trees & ditches rammed me with its knotted stick   my mother filled with guilt about her survival locked herself in the bathroom to cry   it's a sign they kept saying to remind us of what the random collision of molecules the old man in the sky who cares only for ice in the belly not the grieving   i knew then i could never get away wherever i wandered on the green earth this garden this place of deceiving would be there   i knew then in getting lost would be my only finding

3

Mennonite by Chance and by Choice

Art DeFehr

Art DeFehr has studied theology, business, and economics at various colleges and universities, including Goshen College and Harvard Business School. He and his brothers head the furniture factory. Palliser Furniture, in Winnipeg, Manitoba, a firm which their father, A. A. DeFehr built up. Of his Mennonitism, Art writes: "I have chosen to remain a Mennonite because the Mennonite faith represents the best format to deal with the tensions of being a citizen of the world and a citizen of God's kingdom."

What else would I or could I be? Nobody asks a Greek why he is Greek or the Irish why they are Irish, but Mennonites are continually preoccupied with their identity. If Mennonite is essentially ethnically defined, this article can end with this sentence, since both of my parents were Mennonites. On the other hand, there is a unique blend of faith and heritage among Mennonites which permits a range of possibilities and interpretations as to what constitutes the boundaries of the group. What is a Mennonite?

My own starting point is clear: *You don't have to be a Mennonite to be Christian, but you must be a Christian to be a Mennonite!* In order to speak to the question "Why I am a Mennonite?" one must first answer why one has become a Christian, and only then answer why one has chosen the Mennonite path within the larger community of Christian faith.

I was raised in a Mennonite community, attended a Mennonite church and a Mennonite high school. I could have added a traditional Mennonite home but upon reflection it probably wasn't very traditional. My home was a traditional Christian home in that we were raised with the Book, were taught the traditional stories and Christian values, and there was ample opportunity in family, church, camp, and other situations to make the faith of my parents my own. My decision to accept Christ was made at the age of eight at Camp Arnes, a Christian summer camp operated by Christians, most of whom were Mennonite Brethren. I became a Mennonite in the same sense that the children of a Catholic family become Catholic and those of Baptist parents are likely to become Baptist. I chose to become a Christian (although some social scientists may dispute that) but I probably didn't really choose to become Mennonite.

There is a very important sociological factor in the process of entering the Mennonite church which creates the interminable debates regarding ethnicity versus faith. My recollections from childhood contain strong memories of being aware of my ethnicity, but that was only loosely attached to being Mennonite. German was the lingua franca in our home until I attended elementary school, but whereas the neighbors spoke Low German, only High German was permitted in our house. My parents were completely bilingual and my mother had three degrees from American universities. I was aware from an early age that German was promoted to give us the benefit of a second language rather than as a barrier to integration into the dominant culture. We had borscht on Tuesdays, zwiebach on Saturday, raised chickens and pickled cucumbers. Although our home resembled those of our neighbors, my mind never connected these practices with our church. It would be like defining someone who spoke German and ate sauerkraut as a Nazi.

I commented earlier that our home was not a traditional home. Upon reflection on my home and parents it appears that to a certain degree ethnicity was also chosen in our home. Mother had left home at the age of 18, spending time in Moscow and China, and then a dozen years as student and teacher at a variety of American colleges, including Bethel College, but also Moody Bible Institute and the University of Minnesota. During the thirties, when many of her contemporaries were raising families on the farm or working as domestic help in the cities, she lived in an intellectual environment, attended non-Mennonite churches, wore makeup, drove a car, and attended movies. The decision to marry into a Mennonite family and move back into the Mennonite community was deliberate and not without pain. In fact, my parents spent the first two years of married life in a community which did not have a Mennonite church, and consciously established at least in part their own independent lifestyle.

My home environment participated in many of the ethnic practices because they were my parents' inherited traditions but also to blend into the neighborhood. The preparation of food was a necessary evil, so my mother took the path that was most convenient. The German language was also a part of the community, but since Low German was seen as a waste of time, we were not permitted to use it. Our home was also always full of a variety of books—I can never remember when we did not receive the *National Geographic*. Travel was a priority in our family. The trips were always by automobile and the meandering through historical sites, museums, and cultural attractions en route was evidently more important than the destination. Our home and dinner table were often shared with interesting Mennonite and non-Mennonite visitors. My mother enjoyed the intellectual stimulation, and it was her way of being aware and participating in the affairs of the church and the world while retaining a reasonably quiet profile in public.

The ethnicity of our home reflected the traditions of my parents, but also reflected a conscious desire to be part of a community of faith with a minimum of friction. The visitors, books, and travels, as well as a flexible attitude toward traditions, gave me a positive attitude toward my ethnic background. I never felt it was a trap or burden—it was simply my inheritance. Whereas many of my friends resented their parents and traditions, I thank my parents for raising their children in a way which freed me from this resentment. During my late teens I genuinely felt that I could choose to remain within the Mennonite church or choose a different Christian path. Although I probably did not choose to become a Mennonite, I *definitely chose to remain one*.

My decision to remain in the Mennonite church is a blend of sociological and religious factors. During my university years the ties to the Mennonite church and community became very tenuous, providing ample opportunity to consider alternatives. I became very involved with foreign students, spent a summer working and traveling in Europe, studied in Boston, and essentially spent the majority of my university years at a substantial distance from my background. It became evident that everybody else also had a heritage which was to varying degrees either a burden or an asset. It also became obvious that the only heritage I could ever have would be my own. My choice was to live without the benefit of my roots or to come to terms with them. The opportunity to enter the family business was also a factor, since it would make much more sense to live as a full member of the community than to be within it but to have rejected its most important element, the church.

The decision to remain within the Mennonite church was also very substantially the result of placing a value upon certain traditions and religious distinctions. I was never taught that to be Mennonite gave one an edge in the sight of God and it was never part of my understanding of the faith. My understanding of what constituted the religious tenets of the Mennonite church was not limited to the teaching in church or the Mennonite high school, since it always seemed that the present interpretation (and the interpreters) were narrower than the image that came through a reading of church history or a study of the Gospels. My mother became very impatient with church leaders who focused on theological issues which were not relevant to our daily life or took shortsighted positions on emerging social issues. At an early age I gained the impression that the message is greater than the messenger at hand. This raises the interesting question, and one which I continue to struggle with: whether the definition of being Mennonite has an absolute reference point or whether it is simply the sum total of current attitudes and values of those who consider themselves to be Mennonite.

I was encouraged to remain in the Mennonite church because I felt it represented values and theological distinctions which were worth preserving. If it should simply become a vessel for preserving a pseudo-German culture and some East European recipes, it isn't worth the trouble. I am proud of my heritage—both ethnic and religious—but recognize that the linkage with my ethnic traditions is simply personal, and has little to do with the religious values I consider important.

What are the religious distinctions which I consider to be Mennonite? As mentioned earlier these were derived more by example and observation than by teaching. One of the most important elements observable in my parents and many of our Mennonite neighbors was the complete integration of faith and daily life. Integrity in business and social relationships, respect for the Sabbath, and concern for neighbors were evident in every transaction. Although nonresistance was seldom taught as a theory, I was imbued at an early age with the sense that we are citizens of God's kingdom rather than an earthly one. Government should be respected and obeyed but it should not claim our first loyalty. My parents were intimately involved with support of missions. Our basement was the depot for gathering and packaging used clothing and we often were involved with direct assistance to the needy in our neighborhood. I was well into university before I realized that MCC and the Mission Board were two different organizations. In our home there had never been a distinction between the validity of the two programs.

The university years provided opportunity to reassess my own values and to compare them to other value systems. My most critical years were spent at Goshen College and Harvard Business School. This was during the height of the civil rights movement, the start of the Vietnam War, and a point in history where every value and tradition was being challenged by my peers. I participated fully in the spirit of the times, marched with Martin Luther King, painted anti-Goldwater signs, and joined in anti-Vietnam marches. It was during this time that I recognized that the attitude toward prejudice, war, and the disenfranchised that was inherent in my mother's example was refreshingly avant-garde in the turmoil of my university environs.

The position of the Mennonite church on many of these issues was also more defensible and rational than the left/right or conservative/liberal rhetoric of either the rabble-rousers or the established church. The centuries of opposition to violence, the long experience of being a minority, the memories of a refugee past, the experience of being destitute, all gave the Mennonite church a sensitivity and credibility in its response which was often lacking elsewhere. The religious and experiential tradition of the Mennonite church came to be understood as a potentially valuable asset. Although the Mennonite church does not have a monopoly on these values, the emphasis on community and the integration of faith and life tends to preserve and promote these distinctives in a more powerful way. Other traditions may also have great value, but it seemed counterproductive to simply exchange one for another, and lose the deep roots of the tradition I owned in the process.

I chose to remain a Mennonite, but it has occurred to me that what I chose may only be my own definition of what a Mennonite is. Is Mennonite a historical absolute against which one tests present attitudes? Is it a living tradition which changes over time and is continually redefined? If the latter, are there any boundaries which distinguish the Mennonite faith from others? If the Mennonite faith is evolutionary in nature, who is or should be determining the new directions? Is this the role for one or more charismatic leaders, church professionals, or a survey of the membership? Can Mennonite define a diverse set of ideas and people at the same time?

For me, the definition of what it is to be a Mennonite must be consistent with the historical origins of the movement. In my view, the essence of the sixteenth-century Anabaptist movement was the rejection of the mainstream and the willingness to test the frontiers of Christianity. This resulted in new doctrines on baptism and war, an emphasis on community and service, and a redefinition of the relationship between the believer and God. The priesthood of believers provides continual opportunity to redefine the position of the church in regard to changes in the political, social, and technical spheres. Centralized authority will tend to reinforce and follow the mainstream; a decentralized church should always test new frontiers. The Mennonite faith, in its ideal form, provides opportunities for a continuous and radical redefinition of the church, balanced by the anchors of history and tradition.

I have chosen to remain a Mennonite because the Mennonite faith represents the best format to deal with the tension of being a citizen of the world and a citizen of God's kingdom. To be a Christian is to live in tension with the world—and the essence of the Mennonite faith is to find the creative limits to that tension. Unfortunately, many of my fellow Mennonites may understand the nature of being Mennonite in a different way, with the result that the church may fail to meet many of their expectations and mine. Nevertheless, I believe that the creative tension and the ability to test frontiers is an essential element of the church and central to my continued association.

From my earliest days, I can recall always acting in a way which resisted the mainstream, but not cutting my ties completely. I joined the Mennonite church and attended a Mennonite high school but never attended Mennonite church youth programs, rather crossing town to the programs of a non-Mennonite church. I spent more time at IVCF camps than Mennonite camps. After high school I sought intellectual stimulation at university rather than Bible school, but followed that with a year at Goshen College to balance the input. I married a lovely German-speaking Christian girl, but from outside the Mennonite tradition. My daughters are being raised in the Mennonite church, but have different racial origins than their parents.

Whereas others have sought the simplest and least controversial path through life, I have always been drawn to the "road less travelled."

During recent years I have become involved with various social and humanitarian causes. This has included service with MCC, the National Association of Evangelicals, the Government of Canada, and the United Nations. Additional involvement in Canada has included the resettlement of refugees and the founding of the Canadian Foodgrains Bank. Many of these involvements have been both popular and controversial at the same time. In the same way that racial equality was the issue of the sixties, refugees and hunger have been critical issues of the past decade. I am pleased to be part of a church which has produced so many individuals active in Christian missions and service and which has spawned MCC, the Foodgrains Bank, refugee programs, and other initiatives. These programs have been at the frontiers of the Christian church in our time, and yet there are still many untested frontiers. Nevertheless, there is as much tension within the church regarding many of these initiatives as between the church and society, suggesting that the church is not completely of one mind.

The Mennonite church seems to be pulled in three conflicting directions at the same time. There is an element which is oriented to its traditions, ethnic as well as religious. Another segment discounts the value of tradition and desires to integrate spiritually as well as sociologically with the dominant culture. A third element seeks to keep alive the radical traditions of the church in the form of innovative social action.

I am a Mennonite because I believe that each of these three strands has some validity, that there is still room for a person of my convictions within the church, and that there is still an opportunity to redefine the frontiers between the church and society. As Mennonites we need to build on tradition but not worship it, to integrate into society but challenge its values, to radicalize and challenge social policy without forgetting that Christlikeness rather than social reform is our goal.

4

The Mennonite World Is Not Flat and One Does Not Fall Off the Edge

Victor G. Doerksen

Victor G. Doerksen, head of the Department of German at the University of Manitoba, has published widely on German and Mennonite subjects and issues. He is most interested in the "Mennonite imagination," Mennonite history, and German Pietism. While rooted in the Mennonite tradition, he has "been able to look at a number of perspectives on ultimate reality which derive from different traditions." He acknowledges readily, however, that his interest in things Mennonite derives from the fact that he was born a Mennonite.

Mennonites are presumably followers of Menno, although Mennonites generally do not know very much about who Menno was or what he taught. Christians are presumably followers of Jesus Christ, although there are many ways of thinking about who or what "Christ" is. I think that the early Anabaptists and other Reformation radicals like Hans Denck tried, in their own way, to be followers of Jesus. That is why I like to think of myself as Mennonite, although, to be blunt about it, the real reason may have more to do with the accident of birth.

I was born into a Northend Winnipeg Mennonite Brethren (MB) family of eight surviving children. Of these, only one is presently a "practicing" Mennonite for a number of socio-geo-theological reasons. What it meant to be Mennonite then is much different from what it seems to mean today. It meant among other things that the German language was taken very seriously—my first German lessons were thumped into my head by the solid gold ring on the finger of Prediger Franz Thiessen, who as a student had lived with the P. M. Friesen family in Russia.

In our Winnipeg MB world A. H. Unruh was a kind of pope who admonished his flocks to keep their German, as well as their faith, and who established an "index" of less-than-Christian books in the MB Bible College library. The names that I heard in sermons were not those of the Anabaptist "fathers," but rather those of Spurgeon, Erich Sauer, George Müller, Ernst Gaebelein, and of the Great Awakening and the revival movements.

I was converted at the age of nine. After attending a crusade at the old Winnipeg auditorium, I confessed to my older brother that I had wanted to "go forward" and he stood by me as I told my parents of my decision. This remains in my mind as a positive, if very immature, experience. More and more I have come to feel that adult baptism is a good thing, but that the practice of our churches has in most instances reduced it to a socialization process not much different from the rites of passage in other confessions and faiths.

At fourteen or fifteen I remember working very hard one summer in order to earn a bicycle of my own. When I achieved this goal I proudly showed the almost-new, three-gear marvel to my father who remarked: "I wish rather that you had thought about baptism this summer." I was crushed! All winter that wish of my rather stern and distant father weighed on me to the extent that I made sure to attend to that matter the next summer and so I was baptized in the water of the old Bird's Hill gravel pits.

The religious life I had entered into was the inner spiritual drama of the Pietist tradition: it was the journey of the soul to the better land—others had been able to describe it in such exciting terms, I was to find out later—to me it was a rather mundane trip, compared to all the other adventures that my imagination had access to. Even the backslidings did not amount to much, but I was always concerned to stay on what my mother referred to as "the right way." In hindsight, I think my early religious experience taught me more about abstract thought than anything else, but it was no fun then trying to "apply" my faith to real-life situations. Metaphysics and physics were pretty far apart!

The MB church I knew never overtly referred to its Anabaptist past. In the MB high school I learned a little *Mennonitische Geschichte*, but the growth of my awareness was very slow. It was only when I had been overseas as a student and had had time and occasion to look back on my life in Winnipeg, that I began to think consciously about who I was and what this might mean. Involvement with Mennonite Central Committee (MCC) in Frankfurt, with Pax, with AMUS (Association of Mennonite University Students) and with a paper, the *Canadian Mennonite*, followed. Each of these gave me cause to ask questions and reflect on my tradition and its meaning for me.

One experience that sticks in my mind is the meeting I had in Moscow with the then leadership of the Russian Baptist Union, while on a student trip there from Frankfurt. At the instigation of Peter Dyck of the MCC I put several questions before the brethren Zhidkov, Mizkevitsch, and Karev. As it happened, I had my aunt with me, who had come a great distance to see me, and this complication did not help, as Zhidkov, with an appropriate gesture, said something to the effect: We have you Mennonites up to here! (What trouble-makers you are!) I did not know then what was transpiring in the Soviet Union around that time; certainly they were not easy times either for the Baptists or for the Mennonites, but I have ever since felt very close to our many sisters and brothers in the Soviet Union.

When I completed my studies at Zürich the presence there of Professor Fritz Blanke led me to take church history as one of my subjects. With his peculiar sense of humor he introduced me to his seminar by informing the large class that there was present a genuine, live, latter-day Anabaptist! Together with Clarence Bauman, whom I had met at Bonn some years before, Blanke exerted a profound influence on me. Both encouraged me *not* to take up theological studies and at the same time whetted my appetite for that so-called queen of the sciences to the point where reading theology has become something of an avocation for me.

But there is something more that I learned from these and from other good teachers, namely, that one must continually move along one or more lines of questioning, one must feel a sense of probing and criticizing, a sense that is at the very cutting edge of consciousness. It was not enough merely to feel this curiosity (or anxiety!), but rather it was necessary to work toward a clarification of issues, toward a definite perspective which could itself be identified (and identified with). The church too easily dismissed such activity as cheap "sniping from the bleachers," but it is comforting to know that Jesus himself could not afford a grandstand seat.

Frank H. Epp was also a powerful teacher by example, a man who was consumed by a passionate concern for his people. There was never any doubt about where his loyalty lay, and yet he was, particularly in the days of the *Canadian Mennonite*, called a radical and a critic and all manner of bad things. His passion took him to places like Vietnam and the Middle East because he thought that the truth of information would make us free to act responsibly. There was always enough naïveté in Frank Epp to make him similar to Don Quixote and the great fools in Christ of the past, and ultimately to Jesus. Naïveté has been a Mennonite strength, I have always felt, and one which fits them for the kingdom, but it appears to me that our adaptation to modern society has brought out other less desirable inherent characteristics which overshadow the vestiges of that innocence.

In my own professional life I have always been aware of a good measure of naïeté in my own nature and I think it has helped me never to be satisfied with pat answers or solutions, since I doubt myself as much as them. Ignorance can be a good reason for learning and can motivate a journey of exploration. In a sense our experience leads us around in a kind of hermeneutical circle, which is the ideal form for learning. But it is too easy to move around this circle like a transit passenger on whom the familiar signs do not really register anymore. Much of what I consider acutely worth full attention now I have been "familiar with" for years. But the time comes when one must suddenly confront such a "familiar" topic and, seeing it for the first time in a way, deal with it front and center. For this kind of process the image of a journey is not very suitable, since then we would have to admit to going in circles, as does T. S. Eliot in his *Four Quartets*, but perhaps that is a more truthful, if less flattering, imagery.

In any case, while engaged in this kind of searching, I have been able to look at a number of perspectives on ultimate reality which derive from different traditions. For example, I have greatly enjoyed reading books by Catholic theologians (this is not only because I was once blessed by Pope John XXIII!). While in my studies at Zürich, I became familiar with the work of Ramono Guardini because he was an expert on Eduard Mörike, the German poet about whom I wrote my dissertation. This theologian was fascinated by the more philosophical elements in Mörike's poetry, like the dimension of time. Later this theme would preoccupy me for some years. Then I came across the works of Hans Urs von Balthasar, whose five volumes with the title *Herrlichkeit* (Glory) investigate the reflection of the glory of God in human works, particularly of artists and poets. Balthasar, with the typical, immense Catholic education, was able to show me a vast panorama, something like what can be seen on some medieval paintings, and yet to maintain the absolute point of reference outside, God, in whom everything else has its meaning.

And later still I encountered the attempts by people like Hans Küng, David Tracy, and Gordon Kaufman to explore the potential of the human imagination in "seeing God." We think sometimes how mankind too often has limited God by his vain imaginings of the deity, and yet we must recognize how dependent we are and remain upon our own "God-given" faculties of reason, feeling, and imagination. This thinking has led me in my own work on what I have called the "Mennonite imagination." Like many others today I feel that our traditional religious categories are too narrowly theological or "spiritual" and that we must take more "material" elements into consideration in attempting to understand ourselves and our world. For me literature can be a reflection (and thus a record) of a reality that is more than propositional. We want to see, after all, what we are, not only what we purport to be. In our literature—from the Anabaptist martyr songs on—we tell a great deal about ourselves. By studying the imagery throughout the centuries since the Reformation, I hope to read a record of the hopes and fears, the beliefs and doubts, the victories and defeats of our people—apart from the dogma.

This kind of thinking may seem far removed from that of our Anabaptist forefathers, whether they were biblical scholars like Grebel and Manz or the "common people" of the countryside. These folk searched the Scriptures and discerned at their heart the message of Jesus who walked and talked, argued and celebrated with the people of his day and world. He taught love and service. People followed him. He followed the logic of his message to the cross. His followers believed him.

Then Christian theology was born. Theologians like Mark, Luke, and Paul put forward a construction, a way of understanding the life and death of Jesus. Subsequent theologians reinterpreted these things, Augustine, Thomas Aquinas, Luther—and all were criticized, explicitly or implicitly, by Anabaptists, who wanted to get back to the "primitive church"—just as now a theologian like Schillebeeckx searches for the same "receivers of the message of Jesus"—they were radical, probing around the roots of the matter in the best way that they knew how, compelled by the authority and fascinated by the simplicity of Jesus' impossible gospel and eager to prove (that is, to test or try) it.

There is much about the Anabaptists that makes them fascinating to us and to our time. Many of the issues that arose from their Bible study, like nonresistance, are of critical importance in today's world. But just when I think that I can identify with something of that rich heritage, I have to ask myself if it is not a game I am playing: for I am a Mennonite born and that is most likely why I am looking to this tradition. Were I born a Catholic, would I be interested in the Anabaptists? Probably not.

It is highly unlikely that in our institutionalized society any significant body of people would abandon one tradition for another. We are scarcely aware, I think, of how conditioned we are by the institutions which institutionalize us and the conventions that make us conventional. Jesus gave sufficient offense to the institutions of his time to become officially guilty. Our Anabaptist forefathers and mothers also represented an offense to official order. But in time the Mennonite people have always found some form of accommodation with the status quo; today we are a very conventional part of our larger society, apart from the few colorful vestiges of distinctiveness that are multiculturally useful. This raises some very large questions for me about the continuing existence of the Mennonite churches. Indeed, why should our churches retain the Mennonite name when they are concerned to melt into the religious landscape?

One of the consequences of this situation is that we may have to look outside our own immediate world to find the lines that go back to our own heritage. The majority of our people have become conformed to the North American evangelical lifestyle. Creative, recreative impulses could come to us from Tolstoy, from Gandhi, from Martin Luther King, Jr., and Mother Teresa—all of these relating us to our own heritage in a rather roundabout way. But the evangelical mindset of today would rather smear these names with associations of "humanistic communism" than deal with the real challenge which they present to followers of Jesus.

It seems to me that at the present time the real Mennonites, those who are consciously Mennonite, are on the growing fringe of the Mennonite world. The church that I knew is interchangeable with most of the mainline evangelical institutions and that is very different from what the Anabaptists were all about.

One of the great Pietist preoccupations which has remained with us is the felt need for spiritual certainty. Modern evangelicalism has devised its own formulas for salvation and has made "Christ" a part of a formula. These prescriptions are dispensed from the pulpit and through the electronic media (but not sold as indulgences, heaven forbid!) It seems to me that these "plans of salvation" misunderstand and misrepresent the meaning of faith. The Anabaptist vision of discipleship and service seems to me to come much closer to what Jesus was about. The trouble is that it is very difficult indeed for the Muppie of today (who, if he looks in the mirror of Scripture will likely see the "rich young ruler") to find out just who Jesus was and what he said. Between ourselves and Jesus stand two thousand years of Christian theology; perhaps that is what seeing "through a glass darkly" means. . . .

People in another age thought, quite sincerely, that the earth was flat and some religious movements today are reminiscent of flat-earth societies which do not encourage exploration around the rim. The Anabaptists were not of that ilk but were willing to follow their Master to the end of their understanding. I am encouraged by my Anabaptist forefathers and mothers to seek the kingdom, to look to Jesus and to love God and my fellow. My faith has not found a resting place, but it is alive.

5

Mennonite in Spite of . . .

George K. Epp

George K. Epp, an ordained minister in the General Conference Mennonite Church, was born and raised in the Ukraine. After im- migrating to Paraguay after World War II, he and his wife, Agnes, moved to Canada in the 1950s. He taught German and history at the University of Manitoba, at the Mennonite Brethren Bible/Arts College, and was president of Canadian Mennonite Bible College between 1978 and 1983. At present he is the director of Mennonite Studies Centre at the University of Winnipeg. His publications in- clude books and articles on Russian history and German and Men- nonite literature.

*H*ow can a twentieth-century Canadian Mennonite come to terms with his Mennonite identity and how do we explain our choice, if it was a choice? In the growing Mennonite academic community at the universities we could add another question: "Why do so many of us hang on to that Mennonite name in spite of the fact that adherence to the Mennonite church sometimes was not made very easy by the local church or the larger Mennonite community?" The absence of university academics at our conferences is conspicuous, and yet they hang on to the Mennonite name (and I do believe that many do so with growing conviction that this belonging is important). What is it that attracts us to this Mennonite church, in spite of the occasional feeling of alienation? Our individual experiences will determine our answers, but it will be interesting to see whether we do have a common denominator.

Growing up in a Russian-Mennonite village and only vaguely remembering the last church service before all the churches were closed by the Soviet government, my early contacts with Mennonitism could come only through the home. I am sure that the teaching of my parents had some impact on me, but what I really remember are the behavior and actions of family members in that given situation. There was the time when my brothers attended baptismal classes, and I was told that I must not tell anybody where they were going. They were baptized, but I was not allowed to be present. Then my oldest brother was called to enlist in the army, but as a conscientious objector he chose to go through protracted court procedures and then on to a labor camp far away on Lake Baikal. After three years he came home, but we had to pick him up at the railroad station—he was a broken man.

My father was fired by the school because he refused to play according to the rules which demanded that he renounce his faith. Several years later, when the state realized how badly the school system had suffered due to such purges, he was offered his teaching position with one proviso, that he would not talk about his faith. "We will ask no questions, just come and teach." But that stubborn Mennonite said: "If you don't ask me, I have to tell you..." So the better life once more was out of reach for us, and we were poor....

From a child's point of view being a Mennonite was not very profitable. Could not father have compromised just a little bit? But there must have been some powerful glue in that family which kept me from ever considering breaking ranks, although the school made every effort to alienate us from our parents. Only the state deserved loyalty and above all father Stalin, and children were actually rewarded for betraying family members. But such betrayal hardly ever happened in Mennonite families, and my respect for my parents, my older brothers, and my sister was always greater than my resentment about poverty and "being different." It was this family loyalty which helped me through the school years, when pressures of the system sometimes were quite unbearable for children. That Mennonite family was also the base from which you could put up resistance against infections from the left as well as from the right.

I had learned to pray, but I was totally unprepared for the world, when at the age of sixteen the war separated me from my parents and from the Mennonite community. I vaguely remembered some of my father's advice: "We Mennonites do not take up arms." "We do not swear." "Let people know that 'yes' is yes, and that 'no' is really no." "Make sure that you will never have to be ashamed of anything you do."

I really don't know what else I remembered, but even the little I remembered was much for a sixteen-year-old boy whose physical appearance was that of a child of thirteen, while mentally rather mature as a result of difficult childhood experiences. From the age of thirteen this small, undernourished boy had worked as an apprentice to the accountant of a collective farm, and at fourteen he became a junior accountant on that collective farm, working from May to September like all the rest of the children in the village, but with the privilege of working with mature and rather considerate people in the administration. But the point is that from the age of thirteen he had learned to become independent. His income was badly needed in the family.

Now, away from home, I volunteered to work in a field hospital as an interpreter, but since the interpreter's responsibilities would not take that much time, I spent most of the time with the various medical teams, assisting in whichever way I could. It was a privileged position because I had opportunities to meet many interesting people of various convictions and confessions: Catholics, Lutherans, Evangelicals, Orthodox, and members of the Confessing Church. And it was a Catholic theologian that became a kind of father figure for me. He was twenty-eight and I was sixteen when we met and he immediately treated me as a younger brother. He steered me around a number of dangerous cliffs with a peculiar "Catholic" reminder: "You say you are a Mennonite, I think your father would not like this." Never did he attempt even with the slightest hint to draw me into his church. He was from Baden, Germany, and was the only soldier I have met who knew the Mennonites. Although I did not feel comfortable when A. admonished and in his way tutored me, I was not stupid enough to disregard his advice and in time I admired him.

Then there was the evangelical army chaplain who visited us frequently. I discovered that A. and this chaplain had much in common, and it was my privilege to accompany them when they visited Orthodox priests. One of those priests was a learned man and their discussions would go on for hours. I sweated through those sessions, because I struggled with their theological terms, but the experience left a deep impression on me. Here they were of three different confessions, and yet they obviously enjoyed each other's company and thoughts.

Then there was another rather fascinating person that crossed my path. Dr. K., the replacement for one of the surgeons, arrived on a cold winter day. The next morning, casualties were beginning to come in fast and by 6:00 a.m. we had sixty men on stretchers filling every corner and more were coming. I was busy registering and tagging these suffering bodies and then while I was bending over one of the young men the new surgeon's voice came to me through the busy hum: "Would anybody join me in prayer before we start?" I was stunned. I had never heard anybody ask such a question and in that

setting it seemed inappropriate when sixty people waited for the surgeons to save what there was to be saved. One of the soldiers joined
Captain K. It took a minute and then his voice came through the embarrassed silence: "Los (let's go)!" Day after day they were operating
with only a few hours of sleep in between. Never before or after have
I seen so much human blood spilled—so many young lives ending in
a cold grave.

Dr. K. started every shift with a prayer, and by the end of the first
week nobody was embarrassed and his whole team joined him for
that moment. That man was different, and he was the best surgeon.
Top-ranking officers insisted that Dr. K. should treat them. One day,
soon after he had arrived, Dr. K. stopped me. "George, I want to
know a little bit about you," he said. We had many long chats and
then he gave me a beautiful little book—the New Testament. "Don't
save it for after the war, read it," he said. Several weeks later I was
transferred and never again have I heard anything about the fate of
A., the Catholic theologian, or Dr. K., who was a member of the
Confessing Church in Germany. These men were lights never to be
forgotten.

There were other lights along the painful road of wartime
experiences. In Glogau, a town in Silesia (today Poland), more than
10,000 wounded soldiers were being cared for by nuns of the former
convent. They had other help, but these nuns were running the hospital complex, and how! They were everywhere and the touch of their
hands was appreciated by all. But then came the day when the
thunder of the guns of war reached Glogau. The population at that
time already knew what to expect from the invading army. Fear
paralyzed the town and in the hospitals there was only one question
on everybody's mind: "What happens when the nuns leave?" Nobody could be expected to volunteer for an impossible task—there
were 10,000 wounded.

And then the incredible happened. These nuns went from room to
room, comforting those helpless-hopeless creatures: "Take courage.
We are staying with you. We will not desert you." They knew what
was coming and yet they were willing to sacrifice themselves, perhaps
to save some. I was one of the few hundred who were lucky to be
evacuated before the ring was closed. Realizing what it took to make
the decision to stay there in danger of losing their lives and their

dignity, and how great their faith and their dedication had to be, I cried unashamedly as they carried me to the transport.

March 1945. The war was almost over, although the party line was still "Sieg." Now I was safe in West Germany and the only concern I had was the safety of my relatives. Had they escaped? What happened to the families of my brothers and my sisters? What was the fate of my parents? One Saturday morning a young medical student whom I knew came into our room inviting everybody to a communion service. I was surprised, and I did not immediately respond. After all, I was of Mennonite background and not yet baptized. But when the time approached I made it to the church somehow on crutches.

The Lutheran pastor seemed to have forgotten that it was dangerous to mention certain developments. He seemed to ignore the party line about victory and the rest and then he ended his sermon with the statement: "In times like these all of us should turn to Christ." He invited us to participate in the celebration of communion. He was so genuine. Should I tell him that I would like to participate, but that I was not baptized?—but he would not understand. Yes, I remembered that I was Mennonite by birth, but not baptized, yet suddenly I got up and limped to the front to share the bread and wine with the handful of believers, in that moment my closest brothers and sisters. I will always remember that first communion service in a Lutheran church.

In 1947 I was among the first group of Mennonite refugees to go to Paraguay, but not because I was a Mennonite. My name was Epp and therefore MCC or the American screening commission did not find it difficult to accept me, but was I a Mennonite? I joined that first group because my sister and my brother were both of precarious health and with small children, and since they had decided to go, I had to go as well. There was very little thinking involved. I may have remembered my parents when I made that decision, but perhaps I also remembered those nuns in Glogau. I joined that Mennonite group against any rational advice of my employer, Westphalia-Dinendahl-Groeppel. The company was interested in me: "What do you mean you are a Mennonite? What do you know about Mennonites? Here is a future for you." Indeed, what did I know about Mennonites? I had been away from the Mennonite community for four years and had met fine Christians along the way, who belonged to other confessions of faith. I was a believer, but where did I belong if my blood ties were really as insignificant as some of our preachers would have me believe. For the time being my brother's and my sister's families kept me in the Mennonite community.

Eventually a Mennonite girl had a lot to do with my staying in the Mennonite fold. But as we cut our destiny into the jungle of East Paraguay my attitude gradually changed. Here was a group of refugees who at first glance were the same as any refugees that roamed the world, but a closer look revealed a significant difference.

There was above all an impressive cohesiveness and a community spirit which is uncommon among uprooted people. The fifteen years of Stalin terror and war had not utterly destroyed those values that had shaped this community over centuries.

Then there was the surprise in the discovery of a large, caring brotherhood. A telegram had called me to Munich, where I found my brother's and my sister's families and a community of several hundred Mennonites preparing to emigrate to Paraguay or Canada. And there were some Mennonites from Canada, who represented the Mennonite Central Committee (MCC). They had come to help us— because a larger Mennonite community cared for its battered children. That was a revelation to me with an impact. This larger Mennonite community far away in America organized and financed our resettlement and eventually sent teachers and preachers to help us find our bearings, and all, they told us, as a gift from many who loved us—"in the name of Christ." This discovery of a community dedicated to serving others was the most significant single factor contributing to my homecoming as it were, and for the first time I began to identify with the Mennonite ideals of peace and service.

In 1949 I was ready to make a commitment to this Mennonite community, but the slow process of doubting and struggling toward an honest position was by no means completed. During the four years that I had been away from the Mennonite community (age sixteen to twenty), I had developed a fairly strong sense of independence. Thanks to the many lights on my road (including my parents), the two going ideologies of the day had not succeeded in their attempt to mold the young fellow according to their fashion and I was not prepared to give up that independent mind, not even within the church (and I think I never did). But then almost immediately after my baptism the church elected me to the ministry. (I opposed that election, but in those years the church did not ask for your consent—the call of the church was the call of God.) And where I had never waivered when I said no to "left" and "right," I did not have the nerve to say no to the church because of a very persuasive elder who said: "I understand your objection to this election, but before we accept your 'no,' you must show us the man who at this point is better prepared than you." And I looked around in desperation, but we were all in the same boat—we had no theological and not even the most elementary Sunday school preparation. So I postponed my answer and started to work in the church as well as I was able.

I was now married and hoped to solve my problem by continuing my education in Asuncion, the capital of Paraguay. But the administration of the colony pointed out to me that the colony needed every one of us. Would I consider teaching in one of the schools, and of course there was my sister and her children, and my brother whose health was failing. Knowing that leaving this struggling refugee colony which was trying to build a Mennonite community in the jungle was irresponsible desertion, I reluctantly consented to stay. And I set out to investigate my roots, for I had to know why I was doing this. When I left that Mennonite colony almost five years later, I had learned to love and respect those people with all their weaknesses and gifts and their theology of peace and service.

Just before Christmas 1954 we arrived in Canada. Here the question was no longer whether we belonged to the Mennonite community but rather one of adjustment to the American way of life and thinking. At that time Canadian-Mennonite churches were going through a period of strong influences from the revival movement in the United States. Smoking and drinking habits were the criteria according to which Mennonites were divided and classed. I had no problems with the chosen standards, but I found it difficult to swallow the legalism which went with it. And then those divisions! Where was the love of Christ? The incredible self-righteousness of individual groups within the Mennonite church body frustrated me to no end. How could we reconcile this attitude with our professed love of our neighbors and our enemies? And to top it all, we called each other brothers and sisters—publicly—denying each other when we were with our "own kind" of special Mennonites.

In the 1960s Canadian Mennonites began to embrace politics without ever discussing the implications of the new trend which was directly opposed to our traditional position of strict separation of church and state. We never made a statement, but almost overnight we became involved and hardly in a way you would like to see Christian involvement in politics. Our peace position had no bearing on it. Soon we had three political parties (Liberal, Conservative, and New Democratic) within the Mennonite community, and the tensions resulting from this state of affairs affected the church, the body of Christ. Some churches managed to become one-party churches, but the result was in no way more encouraging, for such churches had the tendency to put on blinkers, and as a result political considerations began to color our religious faith. So now we have Mennonite churches leaning to the left or to the right. Can Christ still be ruler of all? Is this Mennonite church not drifting away from our Anabaptist position at the very time when our schools are claiming to have rediscovered true Anabaptism? On what basis can we still claim to be Mennonites in the Anabaptist tradition? Are the major ingredients of Anabaptism, "sola scriptura" plus an unquestioned "obedience to the spirit," still central in our position? Are we not slowly but surely adopting humanism as our real creed? With all due respect for the significant contributions of humanism, it is not a substitute for the foundation of early Anabaptism.

This Mennonite church is also experiencing a very important "cultural revolution." For a long time culture was accepted by one wing of the church but many branches rejected culture as a dangerous force. I am proud of our recent achievements in music, in drama, in writing, in the fine arts, but culture does not make me a Mennonite and in many respects our developing culture is not specifically Mennonite.

Why, then, am I a Mennonite? Those of us who take our Mennonite tradition seriously are frequently tempted to give up on this "peace church," with its endless internal tensions (not to say quarrels). Have we not completely failed our Master when we apply his criteria? "All men will know that you are my disciples, if you have love for one another"; "if you walk in the light, as he is in the light, you have fellowship with one another," etc. The unity question is the most embarrassing problem when we are trying to sell our peace position. And yet the peace position is one reason for my adherence to the Mennonite church, even though we have not clearly defined what that position may mean in our century. We realize that an antiwar position is not necessarily a peace position.

A peace position based on fear of war is merely an extension of our selfish interest. That kind of position tends to oversimplify the issue and above all it does not prevent wars. Peacemakers must know something about conflict resolution and they need much wisdom and courage. There is no simple prescription for peace and we have failed often and in many ways, but in spite of all, throughout the centuries since the Reformation the Mennonite community has been consistent in recognizing the role of the church as a peacemaker and so the principle was kept alive.

Perhaps I am coming to a somewhat paradoxical conclusion after earlier critical reflections on our weaknesses, but the balance sheet of failures and achievements of this Mennonite community is simply in its favor. However divided we may have been theologically (if insignificant peripheral issues can be termed theological), when it came to the practical application of our basic Christian faith and Mennonite conviction, we have been an amazingly cohesive community and especially the Prusso-Russian Mennonite branch has a long history to substantiate this claim. While the tensions between the General Mennonite church (Kirchliche) and the Mennonite Brethren in Russia ran high and differences were never fully reconciled, together they developed a Mennonite commonwealth with admirable educational and social systems which were unique by any standards of that time. When famine struck, when persecution hit the community, when Mennonites decided to find another homeland, when they developed their relief agencies—in all this they were together. Together all the branches of the Mennonite community today are proud of achievements through MCC, Mennonite Disaster Service (MDS), and the Food Bank.

This concept of togetherness has expanded in our century and the only name under which all of us are recognized by the larger community in Canada is simply Mennonite Central Committee and I am proud of it because it comforts me to know that we are actually more united than some theologians would have us believe. And I am not referring only to the achievements of MCC, MDS, and the Food Bank, but also to the accomplishments of our Mission Boards, MB, EMC, GC, MC, Brethren in Christ, EMMC, and whatever their name—Mennonite service-theology is our strongest bond.

The Canadian-Mennonite community has demonstrated an impressive vitality to this point. This community has learned to live with the paradox of being divided for worship on Sundays but united for the work that is to be done in the name of Christ. In spite of its many obvious weaknesses it has achieved an unusual degree of involvement of its members in missions in the broader sense. Every member of this community understands that membership means involvement and giving and serving have become traditions. That is why I am a Mennonite in spite of many misgivings I have about my church. But while I am opting to be a Mennonite, I gratefully acknowledge the positive influences on my spiritual development that came from Christian "cousins"—Catholic, Lutheran, and Confessing Church. I am a Mennonite with strong conviction but without "pious" bias against the "cousins" of other Christian traditions.

6

Between Presumption and Despair: On Remaining Mennonite

Peter C. Erb

Peter Erb, who comes from an Amish background in southern Ontario, teaches English and Religion at Wilfrid Laurier University in Waterloo, Ontario. He has also been a pastor of an Amish church in Ontario. His numerous published articles and books deal with Protestant spirituality, monastic communities in North America, and the Radical Reformers of the sixteenth century. Peter and his wife, Betty, have two daughters.

*T*o respond to the statement "Why I am a Mennonite" is to respond in at least three ways all of which are closely tied together:

1. It may be to respond to simple definition. In this response the emphasis falls on the final word of the statement—"Mennonite." Why I am a Mennonite, i.e., what makes me a Mennonite, why I am defined as a Mennonite, what makes me different from other persons who share my social, economic, and political status but who cannot be defined with the normal use of the term as Mennonites. This response can be formed in one of two ways, either ethnically or theologically. In the case of Mennonites, even those who are not of Swiss or Russian Mennonite stock, the two elements in the definition are inevitably linked.

2. Again, it may be to respond by self-definition. In this response the emphasis falls on the second word of the statement—"I": Who am I as a Mennonite and how am I different from non-Mennonites? This response arises in a particularly intense way in late twentieth-century Canada, where contemporary dislocation of traditional worldviews has forced widespread concern with self-identity in the context of an unsubstantiated national identity.

3. Finally, it may be to respond with an apologia. In this response the emphasis falls on the first word of the statement—"Why": Here are the main reasons why I am a Mennonite, why I think the tradition is an important one to maintain and support. There is in such apologies inevitably a touch of self-aggrandizement and triumphalism, perhaps to be expected of a people which raises its young on the fiber of humility and self-sacrifice.

But for an increasingly great number of Mennonites there is

a fourth response which is primary and which focuses on the second word of the statement—"am": In this form the response presupposes general agreement on the first problem, that of definition, has faced the second honestly, and has thereby realized that the self which has been appropriated is not in keeping with a "self" fitting the definition of Mennonite as generally held. Acculturated to the third problem, the need to offer an apologetic response in the case of all one's activities, such respondents are faced with three choices:

1. to "revive" the present self so that it more properly fits the traditional definition of "Mennonitism," and thereby to "revert" to the earlier position;

2. to "revise" or rethink the traditional definitions of "Mennonitism" so that they more properly fit the present patterns of the respondents' individual lives, and thereby to "divert" attention from the rift between the two positions;

3. or to "convert," to leave Mennonite ecclesial patterns and to choose new ones for which an apologetic response can be given with integrity.

For such persons, still reflecting on the three choices, the response must take the form: "Why remain Mennonite?" It is among this group that I find myself.

Before pursuing the issue in detail, two corollary issues must be raised. First, for some Mennonite and virulently anti-Mennonite commentators reflections on "Why I am a Mennonite" or even on the reduced form of the statement "Why remain Mennonite?" is a "typical" example of Mennonite ethnocentrism. But the question "Why Mennonite?" is no different from the questions "Why Evangelical?" or "Why Roman Catholic?" Others object to the general nature of the topic, seeing in its treatment an example of personal narcissism. Their reaction is typical of our time in which discussion of theological issues is not counted among the acts which mark a mature human being. For such people metaphysical reflection may be acceptable in impractical university lecture rooms but is as visibly embarrassing as dirty linen if publicly considered. This is even the case if the topic is raised in church settings, whereas in liberal circles it is set outside the periphery as unworthy of adult conversation, and in conservative ranks it is reduced to ritual formulae.

Second, the person I am here describing is a real human being, established firmly in a cultural and social network which the person respects and loves and in which he or she is in turn respected and loved. The person is not a disembodied mind for which decisions can be instantaneously made and acted upon, for which truth is a credal statement accepted by an incisive reason and dealt with by a resolute will. Such a person seeks understanding and not knowledge, is not concerned with gaining power over a limited number of facts but with integrating all the facts of his or her environment. We must consider such a person as facing the choices, not as one having already chosen and hypocritically refusing to act.

"Why then remain Mennonite" if one finds oneself with a theological formation not in keeping with that of the majority of his or her co-worshipers? In some cases, facing the onslaught of extraordinary and abnormal circumstances, a personal revival may occur resulting in a reversion to earlier religious structures. But such grace is not granted to all and many who find themselves with a theology foreign to the religious patterns in which they were raised know it is unlikely that their new position, developed over the heat of perhaps several decades, will be set aside. Only two other options appear possible: one can "revise" one's tradition and force it into a form more in keeping with the "new" theology, or one can convert.

For Mennonites "reversion" has manifested itself either in the framework of nineteenth-century North American revivalism or as a return to the physical past, to reconstructed dress and transportation codes of an earlier time. But whether or not "reversion" has occurred, in almost all cases "revision" has. As many Mennonites of the postwar years moved intellectually and at times physically beyond their local communities in southern Manitoba or southwestern Ontario, new circumstances rushed by the demarcations of their early formation and demanded that they reject or radically reinterpret their past. Not even in the traditional occupation of farming was it possible to maintain earlier patterns without demanding a retreat from time behind ever thicker and clumsier fortifications. No Mennonite dialect, for example, grew rapidly enough to absorb the burgeoning vocabulary of diesel engines and marketing boards. Low German could be saved only by the extraordinary energy of a few academics, and Pennsylvania Dutch was forced to plead its case in the Grundsau Lodge.

Some of these Mennonites left their earlier religious world behind as easily as they left their ethnic world while others chose new theological options. For the majority who remained within the Mennonite structure, who participated in what continued to be designated with agricultural metaphors such as church "planting," there were other options. Most chose, with greater or less success and with greater or less personal turmoil, to "revise" their positions, to divide ethnicity from the supposed theological "idea" which it contained and to attempt to apply this "idea" in their new worlds, discarding useless ethnic "baggage." The "idea" to be retained was described in different ways. Those who were more concerned with present fashions used the predominant language of North American revivalism; those who had drunk of the traditional waters more deeply spoke of an "Anabaptist vision," which could be "recovered" or "renewed." In each case there was a move toward a gnostic pattern by which the believer clung to saving truth as comprehensible knowledge. One chose to "know" the Lord or to "discover" what the Anabaptists "thought," and to "revise" one's tradition according to the new knowledge.

But what of those for whom the grace of reversion has not come and for whom new knowledge does not lead to a revised understanding of their tradition? For such the only option is conversion. In the context of the present discussion, it is to answer the question "Why remain Mennonite?" with a sharp "Why indeed?" and to choose and actively participate in another church community, one more in keeping with newfound truth. Without reversion or revision, conversion seems the only option which can be held with integrity.

Even in imagination such believers cannot see themselves reverting to the time of their childhood. It is impossible to do so. The social structures of that period have decayed. There is no longer a milkman with his wagon nor a local baker who delivers cream puffs on Saturday mornings. The ideal of earlier communal life remains unconsciously strong in some, but the patterns which supported the ideal are either lost or prove so fragile that they collapse whenever strain is placed on them. The believers I have here in mind have no interest in reconstructing an earlier "simpler," "purer" community (indeed, they believe such reconstruction to be impossible), and they can suppose no situation in which they would support peculiar dress codes and tightly constrained social conventions.

The path of revision is likewise closed. They cannot with any honesty read Anabaptist or Pietist texts as supporting their present position. There are elements in each which suggest similarities, but even those elements when read in their context uphold a theology radically different from theirs. To revise the texts according to the similar elements alone would be to falsify by historical reduction. Moreover, there is no good reason for choosing some dozen years or less in the early sixteenth century and viewing them as a period of supreme revelatory significance. To further reduce these few years to the works of several and at times divided figures seems equally foolish. For such persons the "Anabaptist vision" can be delineated only in the broadest outlines and then only with extensive "exceptions to." Without a clear sense of what Anabaptism was, there is little chance of its "recovery."

But such Mennonites, as I have here in mind, do not convert. To some of their less thoughtful opponents their remaining is a mark of either cowardice or diffidence, and so it may well be. There are after all great uncles who would never understand, and it may be that the shock of seeing a son or daughter leave the sensible Mennonite world would kill an aging father. It may be; but it is unlikely. Parental or broader family trauma even within close-knit ethnic Mennonite communities does pass, and in any event the Mennonites I have in mind here are not those whose central reasons for remaining are based on cowardice or diffidence.

Why, then, remain Mennonite? The question as I noted earlier is one increasingly asked within Mennonite circles. The question is not "Why do *I* remain *a* Mennonite?"; the need for self-definition as an *I*, *a* Mennonite, has already passed. The questioner here has achieved a religious self-definition; his or her question is not "What do I believe?" but "When one's 'personal' religious position has developed to something clearly different from the 'normal' religious patterns of the majority who define the religion of which one is a member, why remain (actively or passively) within those (Mennonite) ecclesial patterns?"

Autobiographical meanderings are therefore initially to be avoided. Our primary interest is in delineating the religious or theological, not the psychological, reasons for remaining a Mennonite. Second, auto-biographical reflections often lead prematurely to positing one particular answer or to supposing that there is an answer. More pointedly, they limit a question "which is *increasingly* being asked in Mennonite circles" to be the question of one individual, and to sug-gest that if one can reach a satisfactory answer for that individual, the problem will be solved for all.

But autobiography cannot be set aside. Autobiographical delibera-tions have begun even when no dates or places, parents or siblings are mentioned. The autobiographical element is present in merely raising the topic, and the refusal to deal openly that topic contains the same element.

It is therefore with great hesitation (not that I am concerned about the emotional stability of a great uncle, but that I may unduly limit the discussion to my own situation) that I present autobiographical "material" as a case study, to be reflected on not as "true" in itself, but as providing a concrete example through which the problem "On remaining Mennonite" can be discussed.

The Pascalian wager aside, theological discourse has been central for me as long as I can remember. I was born Amish Mennonite in a village in East Zorra township in the middle of a war which marked the middle of our century. Few memories are precise and mine have become less so after reflection on them. But autobiography never functions as an exact science and is seldom intended as such. With this in mind I offer for consideration some "tales."

o   o   o

When I was a boy I sat at the front of the church in a row with the other boys, behind the girls of the same age. We would wait in the back entry until the very last moment before marching in and would challenge each other until either the very weakest or the very strongest of that morning would lead the way. This is my first memory of violence. And I remember sitting at the front of the church, listening for words which would be discussed at length in the community throughout the coming week and which would be initiated with the formulae "I have a conviction . . ." or "There is a matter very heavy on my heart . . ." In such words I learned of further violence.

o   o   o

My great-uncle was opposed to Sunday school but admired a Sunday school superintendent who once told us that he had heard of a young fellow, a "Schtaetzer" (an American, from the States) from the Mennonite seminary at Goshen, who said he went back to his town after many years and everything had changed except the church, and that this was bad. And then the superintendent wondered if it wasn't good that at least one thing stayed the same: "After they took the pegs out of the meetinghouses there were no places to hang your hat, and then people started to wear fancy 'shild-kaps' (caps with peaks and ear-laps) to keep their ears warm—so they'd always be warmed up to hear more gossip, I suppose."

o   o   o

After many years my great-uncle had not brought electricity onto his farm and his friends often commented in laughter. In town I heard A . . . Z . . . say that "Pit must love darkness rather than light." When I told my great-uncle he replied that there were many kinds of light and that some kinds were not light, but only looked like light. "For our age it's not the problem of light or darkness," he said, "but the problem of the right light."

o   o   o

My great-uncle told me that the modern age began on March 14, 1924, when A . . . Z . . . came to church with rubber tires on his buggy and everyone admired them. On the same day he asked me what I was reading. When I told him "Plato" and spoke of "knowing yourself," he said, "A person can only walk four miles an hour and a horse only eight regardless of the smoothness of the tires."

o   o   o

I had a friend in the Mennonite high school who told me that the Mennonites had the best of all the kinds of religion and that we Amish weren't bad, but that we hadn't really kept up with the best ways for our time. My great-uncle told me that there were "our kind of people" and "the other kind of people" and all that really mattered was really being "kind."

And on the same day, on the streets of a nearby city my great-uncle was asked by a vendor of religious wares if he was a Christian. When he answered that he tried to be (to state that one was so great a being as a Christian struck him as an act of the most extreme arrogance), he was told that one could not try, that one either was or was not. Ever after that time, it seemed to me, he was deeply troubled.

o   o   o

One Sunday dinner at the bishop's a friend who went to the Mennonite high school asked the bishop what he thought about the theory of evolution. The bishop had never heard of it. When told that evolution taught that "men came from monkeys," the bishop commented that "when you see the way some of them act, it makes sense" and was untroubled about the possible truth of the theory, except insofar as it seemed to be an insult to monkeys.

On the same day I asked the bishop, "What is truth?", waited for an answer, and was told that the border fences of truth were "probably too far away to find for sure, and all that a person could do was work in the fields. If you spend all your time hoeing at the property line, the weeds will kill out the turnips."

o   o   o

When the decision was finally made that I could attend high school and after the first week of classes had ended, my great-uncle asked me if I had yet seen the devil in any of the books. I answered, "No," and he replied, "That's when he gets you." My great-uncle read whenever he had the opportunity, and sometimes when he did not, but he always called me a "schuler," a "schoolboy," even when I was an adult.

On Sunday when a preacher from the seminary said that all the book-learning in the world was just so much trash, and that only divine wisdom would save you, the "Amen" benches nodded yes, and everyone, except my great-uncle, was pleased. After meeting, in the driving shed, he lit his pipe and said that you can only know the rules of arithmetic by counting apples, and that there were "far too few people counting apples these days."

o   o   o

The Sunday school superintendent's wife once brought eggs to the house and I remember that she rushed in and placed them on the table, tossing words here and there as she did. Among the words which fitted together I heard, "It's not in our tradition." Tradition was often mentioned in our home, but I never knew its meaning and my great-uncle could not answer.

The man who had been to Montreal River told us of the Frenchman from North Bay who didn't want to fight either and who always said he had to "remember himself." I was reminded of his story later when I saw a Quebec license plate. He told us that he had often wondered what the Frenchman meant, and that as near as he could figure it, "it must be like all of us can only sit up right because we're six-month-old babies; it must be like that's one of our parts, and only if we remember what we learned when we were six months old, can we ever be grown up—if we don't remember, we'll just fall over—like if we don't remember our forefathers."

○ ○ ○

The town I grew up in was a happy town. We were given the meaning of the word "fear" and we were not afraid. We understood "truth" and "goodness," "sorrow" and "despair," "poverty" and "pride." The man who gave us the meaning of all these words had once traveled to a place of great suffering and he could tell us the meaning of suffering, just as he could of all the strange words he had met in a land of strangers. He delighted in speaking of that land—the stories repeated themselves on his lips, and passed anew to our ears.

Some in our town delighted in his repetition, some ignored it, some found new words within the stories so often repeated and sought the meanings of these new words and the newer ones which followed them. I was among the latter. I asked the meaning of travel and he told me, and I asked the meaning of his travel and was told. I asked the meanings of all strange words and I was answered. But on a May Sunday, in the back entry when I had been chosen as strongest or weakest to march in first, I asked him the meaning of "stranger"—and he turned aside.

The "tales" may speak for themselves regarding my formation into the Amish Mennonite tradition and my deformation from it. That deformation was not fully my own. As a teenager, a majority of my parents' generation, perhaps embarrassed by supposed barbed remarks about the ignorant Amish from their non-Amish neighbors, gave up their dialect and replaced "Amish" in their name with the faulty geographical designation "Western Ontario." I became Mennonite by the democratic decision of a majority of delegates to a conference, which few among the Amish understood as anything other than a friendly gathering, a way of "keeping in touch" and of helping "those less fortunate than ourselves."

In a sense I was thrown into Mennonitism and it may be that the experience was what first led me to consider the matter of remaining Mennonite, but it is more likely that serious consideration of religious givens and theological choices are rooted deeper in my past. Those whose religious life, like mine, has been formed as an ethnic life and whose religious development is marked by the appropriation and disappropriation of that ethnicity will have a strong sense of the incarnated nature of Christianity. For them decisions regarding the form of religion they are and are to retain is complex since they are far from gnostic presuppositions which distinguish sharply between mind and soul and which speak of truth by axiom and definition. Those with gnostic tendencies can ascertain truth—by whatever hermeneutical principles or contemporary fashion—from Bible, confession of faith, or dogmatic manual, and act according to it. Those who take the incarnation seriously, whose life is shaped according to the revelations of the divine in the concrete history of a single first-century individual and as reflected in the conflicting material and mental constructs regarding that individual over some 2000 years, have greater difficulty.

The tradition in which I was raised taught me a particular respect for the concrete and for the past. One learned mathematics by counting real apples, not by meditating on arithmetical principles, and one learned of truth in human memories applied to present moments, not in theological or philosophical handbooks. But the ideal I held of the tradition forced me beyond the tradition itself. I am a stranger to it; I do not think I turned aside from it, but it reluctantly and sadly turned aside from me when I asked questions of it which it could no longer answer or understand. It required that I always be present to myself, that I integrate the moment that I learned to walk at each moment I walk. It taught me that I can make significant acts in the present only to the degree that I remember the past.

But the remembering of my particular past was peculiar and my present is expanding beyond the full possibility of that remembering. As an Amish Mennonite child I was "poorly" catechized; I had never heard of the Anabaptists and was unaware of the "sixteenth-century turning point." Little wonder, then, that when I began to explore the theological past, I was not initially directed to Grebel and Sattler but to our Christian tradition. *Martyrs Mirror* was too long to read to the end and the introductory section was dry. I began at and never got beyond the section on the Middle Ages.

For all I knew, the Albigensians were "our" tradition, and when I discovered that they were not even heterodox, but another religion, I was not disturbed, but pleased that "my" religion was open to other religious options as well as dissident groups within Christianity itself. There were "our" people and the "other" people, but they were all people. My middle name was "Christian" (it was only later that I was told that I was named after my maternal and paternal grandfathers) and I had a friend whose middle name was "Christian." On being introduced to a boy some four years younger than myself who did not have the same middle name, I recall being puzzled as to his type of religion. When I came to work in a library larger than that of my home, I was naturally drawn to the greatest historical sweep of the Christian tradition, to the patristic and medieval periods in particular, and to a traditional reading of those periods. It was much later that I began to read Reformation and Pietist texts, and when I did, it was always in the context of the broader catholic tradition.

The result was perhaps inevitable; I did not change my theological position, but it grew and my remembering broadened beyond even my adoptive Mennonite parents—until finally, in the joyous days of Vatican II, I was faced for the first time by a well-spoken, intelligent, personable, and traditional Catholic who asked me why I was not a practicing Catholic. I have always found the question difficult to answer and have increasingly felt that it is somehow the wrong question even though there is no doubt that Roman Catholicism, of all Christian "denominations," presents a theological and spiritual position closest to my own. It has formed my thought and continues to do so. It may be that in time it will so completely reform my activities that I will find myself within it, not alongside it, but this is not the case at present. At present I remain Mennonite, not because I am too cowardly or diffident (both of which are deeply bred into all Amish Mennonites), nor because I have serious reservations about Roman Catholicism. My "remaining" Mennonite and my refusal to seek reception into the Church of Rome is based on another foundation.

For those with a Platonic view of existence, the fact of a broken church causes little dismay. For them it is at the most an ecumenical problem, but not ecumenical agony. With docetic simplicity they can posit an ideal spiritual church and speak of it as manifested in this fallen creation. But for those who take the incarnation seriously, who accept without reservation (doubt is another matter) the Chalcedonian "fully God and fully human," such an ideal kingdom floating above a corrupted earth is a denial of Christ. For them the search to find a manifestation closer to the true ideal is a refusal to struggle with the full implications of the broken body of Christ. Their ecclesiastical world is not one in which there are churches or ecclesial communities, gradated in order ever closer to the true church. Rather, they find themselves totally in a human world, able to comprehend only greater or lesser shards from which they must posit or reconstruct the vessel that once was.

This issue can perhaps be made more precise by continuing with this allusion to the grail legend. The grail, like the king whose knights went in search of it, was "once and future." It "once was" but it is no longer anything other than the object of a quest. As a Christian myth, the grail legend directs believers continually to a center of their existence which can be nothing other than ironic. The grail is a grail of this world, a possible, lost, historic object, possible to be found and at the same time transcending all that is earthly. The broken pieces of its history may be gathered in stories of Joseph of Arimathea and its disjointed journey to Glastonbury. As an object it was lost and (to add to the tradition) may well have been broken under a barbaric hoof. The separation of the shards are thus not only the separation of one piece from the other; the very possibility of their history is in doubt. They are divided in time and have forgotten their past.

The persons of whom I have been speaking in this paper and who cling toward the broken grail are obsessed with history. They are not concerned with the conservation of their grandparents' ideals or with reconstructing and restoring earlier times. They are optimistically open to the future, but cannot be defined as liberals. They might best be described as traditionalists. They are at the same time postmoderns and therefore find no difficulty in seeking theological inspiration in individuals as separate, as similar, and as old-fashioned as Newman and Maurice, Bushnell and Scheeben. Not surprisingly, they develop their theological stances by methods open to the paradoxes of human existence, to a human language which can in its simplest form overcome the axiom of non-contradiction—in short, to what is traditionally referred to as "mystery."

The persons of whom I am here speaking are obsessed with history, but not with historical data. Rather, they are focused on the *paradosis*, the *traditio*, the "handed over" and the "handing over"; they are obsessed with present history. A horse-drawn plow which sits on my neighbor's lawn as an ornament is not an object *from* the past but *of* the present, reminding me of a Before slowly fading from sight and reinserting it in my present, while at the same time directing me to possible future furrows and hoped-for harvests. Those who take to the plow cannot look back.

To mend a broken cup with the view to the form of another grail is possible. But what is one to do when there is only a single grail and it is broken? The church is the body of Christ. The body was given once and for all. The event was singular. There are no similar patterns against which to judge it, "to make it right" as it were or, as my Amish Mennonite past supposed, to maintain it in purity, to keep it unsullied from the world. The church is in the world as Christ was in the world, fully reconciling the world to himself. But the church is broken.

And yet, the mere fact of the many broken shards posits the single grail. How can one speak of a single Christianity when historians testify only to christianities? The broken shards drive one to the grail. They shape the wilderness and form the despair as we seek a glimpse of the whole. There is no vision but despair, and the very quest is a presumption. Remaining Mennonite is a conscious act of affirming that denomination as one shard. To leave it is to shout "anathema," but to stay is to live daily with the fear and final anxiety that one day one's more honest, principled, and genuine "fellow-believers" will require one to raise the shout and depart. Whether one has a vision of the whole grail or not, to ride in quest of it is already to leave one's local habitation. And to ride in quest is already to choose a direction for the discovery of the whole outside of the local habitation. To search for a vision of the whole is to reject the proposed vision held by the part.

The shards which remain are only shards, separated from the whole and from their pasts. To seek to become another is to avoid the fact of plurality, of the many pieces which could be assembled in a myriad of sensible forms, but one continues to work toward a single form, presuming it possible to graps it in its perfection while reflecting inadequately on the question of the broader ecumenism, "On remaining Christian." Trapped between presumption and despair no mode of existence is experienced other than that of faith and hope and love. That triune life, seeking to understand the mystery of its own existence, refuses pessimism and develops its optimism in an ever firmer adherence to an imitation of the ironic center of its being: the body of Christ, broken for us.

7

Why I Am a Mennonite

Abraham Friesen

Abraham Friesen, born and raised in Manitoba, teaches Reformation history at the University of California, Santa Barbara. He has published numerous books and articles on Reformation issues, specifically the Anabaptists, Thomas Müntzer, and the Marxist view of the Reformation. He and his wife travel frequently to Winnipeg where their son Eric is studying architecture at the University of Manitoba. During his sabbatical in the fall of 1987, Friesen lectured and did research at the Mennonite Studies Centre, University of Winnipeg.

*I*n the fall of 1957 I had the good fortune to be able to go to Germany for a year's study at the University of Göttingen. I had just completed the third of a four-year honors program in history and German literature at the University of Manitoba. Yet my plans for the future had remained indefinite. I did know one thing, however: physical work was not something I wanted to do for a living. One month at Canada Packers had convinced me of that. Initially, music held the greatest attraction for me, while volleyball, golf, and curling were my main diversions. But because nearly all of the other fellows from my graduating class at the Mennonite Brethren Collegiate Institute (MBCI) in Winnipeg went on to get a university education, I followed suit. It was my good fortune to do so together with my good friend, Victor G. Doerksen, now head of the German Department at the University of Manitoba.

I grew up on a farm just south of Winnipeg, born to parents who had come from Russia in 1926. While my father's family had been able to immigrate intact, my mother was the only member of her family to come to Canada. The rest, because of my grandmother's illness, were forced to migrate to South America. My parents settled near Oak Bluff, Manitoba, today still no more than a hardly noticeable intersection on Highway 3 and the Perimeter Highway that circles the city. We attended the MB Church in Springstein, some thirteen miles away, where my father served as one of several lay ministers. It was there that I was joined to the MB Church at age fourteen, just before leaving for Winnipeg and four years of high school at the MBCI.

In the years that I grew up—the tail end and aftermath of the Second World War—a great deal of anti-German sentiment was abroad. It reached even into the small community we lived in. At home my parents spoke German with us; at church the services were held in German. Had I known of the Mennonite pilgrimage from the Netherlands to Poland during the latter years of the Reformation, or of the later migrations to Russia beginning around 1786, I might have been able to defend myself. I did not, however, and so remained defenseless. I was aware only of the fact that because German was spoken at home and in church I was attacked from time to time in school. How I reacted I no longer recall, but I do know that it warped my attitude toward all things Mennonite in those formative years. I became ashamed of being German and Mennonite because being Mennonite was so closely tied to being German. And being German meant being the enemy of Canada. That did not sit well with me. As a bonus, there was added the natural insecurity of the recent immigrant. All of this left me with very ambivalent feelings about being Mennonite, feelings which—although suppressed during my years at the MBCI—were never resolved. They therefore surfaced again in even more intense form in a heavily Anglo-Saxon environment during my years at the university.

As a consequence, I was more proud of being selected repeatedly as the outstanding player on the University of Manitoba varsity volleyball team during my undergraduate years than for winning a scholarship to study in Germany. I had the good sense to accept the latter nonetheless, leaving for Germany with somewhat mixed emotions. I arrived in Göttingen toward the end of September, settled in, but then was left with a month on my hands until classes were to begin. Before I left Canada, my mother had told me of an uncle of hers in Germany—after some searching she even came up with an address—who had settled there after having come to study early in the century. His name was Abraham Braun. Somewhere I had even read that he was to give the opening address at the Mennonite World Conference to be held in Karlsruhe in 1957. Perhaps he was too "Mennonite" for me! Little did I know! I was later to discover that German Mennonites referred to him affectionately as the "Mennonite pope."

With a month left before classes began and with loneliness quickly setting in, I decided to look up this great uncle of mine and see what the other half of the family was like. At the same time, I said to myself, visiting him in Nierstein on the Rhine would give me an opportunity to see Heidelberg and the Rhine region south of Mainz. (Even country bumpkins from the plains of Manitoba had heard of Heidelberg.) I arrived in Nierstein late one evening totally unannounced. As I stepped from the train the pungent odor of newly pressed wine grapes—which pervaded the moist night air—invaded my tender Mennonite nostrils. Someone at the railroad station, more accustomed to the atmosphere than I, gave me directions and I set out on foot to locate the address.

It was well after nine o'clock when I knocked on the door. The sound of scurrying feet reached my ears and a woman's voice said: "Wer kommt denn so spät?" In a moment the door opened and a woman in her early thirties looked at me. A momentary recognition crossed her face in the dimly lit hallway; it faded, however, upon closer scrutiny. It was Irmgard, my mother's cousin. At first sight she thought I was her brother Christian, returning unannounced from his studies in the United States. But I was not Christian. Nonetheless, that moment of fading recognition told me that I was with family. She invited me in and for the next little while I explained to her and my great uncle where I belonged in the Braun scheme of things. It may have helped that he had been my mother's favorite uncle and that I had been named after him. Without hesitation they accepted me.

During the course of nearly a month that I stayed in Nierstein, I had many opportunities to talk at length with my great uncle about "Mennonite" and related matters. I had never been able to do that with my father. There was an openness about him, a loving acceptance of me with my unresolved tensions that I had not encountered before in Mennonite circles. While he most certainly had the courage of his convictions, he nevertheless possessed a spirit of uncommon breadth. I loved him almost instantly, and he loved me. It became an unspoken bond between us. He became the grandfather to me I had not been privileged to know.

One day, while discussing some aspect of Mennonite life and faith, he looked me squarely in the eye and said: "Someday you too will have to do something for the brotherhood." Since he had given his life to serve the Mennonite cause he had every right to challenge me. But I laughed in response; the "brotherhood" did not hold much meaning for me at the time. By now he was well aware of my attitude, so he responded: "You know, if you intend to throw the whole Mennonite heritage overboard, you should at least do yourself the favor of trying to find out what it is you are rejecting. For what you have encountered as 'Mennonite' may not be the authentic product." The would-be historian in me was cut to the quick. I should have realized this myself! I no longer recall what I mumbled in reply, but I knew I would not soon forget his words.

Upon returning to Manitoba, even though my interests had begun to shift, I completed an M.A. in Canadian History under W. L. Morton. The thesis dealt with the migration of the Old Colony Mennonites to Mexico and South America from Canada after World War I, a relatively safe place to begin my encounter with Mennonite history. Meanwhile, I taught high school at the MBCI, doing penance for the years I had attended there as a student! Already in Germany, however, in response to my great uncle's challenge, I had begun reading in the Renaissance and Reformation, making occasional surreptitious forays into Anabaptist history. The age fascinated me more and more and somewhere along the way I decided to dedicate my life to the study of this era. I was not yet "doing something for the brotherhood," but was I preparing for it? Initially it was Erasmus who attracted me, but the Anabaptists also began to hold my attention. I decided, given the opportunity, to write a doctoral dissertation on "Erasmus and the Anabaptists." To prepare myself ahead of time for that, the summer before I left for Stanford University I spent some time in the Goshen College Historical Library researching the topic.

Thus, by the time I arrived at Stanford in the fall of 1963 to study under Lewis W. Spitz, I had become a Mennonite from conviction. Following Erasmus'—and the Renaissance's—belief that a movement is purest at its source, I had begun to return to the historical source of my faith: I had begun to tread the road back to my spiritual roots. What I discovered there, however, was both inspiring and somewhat troubling. Inspiring were the Swiss Anabaptists with their attempt to establish a voluntary church of "right living" Christians; troubling were Thomas Müntzer and the Münsterite Anabaptists. The first of these, Mennonite scholars sought to keep at arm's length from the "normative" movement; the second, they attempted to explain away as an "aberration." The historian in me rebelled: if the past of my people had its troublesome aspects I had no alternative but to come to grips with them. Otherwise, there was little point to the study of history. Selecting only the inspiring parts of that past would not set me free; only an unbiased understanding of the total picture could do that.

The choice of Stanford and Lewis W. Spitz was a most fortunate one for me. Because it became apparent to me early on that a true understanding of the Anabaptist movement could be achieved only in the broadest of historical contexts, my interests in the sixteenth century had from the beginning been more ecumenical than parochial. And Lewis Spitz provided that context with his magisterial interests in the history of Christian Humanism and the Reformation. Yet it was a class in Modern European Intellectual History by George L. Mosse, visiting from the University of Wisconsin, that turned my attention away from "Erasmus and the Anabaptists" to "Thomas Müntzer in Marxist Thought."

Historiography had begun to interest me during the time I was working on my Master's degree. Books by Herbert Butterfield, Rudolf Bultmann, and others stimulated my thinking on the subject. I became convinced that the historian should know not only how to use his craft, he should also know how others had used it. In a sense, though, the historiographical approach to Thomas Müntzer was a way around dealing with the problem of Müntzer directly; one could, instead, focus on what others had thought of him, tracing how interpretive traditions about him had arisen over time. In the process, however, there were also some very interesting discoveries to be made, especially as I turned to the larger topic of the Marxist interpretation of the Reformation in my doctoral dissertation.

To write the doctoral dissertation I returned to Germany once more, this time to the Institute for European History in Mainz under the direction of the renowned Roman Catholic Church historian, Joseph Lortz. In the meantime my great uncle and his daughter had also moved to Mainz—he being now 83 years of age. They lived only about a block away from the Institute. My wife and I—I had married Gerry Schafer the year before coming to Stanford—were fortunate to find an apartment close to theirs; this allowed us to spend a great deal of time together over the next twenty months. It was precious time, much of it spent discussing Mennonite and related matters.

It was during these twenty months that I really for the first time immersed myself in the primary documents and secondary literature on Anabaptism. Much of the dissertation dealt with the Reformation radicals because the Marxists were so attracted to them. There were a number of reasons for this, I discovered. One was the Marxist acceptance—for their own purposes—of the older Catholic and Protestant interpretation of the radicals as revolutionaries. The other, however, was their recognition that many from among the radicals—for them especially Thomas Müntzer—had sought to reform society. Their affirmation of this pointed to Marx and Engels' own original desire for a more just social order.

While the Marxists took a secularized approach to this problem— witness the secularization of the Holy Spirit in the thought of Thomas Müntzer by Wilhelm Zimmermann, whom Engels used for his reinterpretation of the Reformation—the Reformation radicals, Thomas Müntzer included, had taken a Christian approach. Both, however, believed in the integration of theory and practice. It was for this reason that Marx and Engels' criticism of established Christianity was so severe, as severe as Erasmus and Thomas More's had been in their day. Essentially, what both said was that the church had tailored its theology to accommodate an evil social order; it had become a justifier of the social order rather than a critic. With respect to the Magisterial Reformation, the Anabaptists and Müntzer argued that while Luther and the others had reformed the propositional truths of Christianity, this had not led to a reformed lifestyle. The old dichotomy remained.

Now, I had been brought up on a pretty strict diet of do's and don'ts as a youngster. That there was a little more than a touch of legalism in all this cannot be denied. It was perhaps because of this background that reading Luther on—and others about—his own religious experience had such a liberating effect upon me while at Stanford. Lewis Spitz's enthusiasm for Luther did not hurt either. Luther argued that salvation did not come through human righteousness, but rather through the righteousness of Christ imputed to the believer. Through Christ, God had proferred man the great exchange: in exchange for man's sins he offered man his perfect righteousness. That righteousness alone allowed the sinner to stand in the day of judgment *coram deo*.

On the other hand, however, the Anabaptists had been right as well. Faith without works was dead. "Those who are thus converted," they argued, "have been buried with Adam and baptized in Christ, raised to newness of life, and have a good conscience. And such people may be recognized by the manner in which they express their faith." While Luther stressed the theological content of faith, the Anabaptists stressed its expression. Did emphasizing the first necessarily lead to a neglect of the second, and approaching the problem from the second necessarily lead to legalism? Or was there something else in the equation I was missing?

To this point I had always been able to attend Mennonite church services. When we returned from Germany—and there were now three of us—I took a position at the University of California at Santa Barbara. Perhaps I placed profession above church. In any case, there was no Mennonite church of any kind in Santa Barbara or its environs. Hence we were compelled to look elsewhere. At first we attended a very friendly Baptist church, but the right-wing politics which emanated from the pulpit from time to time did not edify me. Therefore, after six months, we moved to a nondenominational church. Our membership, however, remained in the Mennonite Brethren Church—at first in San Jose, where we had worshiped while attending Stanford, and then, after we became involved in the Center for Mennonite Brethren Studies in Fresno, in the Clovis Community MB Church.

After a number of years in this non-Mennonite church context, two things began to come together for me, convincing me that the Anabaptist-Mennonite position was the only tenable one as far as I was concerned. The first derived from my continuing studies in the Reformation and especially Anabaptist history; the second came from my experiences in the American evangelical churches. Let me begin with the latter. Nearly from the moment we began attending church in Santa Barbara it became apparent to me that the people who attended had little loyalty to any given church. Their loyalty was essentially to themselves. As long as the minister suited them, they stayed. When ministers changed, so did the congregation. Aside from the Magisterial Reformation's concept of the true, the "spiritual" church, there was virtually no concept of what the church was. To be sure there was talk of the "body of believers," but when it came to problems among members of that body, there was rarely any reconciliation. What happened most often was that people simply left to go elsewhere. Furthermore, salvation was considered to be a very personal matter with few, if any, social consequences.

To most, talk of a "Social Gospel" was a Liberal abomination. Adult and infant baptism, too, were practiced at the same time with virtually no awareness of the different concepts of the church each involved. While most of these churches had begun as territorial churches in the age of the Reformation, the separation of church and state in the United States had forced them to become, in effect, voluntary or free churches. Their theologies, however, had remained the theologies of the territorial churches. The whole thing struck me more and more as an anomaly. What was just as bad, as I began to teach classes on the Reformation in the various churches of the city, it quickly became apparent to me that few, if any, even knew why they believed what they did. They had little, if any, knowledge of their spiritual heritage, never mind the changes that had taken place in that heritage since the time of its inception. In effect, they were rootless. And because they were rootless they were easy prey for every new evangelical fad and wind of doctrine that blew across the bows of their rudderless vessels.

It was at this point that a passage in Conrad Grebel's September 1524 letter to Thomas Müntzer became increasingly significant to me. There Grebel argued that the Christian insights arrived at earlier by Zwingli and passed on to them were to be used to transform and reshape the church and society. He therefore wrote:

> In respecting persons and in manifold seduction there is grosser and more pernicious error now than ever has been since the beginning of the world. In the same error we too lingered as long as we heard and read only the evangelical preachers who are to blame for all this, in punishment for our sins. But after we took Scriptures to hand too, and consulted it on many points, we have been instructed somewhat and have discovered the great and harmful error of the shepherds, of ours too, namely, that we do not beseech God earnestly with constant groaning to be brought out of this destruction of all godly life and out of human abominations, *to attain to the true faith and divine practices. The cause of all this is false forbearance, the hiding of the divine Word, and the mixing of it with the human.* Aye, we say it harms all and frustrates all things divine....

The faith of the apostles, they argued, had led to apostolic practices, apostolic ordinances and institutions. There had, in those early years of the church, been a congruence between theology and the way it was expressed, be that in a transformed life, in certain kinds of practices, ordinances, and, yes, even in the way the church itself had been constituted. It was for this reason they were so determined to reestablish the apostolic form of the church. For if the New Testament faith was normative for all time—and everyone said it was— then the forms in which that faith had expressed itself were to be normative as well. The second was a legitimate expression of the faith.

For this reason Zwingli's radical followers rejected his response that "the example of the apostles was not applicable here [in the sixteenth century], for those from whom they [the apostles] withdrew did not confess Christ, but now ours did." They also rejected his argument that Christ had himself addressed new beginnings like theirs, commanding that the "wheat and the tares be allowed to grow until the day of harvest." Since the church had become coterminous with the world, Zwingli, like Augustine long before him, could argue that the field Christ had spoken of in that parable was the church. It had not been so in Christ's time, however. For he had clearly informed his disciples that "the field is the world."

The Magisterial Reformers had attempted to press a new theology into the old medieval forms of Christianity, ignoring the great changes that had taken place in the church after Constantine. But this could only be done by spiritualizing Christianity and making it so individualistic that the external forms did not matter. To a large extent the great Augustine, with his Neoplatonic view of the church as constantly in the process of becoming and his interpretation of the parable of the tares, which he used to justify an increasingly corrupt Roman Catholic Church against Donatist attacks, had been the rationalizer of this position. Theological content, as a consequence, as Desiderius Erasmus and Thomas More both clearly saw, had gradually come to be accommodated to an evil world. Erasmus put it this way in his *Enchiridion* of 1502:

> ... Yet we are living in a world that has grown alien to the world of Christ both in doctrine and in practice....
> Too many of our theologians and teachers only make this matter

worse by adapting the words of Scripture to the justification of their own crimes. In truth Scripture should be a source of that norm of behavior that can correct them. . . .

Erasmus argued that this situation had arisen because the "church" had become confused with the "world." In the same piece he remarked:

> . . . There are too many who think that the expression "world" refers only to those who have embraced the monastic state. In the Gospels, for the Apostles, and for Augustine, Ambrose, and Jerome, the expression means the infidel, enemies of the faith and of the Cross of Christ. It consists of all those who place their care in tomorrow, who strive after riches and sensible pleasures. This world has not known Christ who is the true light of the world. It was from this world that Christ separated not only His Apostles, but all men who would be worthy of Him. How then can we say that this world, everywhere condemned in Scripture, should be associated with Christendom and in its name flatter and maintain our own vices?

Precisely for this reason the Anabaptist attempt to integrate a cleansed apostolic theology with the original form of the apostolic church is so important. They realized that the external forms of Christianity are not irrelevant, as Zwingli asserted. Form must be brought into conformity with content; practice must be congruent with theology. They cannot be held in tension, nor may one regard the forms as indifferent to the faith. They are never irrelevant. Indeed, as Erasmus argued, the forms may well come, in time, to determine the content of theology.

It was this struggle to integrate not only faith and action in a new discipleship, but also apostolic faith with apostolic practice, that was critical. In the past ten years or so this latter aspect has become of central importance to me. The American evangelical churches, heirs to the Magisterial Reformation in this respect, have never done this. Therefore, if we as Mennonites move in their direction with respect to the external forms of Christian practice—and to a certain extent we have already done so—we must inevitably fall prey to their theological tendencies. Rather than move in an evangelical direction, we need rather to return to the Anabaptist model, remove from it those elements that still need removing, and clarify those where they saw only dimly.

In their central concern, however, I regard them as having been right on target. Theological content and the forms in which it is expressed must be congruent. Disastrous consequences will occur if they are not. Discipleship is the personal integration of faith in one's life; that same integration must take place on a corporate level in the experience of the Christian life of the church. The Anabaptists recognized this and church history confirms their judgment. That is why being a Mennonite is important, and that is why I am a Mennonite.

8

Being Mennonite: A Gift and a Choice

John Friesen

John Friesen, a native of Manitoba, teaches history and Mennonite studies at Canadian Mennonite Bible College in Winnipeg, Manitoba. He grew up in a Mennonite community in southern Manitoba in which he formed his first impressions of Mennonite peoplehood and faith commitments. Into this world, in the 1950s, came revivalists, evangelical preachers, urging Mennonites to become "saved." John was both attracted and repelled by these evangelists' methods. "Summer after summer I agonized through the campaigns, refusing to go down the sawdust trail, and yet guilt-ridden for not doing so." He found a "better way" during his studies at Mennonite and other institutions.

Why am I Mennonite? I teach at a Mennonite college, am a member of a Mennonite church, serve on several committees within the Mennonite community, and interpret Mennonite history and identity in the classroom and in print. Most of the time I do not reflect on why I am Mennonite. I am busy being Mennonite.

Thinking about why I am Mennonite causes a flood of feelings, memories of experiences, dreams, and anxieties. I remember my childhood and youth in southern Manitoba, the one-room grade school, life on the farm, the regular farm cycle of seeding and harvesting, playing in a southern Manitoba softball league, attending family gatherings, and singing in the community-wide *Saengerfests*. I was enveloped in a stable, secure Mennonite world of many relatives, close neighbors, and the church.

When I try to analyze the factors which influenced my being and remaining Mennonite, I find that being Mennonite, for me, is more due to a historical process than to a logical or rational deliberation. When I faced issues of identity, when I tried to sort out who I was and what I wanted to become, I did not begin from a neutral position. I was already in the stream of history, with my roots in a particular community. Consequently, an important factor for me being Mennonite was that I was born into a Mennonite home, grew up in a Mennonite community, and discovered my first conscious religious ideas within a Mennonite setting. In a real sense my being Mennonite was a gift. It was not earned, nor chosen, but given. Even though this factor is a truism, and ought to be self-evident, its significance for my own self-identity had to be discovered.

Being born within a Mennonite community gave me a feeling of being part of a people. To be Mennonite was to be part of a large community. In my early experience this predominantly Mennonite community included the people I met in family, church, school, and business, and extended to include people in neighboring towns and villages. This peoplehood within which I felt included was not defined by church affiliation. The peoplehood included people who belonged to numerous Mennonite churches, but the feeling of unity was much stronger than the divisions suggested by church affiliation. This sense of unity and inclusion was strong enough to include even those Mennonites who had joined non-Mennonite churches. This sense of being part of one larger Mennonite community was especially reinforced in the one-room rural school experience. The picnics, Christmas programs, and 4-H-sponsored public meetings helped to create and sustain the sense of unity.

Not only did this sense of peoplehood have very little Mennonite denominational identity, it also had very little theological or historical content. During my early years I do not remember any significant emphasis on the uniqueness of Mennonite theology. I do not remember ever hearing the term "Anabaptist." It was generally known that the forebears of the people in the community had emigrated from Russia sometime in the past. Beyond that, the only reference I can remember being made to Mennonite beginnings, was that Mennonites had probably originated from the medieval sect known as Waldensians. During my teens I tried to find more information about the roots of my community, but the only book I could find in the local bookstore was one dusty copy of C. Henry Smith's *Mennonites in Europe*. The feeling of peoplehood was not shaped by any common, well-defined, articulated Mennonite theology or knowledge of historical roots.

It should, however, not be concluded that the Mennonitism I grew up in was largely or merely cultural. At an early age I noticed that my parents, grandparents, relatives, and many neighbors exhibited very deep religious convictions. Their commitment to God, to the church, and to the Christian way of life was anything but formal and external. It was thoroughly internalized. The people's religious convictions were not articulated theologically, nor verbalized through personal testimonies. Their convictions were, rather, expressed through their lifestyle. Many people exhibited a strong sense of honesty, willingness to share time and farm machinery, and a commitment to peaceful resolution of conflict.

At an early age I was taught by word and by example that in a conflict situation, it is best to resolve the problem peacefully even if you yourself have to absorb a loss. In regards to war, I learned that my community considered war evil. My father and uncles refused military service during the Second World War. I noticed, however, that some Mennonite young men joined the armed forces in both the Second World War and in the Korean War. I saw my family's and my community's disapproval on this way of life, and in the faces of the young men I saw their defiance of the values of home and community.

There was a sense of exclusiveness in the Mennonite experience of peoplehood within which I was nurtured. In the Mennonite Low German expressions of the day, Mennonites were referred to as "one of ours," non-Mennonites as "someone else." Frequently, these references were used in regard to the choice of marriage partners. There was both a positive and a negative side to this differentiation of people. The negative side was that everyone non-Mennonite was given a negative connotation. In reference to marriage, for example, the implication was that it was preferable to marry a Mennonite. This feeling of exclusiveness helped to create, at least in the minds of some, an isolationist attitude which frequently was accompanied by a feeling of superiority.

The feelings of superiority were largely based on lack of knowledge of and acquaintance with people from outside the immediate Mennonite community. On the positive side, since the group had developed a strong sense of identity and group cohesion, it also shared this strong "in" feeling. Being referred to as "one of ours" was the result of a sense of peoplehood. It often seemed to me, though, that somehow it should be possible to develop a strong sense of group loyalty and identity without creating negative feelings toward those outside the group.

Another influence on my being Mennonite was the injection of revivalism into southern Manitoba. Actually, my Mennonite world had already absorbed a lot of revivalism which at the time I did not recognize as such. To me these characteristics were simply Mennonite. The moral standards of my home and community, according to which smoking, drinking, dancing, and card-playing were considered sinful, were at least party due to the influence of revivalism. The Rudnerweide Mennonite Church, itself a product of revivalism during the 1930s, also influenced my religious views. The Rudnerweide Church's Aeltester lived in my school district and he had the closing comments and prayer at every Christmas program. My own church home was the Bergthaler Church, and the Aeltester David Schulz certainly evidenced the influence of a warm pietism in his preaching and pastoral care.

The coming of the revivalists into southern Manitoba in the 1950s, the community-wide meetings, the big tents in the cow pastures, the annual repetition of these revivals, and the styling of these events as "campaigns"—all this injected a new dimension to my religious life. I was both attracted and repelled by these events. I was attracted because all churchgoing people in the sponsoring churches were admonished to attend. I consequently tried hard to apply the messages by the evangelists to my personal life. I was repelled, however, by both the content and the methods of the evangelists and found it hard to find anything of enduring value in them. Summer after summer I agonized through the campaigns, refusing to go down the sawdust trail, and yet guilt-ridden for not doing so.

The effect on me was a rejection of this approach to being Christian and to this method of calling people to faith. Even though I could not articulate my feelings at the time, I was uneasy about the way these campaigns were tearing the fabric of the Mennonite community apart. No longer were we together as a people searching for Christian faithfulness. Rather, in these campaigns one faction was set against another Mennonite faction. The one faction consisted of those churches which participated in the campaigns. Their leaders sat on the stage, mute, but on display, as the evangelists flailed at their audiences. The other faction consisted of those churches whose leaders were not on stage, who by their absence were being judged as not Christian. It was partly for them that the campaigns were being organized so that they too could find salvation. The more frequently this scenario was performed, the more uneasy I became with the implications and the effects.

The campaigns did cause me to do some soul searching. Due at least in part to their influence, I decided to enter theological studies.

To some extent, I was motivated to find a better way than was being exemplified by these annual campaigns.

A strong influence on my being Mennonite was my post-secondary educational experience. My college experience provided the bridge from the intellectually narrower world of my early years, to the larger world of philosophy, literature, and religious studies. The boundaries of my world expanded as I experienced an exhilarating liberation that can probably be experienced only once in a lifetime. During my seminary studies I probed the theological content of the Anabaptist-Mennonite heritage. Here I began to perceive more fully the theological significance of a heritage which in my earlier years I had absorbed and lived, but about which I had reflected very little. Intellectually, though, I found this phase of my studies restricting and defensive. For some reason the freedom boldly to explore and to think new thoughts seemed to be difficult in the studies which probed Mennonite roots. During my graduate studies, in which I was in a non-Mennonite setting, I was forced repeatedly to interpret and defend Mennonite approaches to various issues like peace and war, the church, and discipleship. It was in this setting that I became more firmly convinced of the strengths of my own heritage than ever before.

During my graduate studies in the United States I experienced both the civil rights movement in which blacks were trying to achieve greater social and economic equality, and the antiwar movement in which U.S. citizens were trying to influence government military policy. Intertwined in both of these movements were the issues of peace and equality. For me it seemed that these were also issues which the Anabaptist-Mennonite heritage had believed and tried to practice. I began to see a new vision for the contribution that the Mennonite community could make in today's world. At the same time I was aware that the Mennonite communities frequently fell short of practicing economic and racial equality, or sharing of time and resources, or creating peace, or being reconcilers. And yet, despite the shortcomings, the emphases were there in the heritage, and I felt they could form a basis for addressing issues in our society.

When I was invited to teach at CMBC, my perception of myself within the Mennonite world changed. By accepting the appointment to teach I became part of a Mennonite institution. I was no longer a critic on the fringes, I now perceived the life of the Mennonite community from within an institutional structure. One of the strongest influences on me during the teaching years was the experience of annually teaching Mennonite history and beliefs to college undergraduates. I usually team-taught the course, and the annual analyses and reevaluation of Mennonite identity and history with a colleague and students has been stimulating and invigorating. I became aware that many in the Mennonite community considered history as dead and best forgotten. In my teaching, though, I discovered within the experiences of the Mennonite forebears a vitality, a residual, formative, creative force. This force, I became convinced, could have a continuing, shaping influence in the present and in the future. In my classes I tried to communicate this to my students and was excited when they caught this insight.

My family and I have been involved in a local congregation in Winnipeg. The experiences in this congregation have been complementary to my teaching. The congregation has been a context for experiencing the support of a community of people. The congregation has also been a setting for working through many of the issues of what is involved in being Mennonite in an urban world.

In my present view of myself as Mennonite I acknowledge the continuing influence of my Mennonite upbringing. It provides me with my roots, my sense of "place" in the community of ethnic groups, and a feeling of belonging to a people. Through the years I have come to see that what gave this community its reason to be, its purpose, its drive, were certain convictions or values. These values could be summarized as belief in God, a commitment to a life of peace, a desire to live simply, a conviction that Christian faith must be freely accepted and ought not to be forced or manipulated through physical, psychological, or social coercion, and a belief that the essential values of life lie in establishing supportive relationships among people—in other words, community.

To anyone familiar with Mennonite history, it is evident that Mennonites have not nearly always lived up to their own lofty ideals. Whether we look at the origin of Anabaptism in the sixteenth century, or the experiences of Mennonites in Poland, Switzerland, Austria, Germany, Russia, USA, Canada, or Latin America, from the sixteenth century to the present, the Mennonite experience has been a struggle between noble ideals and human frailties. Instead of allowing people freedom, social or psychological pressure has frequently been applied to young and old. Instead of economic sharing, competition and greed frequently destroyed relationships. Instead of living lives of peace, physical violence has been used to protect life and property, or psychological violence has been directed against the prophets and nonconformists. Instead of creating supportive communities, individualism and selfishness have frequently dominated.

Despite what seem glaring weaknesses in every age of Mennonite experience, there are also strengths. It is these strengths which have attracted me and have given me the confidence that the ideals of the Mennonite heritage have enduring value. When I see hundreds and even thousands of people responding to MCC and MDS appeals for people to share time, money, and expertise, then I feel that the ideals of selfless giving, sharing, and community are still alive within our people. When I see Mennonite churches rallying to sponsor thousands of refugees, refugees who speak strange languages and have different customs, then I feel we are able to reach beyond our ethnic boundaries to be a brother and sister to people from other cultures. When I see some Mennonite businesspeople struggling to develop new patterns of employer-employee relationships in which confrontation can be replaced by negotiation and a sense of common purpose between management and worker, then I feel that the Mennonite belief in mutual support, financial sharing, and community can survive even in a capitalist society. When I see artists, writers, and scholars critically probing the Mennonite psyche, and consequently causing us to laugh at ourselves, or scorning our shams, and our hypocrisies, then I feel honesty and integrity have the possibility of not only surviving in community, but reshaping it into something more wholesome.

So why do I continue to be Mennonite? I continue to be Mennonite because within this historical community it has been possible for me to find those values, relationships, and ideals which I think make life worth living. This is not to say that these values could not be found within other heritages. I am sure they can be found by other people in their own heritage. However, I have been given this heritage, and it is within this heritage that I feel I can continue to find that which is of value.

9

I Could Have Been Born in Spain

Patrick Friesen

Patrick Friesen was born and raised in Steinbach, Manitoba. He attended the University of Manitoba, studying English literature, and later worked as a television producer for the Manitoba Department of Education. He is the founding president of the Manitoba Writer's Guild. His published collections of poems include blue-bottle, The Shunning, and Unearthly Horses. The Shunning was adapted successfully as a stage play.

1

I was born into this. I could have been born in Spain. Barce-
lona maybe, or Seville. If the winds had shifted that night. Or Ireland. When I was 11 or 12 I thought I must have been an Irish foun-
dling. I had the name.

Mother told stories of gypsies who traveled through Altona in small
caravans each year. At night she sang me to sleep with Irish ballads.
She named me.

Father's mother died when he was four. He lost the sight of his
right eye before he was ten. Father used to like Wilf Carter. I think he
even owned a guitar. He stopped listening to that kind of music when
he was saved.

2

It was in a field, trees nearby and behind them, you could hear a
small river. It was a Sunday school picnic. Mother stood at a long
table with other women. They were making *klik* sandwiches and po-
tato salad. They were talking in Low German. Stories of the week,
humorous things they had seen or done. Some talked more than
others. Mrs. P. D. Friesen had the greatest laugh I'd ever heard.

I stood beside Mother. If only I hadn't had to wear that stiff white
shirt, everything would have been fine. A blue sky, soft breeze and all
that familiar talk. I was drinking a glass of lemon-lime Kool-Aid.

Men stood a little way off, at the edge of the trees. A few leaned
against willow and sugar trees. Most stood erect, arms across their
chests. They wore white shirts with the sleeves rolled up. I couldn't
hear what they were talking about.

It was funny how the men stood side by side talking straight ahead.

I think they talked face-to-face during the week. The women were usually in groups. Around tables, around bowls, around the house.

3

I squirmed in the pew, wishing to be outdoors. I learned subversion here.

With friends, I whispered behind my hand, or ducked my head behind the pew, suppressing laughter. We made sly comments about ministers and many-armed song leaders. We jeered at strange flowered hats and ugly, brown or black clothes.

Sometimes everyone stood to sing. Occasionally this was deeply moving. Sometimes everyone got down and kneeled to pray. Once, I remember, someone a few rows away broke wind. Whoever it was, this person was trying to keep it in, you could tell, because what emerged was a long pinched squeal.

I loved the maps at the back of the Bible. I spent many Sunday mornings poring over the names and shapes and colors of these maps. I saw where Jesus walked on water, where Mary Magdalene found the open tomb.

When the words in the air weren't dead, you could usually hear anger beneath them; the kind of suppressed anger that judges and seeks vengeance on all unbelievers. I often heard the word "love," but it never felt like love. I wondered why, because outside of church love was much easier to find.

I loved Revelation. I loved the candles and horses, the river and the trumpets. I loved the whore of Babylon arrayed in purple and scarlet. She had to be magnificent. I thought she was voluptuous and beyond yes and no.

I liked to think I would be safe at the end of the world. I knew there was another life to be lived. The kingdom was within each of us. Then, when I learned heaven was outside someplace, and I, and most other people, had no right to claim it, Revelation became terrifying. It was a threat, a punishment.

Revival meetings were my blast furnaces. Here I learned to conceal emotions. I learned to play tough. I remember the choreography. The frightening sermon, the tear-jerking hymns, altar call, the men watching from the back of the church, or from the platform in front, watching for signs of personal turmoil, watching, then moving toward some troubled person, arm around his or her shoulder, whispering into that torment, cajoling, pushing. . . .

I think most gave in out of fear. Some grew hard. Or, you became sly; skipping, stumbling, lying, cursing, laughing toward a distant day of freedom.

Those voodoo evenings of spiritual violence. No matter what choices were made, how many survived with their spirits full and rejoicing?

4

When I was young, I loved the stories missionaries brought back with them. I soon realized that, although I enjoyed the stories, I didn't like what the missionaries were doing to the people they went to live with.

It seemed unfair to intrude on people in other countries and put the pressure on them to drop their religions and cultures and pick up the new sanctified ones. As if only people who called themselves Christian (who rejected other branches of Christianity) had a monopoly on wisdom and on what led to wisdom.

Like other cause-obsessed people, it seemed missionaries, generally, projected onto others the shadows they could not accept in themselves. So, they went out to war against a mirror. And we, afraid of our own shadows, urged them on.

Today I think about Africans and South Americans who can't find work in their pseudo-Western societies, who don't know anymore what they are, as the new society rejects them, and they can no longer return to what they were.

These, compared to the oilmen and the military, were the soft armies. Wearing their pith helmets and safari shirts. They brought the Word, as they understood it, and this Word fell like a sledge on delicate old worlds.

5

When father was going blind, with bandages on his good eye, he would identify birds I couldn't even hear. He named them as they flew over or hopped among the tomatoes. I thought the birds were in his head; his head an open field where robins tugged at worms and sparrows fell.

Father shot left-handed because of his blind eye. It was confusing, at first, when he taught me to shoot. I would line up my shot but, automatically, close my right eye, as if I was aiming left. I learned to shoot well. Father and I shooting in different directions.

I shot right-handed in hockey, too. I was proud because Gordie Howe was a right-hander. I think the Rocket was as well, but I had learned to fear him.

Father would let me listen to the first two periods of hockey on the Saturday night radio. Then, I had to go to bed. He would turn the radio up just slightly so I could hear the last period from my bed.

The last minute of a game, with Montreal down by a goal, was all the drama I could hope to experience. Father would shift into a kind of terror. "Now they've pulled their goalie, Plante is out, those Frenchmen, those Frenchmen will score for sure. They stick together, they get all heated up, and when they need to get a goal, they always get it."

Father was a Toronto Maple Leafs fan. I liked the Detroit Red Wings.

I played hockey until I was 12. Father would come to some of my games, not all of them. He rationed the number of games he watched because he loved hockey so much. He thought he should control what could easily become an addiction. He didn't shout like a lot of fathers do now.

He was a stark figure standing on a snowbank behind the boards. If I scored, and glanced at him, he would be looking somewhere else.

I knew he was proud inside. I learned not to turn to him.

6

If I met a Mennonite on, say, 4th St. in New York (I would be able to tell by the walk), I would say, "Hey, I know you; let's go and talk."

Then we would go to the corner bar or restaurant and find out who our relatives are and how, exactly, each of us is lost.

7

Choirs can be magnificent. You can lose yourself in a choir; both as a member of it, and as one of the audience. Although solos can go dismally wrong, they touch me in a way choirs can't. Solos are not social. They are high risk. They don't fool you. A choir can fool you.

8

I would be happy to remove guilt from my human lexicon. Maybe next time.

9

I was about seventeen. Ralph and I were talking theology. I must have been in an obnoxious mood. I said that maybe hell existed. Ralph got very angry at this. He wasn't angry about my believing in hell; he knew I didn't really believe that. It was my "againstness," how I had to be "other."

There is a Low German word for this. It says something about me.

Later, it may have been the same day, I grabbed Ralph's hat and threw it into a tree. He grabbed mine and threw it too. We laughed.

10

I confess I touched myself. Someone said I would be short.

I confess I thought of making love. I imagined it. I longed for it. I didn't long for moral perfection nearly as much.

I wanted to talk all night with a woman and fall asleep in her bed. I wanted to travel with her.

I wanted to ravish her, and I wanted her to ravish me.

I heard of an old dying man in the town hospital who disgusted his children by touching himself beneath the sheets when he thought they had left.

I confess I am a kind of virgin, again and again. This is one way I am renewed. It is how I become part of another; it is how I am myself. There is nothing new here. It is one of the ways I worship.

I confess I love life in spite of what I often am. There is something insatiable beneath my routine. Maybe, one day, I'll pick all the locks.

11

I have learned this: when I say "you," I might mean someone I am addressing, or I might mean my lover, god, or my children. When I say "I," I might mean the same thing I mean when I say "you."

12

Menno, I've got an angel in my ear she's talking everything holy the willow and lamp the cat watching from the shed roof.

13

Ralph and I used to visit, occasionally, with a member of our home church. He must have been maybe eight years older than us. We could talk about anything with him. He had a marvelous library.

I borrowed *The Dynamics of Faith* by Paul Tillich. I had never read anything like that before. A landmark for me. I think I first read Kierkegaard here, as well. I didn't enjoy him much. The lack of interest was because I didn't feel any connection with his mind.

Thinking about it, now, I know I had a similar reaction to writers like Sartre and, at least partially, to Kafka. I wondered what it was that held them back. As if each of them came to a barrier on the street and spent the rest of their lives playing on it.

I did enjoy some of Kafka's short stories. "The Country Physician" was crazy, and it struck home. I loved the horses looking in at the window.

Although I first read Graham Greene's *Brighton Rock* in this library, I read primarily nonfiction. Buber, a little Bonhoeffer, various German philosophers, writings by, or about, people like Bakunin, and so on.

At the time many of these books were fresh, friendly breezes to me. There were so many possibilities. One could do wonderful things with the mind. When hitched to feelings and desire in a young man, it seemed ideas could go anywhere. I was eclectic and never learned to separate out the systems these writers might have. I took what I wanted, an idea, a series of ideas, an image, a word even, and I fused it all together. It made sense to me.

I guess some of these writers, especially philosophers, eventually made me laugh. I wondered how they could claim to be utterly objective, how they could say their lives were somehow separate from the linguistic products of their minds. Poets, usually, didn't bother with that kind of schizophrenia.

Gerard Manley Hopkins' "Carrion Comfort" left me stunned.

Our friend was a compassionate man with a fine intellect. I learned from the books in his library but, more importantly, I learned from him. I think I am only beginning to apply some of his lessons; how to let the ego have its place, but its place only; how to tolerate the worst, as well as the best, in people; maybe, how to slough off words like "worst" and "best."

He kept his fairly serious difference with the church private. When we asked why, he said he believed in the brotherhood. He was not better than the next man, he said. He didn't have a corner on truth, and there was much to be gained in submitting oneself to a union of fellow believers.

I guess I never fully understood this. Still, I had great respect for him.

14

A Zen master once told a student who was busy "being right" by quoting the Buddha to shit on the head of Buddha. This was not to be done with any hostility, but with affection.

15

I love those voices that talk of the real world, not the one we have manufactured out of ideas, authority, and arrogance. That world has its barking voices, its reason, and its icons. But I love those voices that will not be committed to any cause but continue to speak what no one speaks and hold sacred the world that falls in the cracks.

Until they are silent.

16

I have been ashamed of my heritage. I have been proud. I have been confused by this heritage. What is it? What was it? Why, given their spiritual and social heritage, do most North American Mennonites appear to be socially conservative, materialistic, and nonpacifist? What about the Mennonite terrorist the West German police shot? Was she the truest Mennonite? Was she our shadow?

Religiously I'm not Mennonite. In other important ways I am. Some days I feel Mennonite, other days not. It doesn't really matter.

I was born into this. I could have been born elsewhere to different people. That's how it goes. I could have been born in Spain.

10

From the Cloakroom to the Lecture Hall

Hans-Jürgen Goertz

Hans-Jürgen Goertz was a pastor of the Mennonite church in Hamburg, West Germany, and at present teaches history and sociology at the University of Hamburg. Of West-Prussian Mennonite background, he has been a leader in reinterpreting Anabaptist-Mennonite history, emphasizing the anticlericalism among the early Anabaptists and the "multiple origins" of the Anabaptist movement. He has published numerous books and articles and is a coeditor of Mennonitische Geschichtsblätter, *a German-Mennonite journal.*

I do not know what caused the editor of this volume to put the question to me: "Why are you a Mennonite?" It was not concern about the welfare of my soul which brought on a request for me to re-think the ecclesiastical-confessional basis of my existence. We don't know each other well enough to have taken such a brotherly responsi- bility for one another. He must have had something else in mind. Perhaps he is bothered by the thought that Mennonitism is gradually losing its power to attract persons and to hold them together, to fill their lives with meaning, and he might be trying to discover how others with similar feelings come to terms with this experience—as an orientation and a comfort for all concerned.

This kind of experience was foreign to our parents and grandparents. I am thinking about the West-Prussian churches which are my background. There were indeed occasional black sheep which broke out of the fold or were thrown out: misbegotten sons, ec- centrics, and others whose careers led them out into the world and not back. But in the main our fathers and grandfathers had no prob- lems with their church. They harnessed up to go to the church ser- vice, listened to the preacher, and looked forward to the time spent in the cloakroom. Not much has been written as yet about the cloak- room, and yet it was an important place. Here they laughed and cried, joked and comforted one another. Here fathers watched for suitable mates for their sons; mothers critically assessed potential sons-in-law; boys and girls formed their first tender attachments. Here hog prices were discussed alongside reflections on how well Ohm Reimer and Ohm Thiessen had presented the Word of God to the consciences of the congregation. In such an atmosphere and in the course of centuries the sacred and profane had thus been mixed, creating a comfortable milieu in which almost everyone felt at home. The cloakroom was a symbol of this Mennonite coziness.

Unfortunately I was not able to experience this cloakroom atmosphere at firsthand. When that was still in full sway among the Mennonites I was of preschool age. I don't even know whether my parents had attended church at all with their children. Our family lived apart from the Mennonite congregations, in the diaspora so to speak, and my parents belonged to those upwardly mobile persons who put the books *Mein Kampf, Werewolf,* and *Volk ohne Raum* on their bookshelves. They are still recognizable on an old yellowed photograph of the sitting room interior. Presumably these books were not read; the administrator of the government estate in occupied Poland had other things to do. Neither was it opportune to attend church. It is interesting, though, that when all manner of things— necessary and unnecessary—were loaded onto the wagons for the trek to the west in the cold January days of 1945 those books remained behind. But what was taken along were the memories of Mennonite life along the Vistula. That is what we heard about in the long refugee conversations and it is from these that I know of the cloakroom and its meaning.

The first Bible stories that I can remember I had heard before that flight. An aunt, who was recovering from a serious illness in the country, told them to me and my brother and sister. She was active in a Lutheran kindergarten and close to the position of the "Confessing Church," a movement opposed to the Nazi regime. It was not easy for her at that time to take her stand on a West-Prussian estate. She had to endure derision and make some concessions. Perhaps the crest of the Hitler Youth which she gave to me was one such concession. My pride in possessing this crest was short-lived and became a source of pain for me; a Hitler Youth saw it on my shirt, tore it off, and gave me a severe beating. I was still too young to decorate myself with this symbol of a youth dedicated to the Führer. The son of the "Panje" (Lord or Sir) was beaten up by a Pole. He was called "Bienek" and hated me. I cannot remember my own feelings about this. I wanted to belong—and was not allowed to. A strange little martyrdom!

After the end of the war we lived in a little village on the edge of the Lüneburg Heath. Only occasionally a formerly West-Prussian

Mennonite minister would come along and gather the scattered sheep for an improvised church service in the living room. Here I sensed something of the atmosphere of the peasant religiosity of the Vistula Mennonites: a crude biblicism and worship without pathos or ceremony.

We naturally attended the services of the Lutheran village church. This church was of the Wilhelminian Era, countryside brick gothic; its bright windows, the crucifix over the altar, the power of the organ and the small stern superintendent, who also came from the east and bore a Polish name—these attracted us. And here were the clerical collar and robe; here were rhetoric, pathos, and ceremony!

This superintendent took me into the discipline of his confirmation instruction. Of course he had problems with an unbaptized "heathen" like me. In these classes I learned Bible verses and songs. Soon I knew the lesser and greater prophets and I could rattle off the names of the evangelists and the Pauline letters. But after this instruction I was baptized by a Mennonite elder, who had to come to our town for this purpose. He was a friend of my grandfather and had officiated at my parents' wedding. I had to learn the questions and answers of an old Mennonite catechism which he conscientiously had me recite and he was able to communicate the Golgotha-seriousness of baptism to me. Dying with Christ has remained more deeply impressed on my memory than resurrection with the Lord. In the Epistle to the Romans Paul speaks of both. In the Lutheran Church I learned something about the communal nature of the Christian faith; in the Mennonite baptismal service I learned something about the singularity of Christian existence. According to the textbooks of the two confessional doctrines, the order should have been reversed.

This determined a confessional double life for me. This kind of life was influenced in the first instance by sporadic retreats of North German youth groups which were often under the psychological influence and pressure of North American evangelists, who were attempting to "re-educate" German Mennonite youth in the direction of revivalist fundamentalism. This most probably did not do permanent harm to me but rather fed and strengthened a renewed consciousness of the singularity of the Christian existence. At the same time I was given food for thought by the sermons in the Lutheran church in the town to which we had moved and I was fascinated by the intelligent religious instruction offered at the high school there. That instruction took a critical approach, which in turn made it easy for me to choose to study Protestant theology at the university.

There I was quickly drawn into the controversy which had arisen concerning "existential theology." Although I had spent a semester at Tabor College in Kansas, the academic capital of Mennonite Pietism in North America, I was not immune to the effects of modern theology. On the contrary: I had returned to Germany disappointed by some bigoted characteristics of Mennonite Pietism and I opened myself to the program of demythologizing, a program which represented a symbiosis of theological liberalism, dialectical theology, and philosophical existentialism which was opaque to students. What a confusion of ideas we had to deal with! We needed to acquire the tools of theology and at the same time we were supposed to take sides in matters of ultimate importance. This was an impossible demand. In such situations one needs teachers who can be trusted. For me these were the so-called Bultmann-Schüler and those systematic theologians who had withdrawn from confessionalistic theology and were in conversation with philosophy, literature, and art.

These studies had estranged me from the reigning spirit of the Mennonite world. But together with other Mennonite students of theology I kept in touch with our congregations. We spoke up at youth meetings and camps and tried to apply with missionary zeal among our Mennonite people what we had ingested in the lecture hall but certainly had not digested. Experienced ministers and elders, primarily from South Germany and Switzerland, from France and North America, felt themselves challenged and consequently put us in our place.

They discussed with us, though often not with us so much as against a Modernism which they knew less from their own reading than from conservative polemics. The cloudy rationality of the students clashed with the prejudiced irritability of the preachers. Such discussions were doomed to failure. In hindsight I regret that almost no one among the elders had the pedagogical wisdom to look upon the new theological development among the young people with forbearance. We matured without Mennonite fathers and were suspected of heresy. But these bitter discussions had a good side.

They were a field on which we measured our strength while keeping in touch with our congregations—as unloved but not as lost sons.

As the end of my studies beckoned, the question became acute: should I seek theological work in the Mennonite world or should I change denominations? In that situation I made significant contact with North American doctoral students who were writing dissertations on the Anabaptists at various universities and were in conversation with theologians of the state churches about the peace question, including our own teachers. They dealt with Anabaptism in such a way that it could provide arguments for the discussion of peace and war and the ecumenical dialogue in the churches of today. This gave me a new impetus and caused my doubts about my confessional membership to fade. The proclamations of the evangelical (state church) theology were no longer strong enough to justify a separation from the Mennonite church.

The topic of my dissertation at Göttingen was, however, not on the Anabaptists. I felt that the danger of its being affected by my own theological predisposition was too great and so I chose a subject that belonged neither to Anabaptism nor Lutheranism but had a relationship to both: the theology of Thomas Müntzer. The philosopher Ernst Bloch, to whom I am grateful for valuable suggestions, has called him the "rebel in Christ." I was interested in how Müntzer absorbed the social challenge of his day theologically and developed it into a "theology of revolution." A few years later the theology of revolution was discussed around the world, although that discussion had other roots.

I could not have anticipated that I was preparing myself for that discussion and that I was on a theological path which enabled me to open myself to the social and political concerns which during the sixties became the order of the day in church and society. Increasingly I moved to the "left," strengthened and supported by my acquaintance and later friendship with Johannes Harder, who in those years began to carry the message of "religious socialism" into the Mennonite world.

By this time the Mennonite congregation at Hamburg and Altona had offered me the position of minister in this city church of long tradition. This congregation was enlightened if not "liberal" and I accepted the invitation. It was easy to combine the exegesis of Scripture that I had learned in the theological faculty with a confident representation of the Anabaptist-Mennonite tradition in my public work. At the same time I was able to continue the confessional double-life to which I seemed predestined, although certain elements of the Anabaptist tradition and ideas about the then contemporary Mennonite situation asserted themselves more strongly. But without this double source of inspiration I would have become a minister "of the sad variety."

I was fulfilled by my church work and I found a resonance even though I began to raise problems which are usually not discussed in this context. One such problem was the notorious *Ostdenkschrift*, a proposal of the Protestant German state church which attempted a reconciliation with our Polish neighbor before this became a political initiative. This document understandably aroused some strong reaction in a congregation which consisted largely of refugees from the eastern territories. It was a great deal to expect that such people would give up legal claims to what had been their homeland. Other problems were caused by the fact that I invited a black civil rights activist from the Mennonite group in Chicago to preach a particularly well-publicized sermon. One member left the church in protest; he could not accept a black behind a Mennonite pulpit. I also began to formulate thoughts about the position of the Mennonites in the Third Reich—not always with elegance or empathy, but honestly nevertheless.

Within that congregation it was possible to put aside misunderstanding which necessarily arose and to heal wounds by preaching, singing, and prayer. This was more difficult in the wider Mennonite world. For a number of years I was entrusted with the editorship of an international Mennonite church paper. Here too I tried, with the support of likeminded friends, to achieve an opening in the Mennonite public for discussion of topics in theology, politics, and society. If the Mennonites were truly a faith community with spiritual resources for the whole person, then it would be necessary to be able to speak about everything. But this thinking ran into serious opposition. An editor with greater talents of compromise might have been able to achieve more, but at the time it seemed to me that confrontation was the only way to make these urgent questions into topics of serious conversation.

I was threathened with censorship so early in my career that I was not able to contemplate a change of course. As far as I was concerned, it was a principle question of freedom of thought and expression. I didn't want to recognize that a small religious community which had suffered the intolerance of the established churches for centuries now would turn the same intolerance against itself and would be unwilling to tolerate self-criticism. In the end I lost the confidence of the editorial board of the paper and resigned the editorship. I am left with a feeling of sorrow about the fact that it was not possible to discuss all those matters of concern in an open and preliminary dialogue and that at times even those who considered dialogue a *nota ecclesiae* of Anabaptism would be reluctant to engage in dialogue themselves. They did not put in a good word for a German periodical that would be open to dialogue.

With this sorrow I began to move away from practical work in the Mennonite sphere and toward scholarship. At the height of the student unrest of the 1960s I took up the position of academic assistant at the Ecumenical Institute of the University of Heidelberg and at the same time took up duties at a student residence in which German and foreign students of various confessions lived, studied, and worshiped together. In this way I could carry forward my practical and ecumenical experiences on a different plane. After five years of pastoral work, I could begin to think through theologically with some detachment what was happening among the Mennonites.

After this my preoccupation with Anabaptism became more intense. The volume *Die Mennoniten* which I edited in 1971 (a Lutheran bishop had given me this task) was a product of my Anabaptist enthusiasm, which now, however, also set in motion a critical process of inquiry. My eyes for an Anabaptism that was not nearly so homogeneous, so peaceful, and theologically attractive as has been supposed for purposes of church work and ecumenical discussion, were opened not by church historians but by secular historians. The emphases in my confessional double life began to shift. The basis of a vocational engagement with the Mennonite church structure had broken down; fortunately, I was no longer dependent on such a basis.

While I was working on a systematic study about pneumatic problems in Protestant theology around World War I, I collected a volume of essays by historians and theologians commemorating the beginnings of Anabaptism 450 years earlier. This volume, which appeared in 1975, was called *Umstrittenes Täufertum* (Controversial Anabaptism). It did not only make friends for me in the Mennonite congregations. But many did become aware of the fact that a change was occurring in Anabaptist studies which would have consequences for theology, a change from an idealized picture which gave temporary relief to our confessional situation to an image of Anabaptism which was historically more plausible.

Perhaps I would not have been open to this new image of Anabaptism and would not have become involved had I still been locked into pedagogical pressures of pastoral work. It was an experience of freedom for me to see that distance aids our vision. Subsequently I only continued my editorial work with the *Mennonitische Geschichtsblätter* and contributed occasional critical articles on topical questions in Mennonitism. This brought me to the fringe of the congregations and I became an outsider. This was a position I had sought since I needed it in order to deal critically with my confessional background, but it was also a position into which I had been pushed. I was told that Menno Simons had loved his church, while I had only criticism to offer, as though criticism were not also a form of love.

Gradually I was driven a step further. I left my position in the theological faculty, in which a Mennonite systematic theologian has no future, and turned to social and economic history. But I did not give up my interest and my work in the area of Anabaptist studies. On the contrary, I think sometimes that it was precisely my work on Anabaptism and Thomas Müntzer which helped me to find this new field of interest. A few years ago I published my book *Die Täufer*, which arose out of a combination of church and social history and which can be read as a critical coming to terms with my confessional background. It is also a homage to those women and men who found the courage to exert a critical influence on church and society from the fringe. If we are serious about Jesus Christ as the center of the church, then we all stand on the fringe and then there are only outsiders in the church.

And so my way led from the cloakroom in West Prussia via the pulpit of a Mennonite church to the lectern of a university—and in the end I have remained a Mennonite.

If I consider how this has come to be, then I am sure it is not due to the vitality of Anabaptist-Mennonitism in answering ultimate questions of concern to us. I cannot discern any such vitality. If I had been dependent on that I would be elsewhere today. It was my confessional double life which prevented me from expecting too much from Mennonitism and enabled me to remain true to it in my own fashion. In its beginnings Anabaptism embodies a wealth of Christian existence which cannot be used up in one lifetime: with Hans Denck I could be a religious individualist, with Conrad Grebel an uncompromising biblicist, with Johannes Brötli a believing revolutionary, with Michael Sattler a pious pacifist, with Jacob Hutter a radical communalist, with Menno Simons a concerned evangelist, with David Joris an anarchic aesthete.

Those are all variations of Christian existence. As long as they give me food for thought and do not jealously forbid me to listen to and receive from others what they believe, think, and say, and above all do not prevent me from hearing behind all of them the voice of him who is the truth and life, I will be true to this faith of my fathers. That is my attempt to deal ecumenically with my confessional adherence and tradition.

(Translated by Victor G. Doerksen)

11

To Be or to Become a Mennonite

Johannes Harder

Johannes Harder, born in a Mennonite settlement on the Volga River in 1903, was an eminent man of letters, novelist, translator, editor, teacher, sociologist, theologian, minister, and Christian activist. Until his sudden death on March 7, 1987, he enjoyed a vigorous retirement near the picturesque village of Schlüchtern near Frankfurt, West Germany, with his second wife, Gudrun. Author of a dozen books, including eight novels, he was a rare human being who was both passionate and steadfast, possessed of a mind that was forceful and shrewd, and a heart that was simple and spontaneous in its love for people.

1

*T*he smallest of the religious groups of the Reformation, the Anabaptists, has not had or created fewer problems than the large bodies (Calvinists and Lutherans) which exited from the Roman Catholic Church.

Those who confess being the radical wing of the Reformation should be prepared to ask probing and self-critical questions about themselves in view of their many transformations in a changing environment. Who are we anyway, we heirs of the Anabaptist movement, who bear the name "Mennonite"? Perhaps we have testified too much in our history and thought too little.

I will try to articulate the reservations which occurred to me when I was thinking about this; my first questions were about myself, so that this questioning and criticism includes considerable self-probing and self-criticism.

I will begin with doubts about the legitimacy of the name "Mennonite." May a confession which is based on the Bible refer to persons in this way? Are not such names used in our midst in a variety of meanings and interpretations? Goethe said: Names are but sound and smoke.

I ask about the meaning and nature of a confession. Isn't it true that I can only confess what I have recognized and that that kind of knowledge is the result of study?

Confession is something given, it is never an achievement or possession. It can never be more than a reply, an answer to a particular call, whether this comes to me from the Bible or whether by means of our fathers. Confession is then no personal statement, for it is spoken with others who have convinced me and who oblige me to pass on my insight.

2

With his confession a person comes out of himself and speaks in the chorus of those of like mind. All my life I have suffered from the fact that our sermons were mostly individualistic and that our faith was that way too ("How will *I* be saved?").

As true as it is that in the biblical message everything begins with a single person and by *the One*, the New Testament reaches far beyond me and marks the beginning of a salvation history for *all*; for it is a matter of universal restoration of the world. ("For God so loved the world."—John 3.) One person is called by another; there is a chain of invitations carried along as in a relay race. The called are gathered and become the *Gemeinde*, which transforms everything that is.

The Anabaptists did not invent the idea of the *Gemeinde* as the most intensive form of human society. They understood themselves as a continuation of the disciples of Christ, as convinced and convincing students of the early church. *Gemeinde* is neither organization nor institution, but rather an *organism*. A believer is always a beginner and a student of the biblical ABC, one who is becoming, a person on the way to the message of Jesus, to the kingdom of God, into which he enters with his confession. Just as the single person is sociologically only a particle of a larger whole, so the *Gemeinde* is an avant-garde, a proclaimer and prophet for the kingdom of God on earth.

That is why there cannot be any perfection among the disciples. As faith grows, so too does the openness for a progressive revelation. Whoever interrupts this living process and does not participate in the gathering is in opposition to all the prophets and apostles.

God turned to the world and that is why conversion (turning around) is possible for every person. There are many, all too many, amputees attached to the body of Christ who against their own will oppose the unifying Lord (John 17), whose arms embrace the whole world and resist every separation between brothers and sisters.

I am speaking of the divisions and controversies within Mennonitism. The virus of separation must be in our blood; otherwise it would be unthinkable that from the beginning we would have fallen prey to so many dogmatic arguments and even enmities. Whoever thinks that he might have more knowledge and confession to offer should ponder the unlimited patience of God. As one's faith grows, so too should grow the ability to carry the brother and tolerance.

As time goes on I can less and less find my way clearly among the dozens of "directions" (movements) in our faith community, some of them very judgmental in character. Difference within the character of a particular *Gemeinde* may well be a strength, as long as it does not become separation, accompanied by judgment and damnation, which is a kind of spiritual sickness. Why should we not live in different houses, as long as they are not fortresses from which we shoot Bible quotations at one another. Are there not differences and tensions enough in our social and political world? Should we not seek to bring our world peace by our unity and forgiving spirit?

The schism in the Russian Mennonite church of the 1860s, which I have gotten to know in its consequences, leads me to ask whether the pious hubbub which took over both the mother church and those who left, did not have its roots in self-righteousness or pride. Is the Bible a textbook for fighting and bickering? I do not want to say anything against an honest insight which may have moved some to take their leave of the mother church. I wonder though why these refugees from the church broke out in spite and condemnation and—probably not incidentally—bound their new groups to names, concepts, and places, as though there had been a relapse into the age of the Pauline letters of admonition.

Were not our fathers—not to speak of the Bible—anti-clerical and anti-sacramental? But here dogmatic formulations arose as in papal times. I cannot imagine that these scenes of separation made either the mother church or the new groups happier. Is it any surprise if we have been looked upon as sectarians from the beginning and denounced as such?

3

The question arises whether our differentiations and differences might not also have ethnic causes. The fact that the Anabaptists came from Switzerland, the Low Countries, Tirol, Alsace, central Germany (Saxony, Thuringia, the Harz), and even Poland, could be an explanation. Different customs and practices and differences in character appeared and were absorbed. These differences were harmonized by gradual socialization within ordered settlements, but also perhaps by the common teaching in the *Gemeinde*.

My confession of unity, which is more than mere harmony in the sense of agreement (consensus?), should not be misconstrued as a contradiction of my critical commentary. I am mindful of the words of Dostoevsky: "All are guilty toward everyone" (obliged toward everyone?). That makes it necessary to share the guilt for the fragmentation in the knowledge that one has loved and hoped too little. Historically that means: "The sects are the sins of the church."

4

If the Anabaptists wanted not only to formulate faith *dogmatically* but also to practice it *ethically* and thus have their confession known as a reality and actualization, then in historic hindsight there are fateful breaches to be observed. If ethics (teaching of the good) is more than moralism or mere humaneness, then it is the development or translation of truth into reality. Faith is life in which the Word is translated into the whole existence. In this way the dualism, the juxtaposition of this world and the other, of preaching and praxis, of God and man, is overcome.

The times of persecution robbed our fathers of the chance to become socially active. They were always isolated and excluded from public life. This fact intensified their living together as *Gemeinde*. The enmity that surrounded them strengthened their belief that Christian life meant an absolute lack of enmity. Their refusal to participate in countermovements and their rejection of force, their "nonresistance," were a part of their decision for the cross, in which their discipleship became visible. Where love degenerates into a Sunday habit and does not apply during the week, a contradiction arises between the statement of faith and the evidence of praxis; this separation is unbelief.

My generation in Germany had to pay dearly for the conflict between teaching and living which had become obvious in the nineteenth century. After the periods of persecution and flight the Mennonites fell prey to a gradual *conformity*. The ground on which this began and prospered was above all Prussian and then Pan-German nationalism. Recognition and thankfulness for received toleration and asylum led, in the course of economic and cultural development, to a secularization process from which the successful Mennonite farmers could not be excluded. They were caught up in this development after the urbanized groups (in Danzig, Elbing, etc.) had accommodated themselves to the general lifestyle.

These heretofore homeless wanderers discovered the land they had cultivated to be a "Fatherland"; their Prussian surroundings taught them patriotism upon which nationalism arose, which in turn misled them to disregard their Mennonite principles. Their fall into the "world" they had so long mistrusted occurred in 1934 when their leaders, without the concurrence of their members, sacrificed their nonresistance to Fascism. After the war (1945) a rethinking began; a Peace Committee was formed, which is having a growing influence in the *Gemeinde.*

With some astonishment, and yet thankfully, I see that in the meantime the Anabaptist heritage of nonresistance has been taken up by not a few of the official churches and the ecumenical movement. More than that: in West Germany the peace movement has been joined by unchurched young people with idealism and a willingness to sacrifice. They are committed to what Nietzsche called "faithfulness to the earth." They are followers of Mahatma Gandhi, Leo Tolstoy, Martin Luther King, Jr., and others who have called them to peace and peacemaking. We should not consider them with suspicion; rather, we should outdo them with an even greater confession with regard to peacemaking. But that would mean that we Mennonites would at long last once again proclaim from the rooftops what has been whispered into our ears (Matthew 10:27).

5

I continue to meditate on my relationship to the traditional community of faith by comparing it to the biblical tradition. My questions continually run into questionable circumstances in the relationship between our heritage and our reality. For example, baptism, which has gotten into a bad way no less than has nonresistance. Baptism was the confession of "mature" Christians; never a sacrament, that is, an act holy in itself, but always only a *sign* of obedience to Scripture. I can recall how in some Russian Mennonite churches baptism was given the adjective "holy" as though it was to be understood in a sacramental sense. Holy means "belonging to God"; God himself is the Lord of baptism, his Spirit is the Baptizer. And so the transfer of the character of holiness to an act appears problematic to me.

It is something else when God speaks to persons in an act of the *Gemeinde* through the Word or through images and symbols. The baptismal candidate can express himself only in a fragmentary and incomplete way as to what has happened to him, whether he uses his own or biblical language. God himself, not a tradition, however good, has accepted the person; this adoption is beyond our asking or comprehension. That is why baptism is an exaltation out of indebtedness and at the same time a humbling before the rightful Lord. That is the way the Lord of baptism opens the door to the *Gemeinde*, which is his consulate (representative) on earth. Baptism is a testimonial to the candidate of his decisive call. Through baptism in and of itself nothing is changed in the candidate, but it testifies that the Spirit has changed the mind of a person and directed him to others.

The teaching on baptism is a serious matter for me, but I want to inquire about the practice. I know of cases where it is "passed" as a kind of exam after a training process. Or it is considered a rite of passage out of childhood. Or baptism is seen to be part of a perfect life. Such misunderstandings lead "free" churches to become "state" churches, which set baptism as an entrance requirement for full membership. But already Luther knew: "Water alone will not do it."

6

To me it is more than a mere linguistic peculiarity when we speak of *Gemeinde* instead of *church*. Church has been a compromised term since the year 325, when those who had previously been hunted down became legitimate citizens and the church became an accomplice of the state whose cooperation was necessary for domestic order. In such a combination the church became a co-ruler of the people and a persecutor of those of contrary mind. In the various forced christianizations, in the crusades, and in the burning of heretics and witches, the church took upon itself the role of protector of the monarchy.

It must be said to the shame of the Christians that it was not the church, but rather secular forces, the Enlightenment, political revolutions, and the Liberalism we find suspect, which did more for humanity and freedom than the Christian confessions. I am happy that the belief in nonresistance which we have treated so ignobly in the recent past was able to protect us from many errors for long periods of our history.

And yet this light too has its shadow. Through it we came to frown upon secular life and to shun the world. In our history we contented ourselves with a modest mission activity and largely lost sight of the world, that world which was the address of Jesus' message and which will be our "place of work" until the end of days. To be not "of" but "in" the world has become for us an inward-directedness and simple piety of the heart. Thus it was overlooked that we had come into an insoluble contradiction to our confession, since we all participate in all areas of the world, in events and developments in economics and business, cultural and other (perhaps destructive) kinds of progress, competition and even political actions.

I have never been able to understand our fear of the world. We preach about sin and guilt, which we correctly apply to ourselves personally and for which we seek individual forgiveness. At the same time we are, consciously or not, caught up in an unending chain of producers and consumers, and we act in this context, positively or negatively influencing these relationships. Whatever happens in the field of politics—what have I done for or against these things due to my Christian character? If we think we are not involved because of a passive attitude we are deceiving ourselves and we will be shown to be fools or hypocrites. Our relationship to property and our handling of money is dealt with in the New Testament and does not arise only in the judgment day.

We German Mennonites were awakened out of our sleep by thirteen years of Fascism; whether as cowards or traitors, we stood before a court of judgment which even today some will not comprehend. The light on the hill that is to shine in darkness, the salt of the earth that is to protect from spoilage, these are not the exclusive tasks of the *Gemeinde*. The *Gemeinde* is either a prophet or a dumb dog (Isaiah 56:10). To say it even more clearly, we do not need first of all to become political; we are political every day and we need to counteract errors and inhumanities everywhere and at all times. Indifference is lack of love in the New Testament.

7

Finally I ask myself whether, in this welter of questions and questionable situations, I still may be called a Mennonite. I can do this only insofar as I am beset with disquiet at the fact that in reading the good news I always find myself only halfway, on a road on which I am not to rest or philosophize but rather be continually driven forward by the hand of grace.

The Bible I read is a critique of me and my worth. I wanted to have said that here.

I confess that I am not yet a Mennonite, but there is nothing I would like more than to become one. That is why I have every reason to call myself into question with every criticism uttered on these pages. I am content that we are forgiven; that is, we have been forgiven so that we can in turn give ourselves to this wicked world, which God loved so much.

(Translated by Victor G. Doerksen)

12

Apologia Pro Vita Sua

Gordon D. Kaufman

*Gordon D. Kaufman is a Mennonite theologian and a professor of
divinity at Harvard Divinity School. He is no doubt one of the
very few original thinkers that the Mennonites have produced.
Daring, innovative, at times controversial, and radical in the true
sense of the word—exploring root issues—he has written articles
and books on contemporary theological and ethical questions.
Such book titles as* God the Problem *and* Theology in a Nuclear
Age *indicate the areas of his concern. Kaufman argues that unless
Christians rethink and reinterpret old symbols and categories they
will have little impact on modern society.*

Why am I a Mennonite? Largely, I suppose, because I was born into a Mennonite home and raised in a Mennonite community. This is a rather un-Mennonite answer to the question, inasmuch as Mennonites have long prided themselves on their rejection of the view that Christian faith can be largely a matter of one's religious inheritance, insisting instead that only through a self-conscious decision and confession of faith may one become a Mennonite. But it seems to me quite unlikely that I would now be Mennonite had I not been exposed to this understanding of Christian faith from early in my life, my selfhood being shaped to quite deep levels by Mennonite attitudes and beliefs.

I am not attempting to suggest that Mennonite convictions and attitudes belonged only to my childhood and youth and that I have now outgrown them. On the contrary. As I want to show in this article, I believe they go to the deepest levels of my sense of self-identity and have in many ways informed my thinking and behavior throughout my life; I affirm what seems to me a basically Mennonite stance in my living and in my work as a Christian theologian. (The fact that, as I suspect, most of the contributors to this volume were also born and raised in Mennonite communities may pose some awkward questions about our long-cherished conviction, that to be a Mennonite somehow involves personal decision and commitment in a way different from most other Christian groups.)

I grew up on a Mennonite college campus (Bethel College in Kansas) in the home of the president. From my earliest days, therefore, I was exposed to a broad range of intellectual and cultural activities as well as to peculiarly Mennonite interests and concerns. My adolescent years in the late thirties and early forties were a time of great patriotic emotion (connected with the onset of World War II) in Newton junior and senior high schools which I attended, and this helped to give me a strong sense of what it meant to be a Mennonite. I was firmly convinced of the correctness of the Mennonite understanding of Christian faith: we were a community set over against the rest of the world, including the other churches that claimed the name "Christian"; we were the "true believers" who took our faith with genuine seriousness. With my broad cultural interests and my strong Mennonite convictions it is hardly surprising that I gradually came to think of myself as one who might someday be engaged in mediating Mennonite understandings of life and its proper conduct to the wider culture, as well as seeking to introduce broader intellectual and cultural interests and concerns back into Mennonite circles. It is, thus, in these early formative experiences (together with my nearly three years in Civilian Public Service during World War II) that I find the origins of my eventual decision to become a Christian theologian and teacher.

It is to this same Mennonite background that I trace many of the major emphases in the understanding of Christian faith and theology to which I have come in the course of my professional life—as surprising as this may seem to some religiously conservative persons acquainted with my work. I cannot but think of myself as through and through a Mennonite Christian—a Mennonite trying to find his way in the baffling intellectual complexity of the modern world. In the remainder of this short article I would like to elaborate on these statements a bit.

Mennonites have always had powerful convictions about what is right and what is true, convictions that they believed were directly grounded in God's will for human beings as seen in the life and teachings of Jesus, convictions that enabled them to endure great hardships, migrations to remote parts of the earth, even martyrdom if necessary. As an heir to this tradition, it was clear to me as a teenager that the understanding which many other Christians had of Christian truth and of the requirements of the Christian ethic was simply wrong. In particular, those Christians who rejected pacifism either misunderstood, or were ignorant of, the real meaning of Christian faith.

I was strongly impressed, for example, by a seventh-grade math teacher of mine who spoke with confidence about Jesus' teachings but was quite surprised to learn (from me) that Jesus had told his followers to "love your enemies." What was one to make of such obvious ignorance? It seemed apparent to me already in that early period that questions of truth and right are not simple ones, that it is easy for persons to be completely mistaken even when they supposed they understood what the truth was. "The majority is always wrong," was a phrase that expressed this sentiment well to those who lived within our minority community on the Bethel campus. Thus, from an early age the problems of illusion and misunderstanding began to grip my consciousness. This awareness was ultimately to express itself in my ideas about the relativity and the questionableness of all human convictions regarding right and truth.

A second way in which my Mennonite background influenced my later thinking was in its emphasis on the primacy of *life* over belief for Christians. The sort of life one lived—the way in which it manifested true "love of neighbor" and "love of enemies"—was the real measure of one's faith, not the sort of verbal assents that one was willing or able to give. Nominal or verbal Christians were not true Christians, as we understood the matter. I have retained this emphasis on the priority of moral values and moral performance over truth-claims throughout my life; and this also shows up in my theological work with its central claim that the "truth" of our "imaginative constructions" is finally to be tested in the quality of life that they bring forth.

Other experiences, of course, also played a part in the way my later theological position was gradually to develop out of these early perceptions and convictions. As a result of my Mennonite upbringing, I chose to be a conscientious objector in World War II. During the period I was drafted (1943-46), I spent over a year working in the Ypsilanti, Michigan, state hospital for the mentally ill, and this experience further reinforced my questions about matters of truth and of experiential certainty. For many months I worked on a ward full of senile old men, and it was part of my responsibility to feed them, to clean them up when they were incontinent, and the like. Many, of course, were living in the world of their memories, and were completely unaware of what was going on round about them. Charlie Wilson was such a person.

Charlie had evidently managed a small grocery store for most of his life, and though he was sitting in a chair all day long in our ward, dressed in a sheet because of his regular incontinence, he usually thought he was still at home in the grocery store, picking up a can of coffee for Mrs. Jones or five pounds of sugar for Mrs. Smith, ringing up their bills on the cash register and counting out their change. All of this was obvious to those of us who were ward attendants, because Charlie talked aloud to his customers as they came by, and we could make out quite easily what he was saying to them. It was clear that as far as Charlie's consciousness was concerned, he was still living in the world in which he had lived most of his life; he had little awareness of being in a mental hospital, completely unable to care for himself. If I was spoon-feeding Charlie, and it was necessary for him to respond to me in some way, he took me to be one of the customers with whom he was dealing; only very rarely did he recognize that he was being cared for in a hospital.

All of this raised further questions for me about the trustworthiness of our personal consciousness and experience. If Charlie could be so mistaken about the world he was living in and what he was doing, how could I be so certain of my world that I was living in and of what I was doing? It seemed obvious to me that Charlie was wrong, that he was simply living in a dream; but who was to say that I was not also living in such a dream world? Perhaps Charlie's was the true world, and mine the dream? How could one know? It was clear to me that subjective certitude about even our most fundamental convictions regarding reality and truth was no sufficient proof of their validity.

What criterion, then, can there be for truth, if even our own experience and consciousness must be put into question? Only one occurred to me. If I did not continue to spoon-feed Charlie on regular occasions, he would die. That is, if Charlie were left to live in *his* world, he could not survive. In contrast, I was able to continue to survive in mine, and to make it possible for Charlie to survive in his. *The ability for life to go on*, then, seemed to be the ultimate test of our consciousness and our experience, not simply what appeared to us as certain or true in that consciousness and experience itself. If our ideas enabled us successfully to continue to get around in the world and to survive, they had a certain validity; if they did not or could not, that was a sure sign they were invalid. A kind of pragmatic criterion, it became clear to me, needed to be applied to all of our certainties and convictions; experience and conviction themselves, no matter how powerful, were simply not adequate to assure truth and right. Thus, questions of truth and reality, of illusion and delusion, became important for me from an early age, and they have never left me. My work all the way to the present has been informed by them.

During that earlier period of my life, however, I did not have serious doubts about fundamental moral issues. It was clear to me, for example, that love of neighbors and of enemies was required of all humans; these Mennonite pacifist convictions seemed to me quite certain. Though I had many doubts throughout this period about the existence and nature of God (doubts which have remained with me in some form down to the present), I had almost none about the sort of life we humans should live. The Mennonite priority of morality and life over matters of belief or truth gripped me quite deeply.

When I went to Yale Divinity School, however, these moral certainties were also to be severely shaken. This was shortly after the conclusion of World War II, and there were many veterans present in my classes. Yale was an exciting place to study, and questions of social ethics were at the center of everyone's consciousness, with Liston Pope and Richard Niebuhr as highly respected teachers. Neither Pope nor Niebuhr was a pacifist. Both were strongly convinced that there had been a Christian obligation to fight Hitler, and they had worked out powerful moral and theological rationales for their positions. Reinhold Niebuhr also was widely read and much respected among students and faculty alike, and his anti-pacifist stance was persuasive to most persons at the Divinity School. It became necessary, therefore, for those of us who had been pacifists during the war, to think through these fundamental questions of Christian ethics afresh.

For the first time I began to see that there was a real possibility that the Mennonite position on war, which I had taken to be so certainly true, might be mistaken, even self-serving and hypocritical. Although (along with some friends with whom I regularly discussed these questions) I managed to work my way through to a modified pacifist position, I would never again be able to have the kind of rock-sure moral consciousness which had earlier been mine. Morality like truth, it now became clear, was relative, questionable, uncertain. There was no sure point anywhere—in consciousness, experience, or religious tradition—on which one could depend. How then can humans live? Must we be condemned to nihilism and despair? or to outright arbitrariness? This problem became the focus for my doctoral dissertation: to seek to understand this relativity and contingency of all our truth- and value-claims in the hope of ascertaining whether some kind of viable framework for orientation in life and the world (i.e., a valid "metaphysics" or "theology") could be constructed.

As I have tried to suggest, the overwhelming relativistic consciousness which by this time was mine did not have its origins in my years at Yale. It had been prepared for in my earlier experience as a member of a cognitive minority (a Mennonite in wartime) and in my reflection on the delusions of mental patients; I had been thinking about these issues for a long time, and they not infrequently showed themselves. For example, while I was enrolled in a masters program in sociology (1948) at Northwestern University (Evanston, Illinois), I remember writing a paper for the interdepartmental anthropology-sociology-psychology seminar. It dealt with the psychological and cultural relativism commonly affirmed by many social scientists, but it drew the conclusion that this relativity of all perspectives implies that our perspectives also—as psychologists, sociologists, and anthropologists—must be regarded as limited and in question. This conclusion, however, was unacceptable to my teachers: they took everyone else's thought to be relative in various ways, but not their own. I remained convinced of the correctness of my conclusion on this matter, however, and that deepening conviction fed into the problematic on which I determined to work in my dissertation (completed in 1955).

The important thing that I learned at Yale Divinity School with regard to this issue—particularly from H. Richard Niebuhr—was that precisely because of the relativity of all our experience and thought, we have no choice but to live out of the tradition of value and truth which has formed us, and which has made available to us such goods as we come to know in life. We can, then, decide to live gratefully and happily out of tradition, which may even be seen, quite properly, as God's revelation to us and salvation for us. In this way I got my Mennonite-Christian faith back once again—but deeply changed. It was now no longer possible for me to accept tradition uncritically; but it was not necessary, either (as some existentialist philosophers might insist), to reject the traditions I had inherited in defiance and despair, simply because they were historically relative. My dissertation, which explored the problem of relativism and its anthropological roots and necessity, on the one hand, and, on the other, attempted to show how Christian conceptions of human historicity could interpret and render meaningful such relativity, was an attempt to articulate for myself a way of dealing with this problem, rooted in such deep levels of my being. It turned out to be a work which laid down major lines along which much of my later theological thinking was to develop. I had already begun to understand that all our conceptions of self and world and God are our own "imaginative constructions" (though I did not realize at that time the full implications this notion has for theological work).

For the next fifteen years or so I assumed that the task of theology was simply to work out (imaginatively) a Christian understanding of the world and humanity and God. My basic perspective on these matters (an obviously Mennonite one) was initially sketched in a series of Menno Simons Lectures delivered at Bethel College in 1959 and published as *The Context of Decision* in 1961. In subsequent years I worked out the main lines of this position in lectures on systematic theology at Vanderbilt Divinity School and Harvard Divinity School, and in 1968 published *Systematic Theology: A Historicist Perspective.* I tried to show how all the major concepts of the Christian theological vocabulary fit together to give a picture of human life as historical through and through, but nonetheless as under the lordship of "the God and Father of Jesus Christ"; and I tried to show how the concept of God as understood by Christians was put together by means of an imaginative synthesis of a number of central metaphors (father, lord, creator, son, servant, word, spirit, etc.).

I was particularly proud of the fact that the conception of God which I worked out included a doctrine of God's "nonresistance" in counterpoint with the more traditional doctrine of God's "power." In this way, I believed, I was grounding in God's very nature the central emphasis of the Mennonite version of Christian ethics, something that, to the best of my knowledge, had nowhere previously been so boldly attempted. At a good many other points the Mennonite background of my interpretation of Christian faith was also clearly visible. My intention with this book, however, was not to set out a Mennonite theology as such, but rather an interpretation of Christian faith which (though it incorporated Mennonite insights and perspectives) would be illuminating and helpful to a much wider circle of Christians. In all of this I was well aware that I was engaged throughout in an "imaginative construction" of the Christian worldview. Since it seemed to me clear that this is precisely what Christian theologians had always been doing, it was justifiable for me to proceed in this way also. What I did not yet understand was how radical were the implications of this conception of theology.

By the time I had published my *Systematic Theology*, I was already beginning to feel many problems in it; these were centered particularly on the concept of God, and on the question of what we mean when we speak of God. (The neo-orthodox claim which I had found myself able to accept for a time—even to take religious comfort in—that the business of theology was to deal with the supposedly objective "reality of Christian faith," not with the doubts and half-hearted personal beliefs of the theologian, had for some years been becoming increasingly untenable for me.) I decided, therefore, to write a book of essays to address these problems in a kind of series of long footnotes to my *Systematic Theology*. These essays, brought together with my most recent reflections on the nature of theology and the problems of "God-talk" in *God the Problem*, were published only four years after the *Systematic Theology* (in 1972), but they represented much better my deeper perception of certain central theological issues. (The *Systematic Theology* was substantially completed at least three years before it was actually published, so the distance between those two books is greater than the copyright dates suggest.)

The essay in *God the Problem* which most clearly shows the new directions in which I was moving was the one on "God as Symbol," written shortly before the manuscript was completed. At the same time that I was working on that essay (in England), another piece took shape for me very quickly; in a matter of just a few days I put together a draft of "Theology as Construction." This piece excited me very much because I felt I was now at last getting clear in my mind what was actually going on in theology. This essay was the basis for the middle chapter of my *Essay on Theological Method* (1975; rev. ed. 1979), the chapter that for the first time attempted to show why all theology must be imaginative construction, and what that means for theological method.

For our purposes here it is important to note that in that book, especially in the Epilogue, it became clear once again for me that the principal criterion for testing theological assertions was not their putative claims to truth, but rather their pragmatic fruitfulness for ordering human life in a humane way—a central Mennonite theme (as I have already mentioned) which had been of importance to me for many years. Now, as I developed my understanding of all truth-claims and moral claims as imaginative constructs with the aid of which we humans find orientation in life and in the world, this Mennonite theme found articulation in terms suggested by American pragmatic philosophy.

The year after the *Essay* was published was spent in India. This was important because it helped to confirm the direction in which my thought was moving, while at the same time persuading me that we in the West must take much more seriously the religious and philosophical traditions of other cultures. Ninety-eight percent of India's 600 million people have virtually no understanding of or interest in the Christian God; their lives are ordered by quite different metaphysical, religious, and moral principles. The experience of living in India showed me once again that human beings are capable of creating many different ways of understanding the world and many different forms of life, seeing each from within as right and good and true, and ordering their lives and their thinking accordingly—something I had already begun to realize in a much less sophisticated way as an adolescent.

It has become increasingly clear to me in recent years that the different religious traditions are all great imaginative constructions of the human spirit, through which men and women have found ways to order their world so they can live in it and find some meaning within it. Is there any way to assess these various schemes for shaping and ordering human life, and to choose among them? Witnessing the massive degradation and suffering in India served to reinforce further my conviction that all religious, social, and cultural systems must be judged not primarily by metaphysical, epistemological, or specifically religious criteria but by a *moral* one—what I have come to call the criterion of "humanization," the fullest and most equitable possible realization and development of the human and the humane.

Once again my Mennonite convictions about the importance of relieving human suffering, of assisting others toward a fuller realization of their basic human worth and well-being, proved central to my theological and philosophical reflection. (Elaboration of some of these distinctively Mennonite themes can be found in a collection of essays and speeches which I published in 1979 under the title *Nonresistance and Responsibility and Other Mennonite Essays*.) The experience in India helped me to see that my notion of theology as imaginative construction should be conceived more fully within the context of an understanding of all human religious activity and institutions, ideas and practices, as an expression of the basic human need to find orientation in life.

The response that I got to my ideas about theology from Indian students and colleagues was very encouraging to me: in particular, my understanding of theology seemed to free Indian theologians to develop their own indigenous theology in significant ways which had not been encouraged by the more traditional view of Christian theology as essentially translation of a received tradition (revelation). Two essays written in India (and dealing with some of these matters), together with a number of other essays during the next four years, became the basis for *The Theological Imagination: Constructing the Concept of God* (1981), which tries to give some notion of what a Christian theology would look like if developed self-consciously as a work of imaginative construction, with humanization as its ultimate governing principle. This book, of course, represents only a series of fragments and glimpses, but it does help to make more concrete and visible the intentions expressed in the *Essay on Theological Method*.

The appearance of my most recent book, *Theology for a Nuclear Age* (1985), further shows the constructive possibilities opened up by my methodological proposals, while at the same time making evident the continuing importance to me of what are fundamentally Mennonite issues and themes. In this brief work I argue that since the occurrence of another great war may well signal the end of human life on earth, the advent of the nuclear age has made warfare no longer tolerable as a means of settling disputes among nations. We have, thus, entered a new historical era in which we must find ways to replace our present all-too-free use of compulsive power to achieve objectives—whether with respect to our neighbors or with respect to the natural environment in which we live—with patterns of interdependence and mutual caring.

It now becomes clear that a willingness to give ourselves, whether individuals or nations, for the sake of the well-being of all (even our "enemies") is requisite not just for religious salvation but for bare human survival. So the death on a cross of the one who "came not to be served but to serve, and to give his life as a ransom for many" (Mark 10:45) becomes a paradigm, in a much fuller and more radical sense, of what is essential to human life, than any of us had realized before. Thus, this book directly expresses what is basically a radical Mennonite vision of what is essential for human salvation.

This book also makes clear, however, the extent to which I have found it necessary to depart from the more traditional Christian—and thus traditional Mennonite—ways of speaking about God, the world, and Christ. For the highly personalistic and political metaphors and images, which have been so central in most Christian thinking and faith, seem to me now to be seriously misleading in their import. Indeed, in my view they contribute directly to our inability to come fully to terms with the religious dimensions of the problems that today confront us. Instead of the old hierarchical and authoritarian patterns of order and of religious thinking, reinforced by an uncritical reliance on the Bible, we need to move to quite different ways of thinking about God and humanity and the world.

I cannot develop these ideas any further here, but my point is that the advent of the nuclear age calls us as much to reassess our religious traditions as to reconstruct our ways of ordering human life. A radical application of the pragmatic criterion of "humanization"—that quality of life is more important than claim to truth (a basically Mennonite principle, as I have suggested here)—must lead ultimately to a deconstruction and reconstruction of what have heretofore been central Christian beliefs.

Why do I still consider myself a Mennonite? Because the deepest, most powerfully defining principles of my theological thinking derive, as I see the matter, from a radicalization of what is basically a Mennonite understanding of Christian faith. However far I may have departed from many traditional Mennonite views, and however constrained I may feel to criticize and reject much that today calls it-self "Mennonite," there is no other strand of Christian tradition with which I so directly and wholeheartedly identify myself.

Though, as I said at the beginning, I am a Mennonite largely because I was born into a Mennonite family and community, this is not a matter of merely nominal interest to me: I am a Mennonite also by deep conviction. The most fundamental commitments in terms of which I seek to order my life, and which underlie all my theological work, appear to me rooted in a basically Mennonite-Christian understanding of the problems and the possibilities of human existence under God.

13

Fig Leaves and Anabaptists

Walter Klaassen

Walter Klaassen was born in Saskatchewan, where he attended Rosthern Bible School and Rosthern Junior College. His advanced studies took him to McMaster University in Hamilton, Ontario, and to Oxford University in England. He has published numerous articles and books on Anabaptism and subjects from medieval history. Klaassen was until recently the editor of the Conrad Grebel Review. *After teaching for many years at Conrad Grebel College in Waterloo, Ontario, the Klaassens moved to near Vernon, British Columbia.*

The audience were Danforth Associates, some hundreds of us. The occasion was a retreat on the east shore of Lake Michigan for inspiration and reflection on how better to serve our students. The speaker that afternoon was Paul Holmer, theologian, from Yale Divinity School.

The address was over and it was question period. It started slowly as these things often do, but suddenly there was electricity in the air. A psychologist in the back row laid a trap for the theologian whom he evidently regarded as somewhat simplistic and naive. "Dr. Holmer," he asked in mock innocence, "why are you a Lutheran?" Dead silence for what seemed like a long time. (Why are you a Lutheran? Why naturally, because it is the most faithful expression of Christian faith in its theology, church polity, and liturgy?) The psychologist at the rear could already see the hapless professor struggling in the relativity trap that had snapped shut on him. But his glee was short-lived. Dr. Holmer saw the trap the moment it was set and harmlessly tripped it with the words, "Because my mother was!" There was a lot of laughter and clapping.

I am a Lutheran because my mother was.

I am a Mennonite because my parents were.

I suspect that most of us who share our stories here would have to begin with that simple acknowledgement. Although our psychologist did not catch his prey that day and was robbed of his anticipated lecture on the relativity of all religious confessions, the answer he was so anxious to give was correct. Up to a point. Up to a very considerable point.

For there was nothing trivial about the Mennonite tradition in which I was raised. Consciousness of it came chiefly from grandfather and father. For the sake of that tradition, the values and the truths it embodied, my great-grandfather had emigrated twice, my grandfather thrice, and my father once. From Tiegenhagen in Prussia to Köppental near Saratov on the Volga to Chiva in Turkestan to Bessie, Oklahoma, to Eigenheim near Laird, Saskatchewan. Five major moves within sixty-five years, an average once every thirteen years. That kind of mobility makes for minimal dependence on the *civitas terrena* and maximum hope in the *civitas dei*. The tradition of my Mennonite ancestors was seen by them as part of the search for the city which has foundations regardless of whatever mundane motivations there might also have been.

I absorbed, then, an ethos of pilgrimage, which implied the constant readiness to pack and move, to abandon earthly possessions and the graves of the ancestors in obedience "to the heavenly vision." I absorbed the conviction that even in the twentieth century we were part of the church of the martyrs and that we could be called upon to surrender life itself at any time. I imbibed a sense of pride to be a member of the chosen few, and avidly read anything I could find about the thin thread of the faithful witnesses from apostolic times to the present. I found these things in the book by Cornelius H. Wedel, *Abriss der Geschichte der Mennoniten*, which I first read when I was perhaps eleven or twelve years old. It was a book my father had used in school at Meno, Oklahoma. All this was reinforced in many different ways also by the church, a fact that is perhaps not surprising considering that grandfather and father were ministers and an uncle, brother of my mother, was the bishop.

It is important to add here that I received the tradition in which my own family had such a visible part, with eagerness. I loved it and wanted to be part of it. And when I was baptized at age seventeen I knew that I had made the whole story from the time of Jesus to my own imminent call to be a witness by refusing military service, my very own. I was a Mennonite; I was sure of it. I loved it. It was a gift to me from my parents. But had I been born into any other Christian stream I should likely never have been a Mennonite.

The time came, however, when I tried to lose this gripping, tenacious tradition. My two years in Rosthern Junior College were very important to me because that was where I first found out that I could have ideas of my own. One Sunday morning as I walked from church with my revered teacher, Peter P. Rempel, he asked me: "Well, Walter, did you agree with the preacher this morning?" I had no answer because it had never occurred to me that I could disagree with the preacher. It's hard to imagine now, but I was twenty-one years old, and the idea of challenging the preacher's Sunday morning sermon had never entered my mind. Peter Rempel gently began to ask some questions of his own to suggest that one could so disagree without thereby becoming disloyal or committing a sin. That moment was really my intellectual birth.

After I graduated from high school I applied for and got a position as a ward attendant at the Saskatchewan Training School, an institution for the mentally handicapped, at Weyburn, Saskatchewan. It was the beginning of my life as Walter Klaassen for, apart from a cousin who was also working there, no one knew me as a Mennonite, as a member of my home church, or as the son of the preacher H. T. Klaassen, who lived with his family three and one half miles north of the church on the Carlton Line. I had walked out of one of life's rooms into another. The light was different there and so was the furniture.

The job I had gave me plenty of time to pursue my major interest which was reading. I went to the local library and found there a box of books that were being disposed of for twenty-five cents each, and I started my library. One purchase was *A Guide to Understanding the Bible* by Harry Emerson Fosdick. Apparently I was ready for that book, for my intellectual faculties sprang to life. I devoured it. Certain questions about the Bible and the interpretation of it with which I was familiar had evidently been incubating, and the friendliness and simplicity of Fosdick's book hatched them out. It was intoxicating! I was walking on air, and then I looked for other books by Fosdick and similar writers and read them all.

There was no Mennonite church in Weyburn, and I did not mind. However, it never occurred to me to stay at home on Sunday mornings. I began shopping around and began with the United Church. Everything was new. The church was more elaborate than ours at home, and the preacher, Rev. Dr. Leitch, wore a brightly colored gown in the pulpit. He talked one Sunday morning about "those of us in the Puritan tradition." Whatever could that mean? I went to the encyclopedia at the library and found out. I genuinely liked the hymns they sang, the poetry, and the music. "My God, I love thee, not because I hope for heav'n thereby. Nor yet because who love thee not are lost eternally.... Therefore I love thee and will love, and in thy praise will sing solely because thou art my God and my eternal King." Oh, the joy of this discovery, to love God just because he is God, for no other reason. As I had embraced demand and obedience at my baptism, so I now began to accept and adore the grace of God.

I continued to shop and thought I'd go to the Baptist church. But I stopped over at the Presbyterians instead. They did not see me there, so next Sunday at eleven, I was at Calvary Baptist Church. There I was noticed. I've never enjoyed invisibility for long, and I've always had trouble in a church where a stranger represents a spanner flung into a smoothly functioning machine. I quickly became acquainted with the Baptist pastor, who recognized the struggle I was just then undergoing.

In my excitement about my new discoveries concerning the Bible I had written to my father describing to him my newly hatched convictions. His response was high alarm, and he implored me not to go down that road. He was, however, defenseless against me, for his reading had been mostly in fundamentalist literature. Thanks to Fosdick, the arguments he found there against my incipient "modernism" were already familiar to me. I had discarded them because I had found them wanting. My father begged me not to desert the tradition, to remember our martyr past. Had I not committed myself to the Christian ministry? Was all that to be thrown over for some new-fangled ideas that already stood condemned?

Our confrontation developed into a battle between what it meant to be a Mennonite and whatever it was I was after. It had not occurred to me that my views could be incompatible with being a faithful Mennonite. I argued that there were Anabaptists, like Hans Denck, who were on my side. I had learned my lesson from C. H. Wedel well, being especially attracted to Denck's tolerance of other viewpoints, and pushed the matter with my father. I was using his own ammunition against him; he had, after all, introduced me to Wedel and encouraged me to read his books. All my father could do was to insist in his dismay that I was denying my own history with the way I had chosen to go.

Then I said to myself: if I have to choose between being a Mennonite and my religious and intellectual liberation, then I choose the latter. And that is how I came to separate myself from my tradition formally. The understanding I needed at that time came from the Baptists I now associated with, and soon I took the formal step of becoming a member. Very deliberately I requested my bishop uncle to take my name from the membership of the Eigenheim Mennonite Church. I was no longer a Mennonite. I was now a liberated Baptist.

But separation from so powerful a tradition exacted its price. I developed a duodenal ulcer with which I struggled for 30 years. Twice I went to the hospital in danger of my life. In retrospect, I cannot see any way along which the deplorable and painful break with my father could have been prevented. Now that I am a father of sons myself I have begun to have some understanding for the desolation and pain I caused him. Liberation, maturing, becoming a person in one's own right, is rarely achieved without suffering.

For fifteen years I was formally a Baptist. I had my whole theological training under Baptist supervision. It was a gift for which I am profoundly grateful. I met with and was influenced by good scholars as well as first-rate preachers. The gospel of God's grace became very important to me, but the imperative to action and obedience always asserted itself as well. In England, where I had gone for graduate studies, I was deeply impressed by the quiet, puritan dignity of Baptist worship. I reveled in being associated with some of the most prominent biblical scholars of the time, among them H. H. Rowley, George Caird, and C. H. Dodd. And never will I forget the many Sunday evenings spent at the University Church of St. Mary participating in evensong. I thrilled to the dignity and rhythm of the evensong liturgy. But, along with hundreds of students, I went there primarily to hear famous preachers like the brothers John and Donald Baillie from Edinburgh. Often I attended morning mass at Pusey House Chapel, where I encountered high church Anglicanism at its best both in the sung liturgy as well as in the profound intellectual piety of Pusey and Newman that was still very much alive after a century.

I loved that stimulating church setting of Oxford so much, I could easily have been persuaded to stay there. I was participating in and also appropriating for myself a church tradition that included as normal careful thinking and loving God with the mind, but which was not simply cerebral. For this work of the mind merged seamlessly also with an ancient mysticism, the recognition that God is infinitely beyond all human thought and perfection and that this mystical work of the mind leads in the first place to adoration. Obedience, I learned, is a by-product of adoration.

The experience also gave me a growing and lasting appreciation for the liturgy of the church. I learned that the basic parts of the eucharistic liturgy antedated Roman Catholicism, having been developed in the first century and a half of the church's life. I loved the collects and memorized them in order to possess that humble beauty. This was all a long way from the Eigenheim Mennonite Church.

One should never suppose that when a change of traditions takes place the old one is expelled to make room for the new. What happens is that the old one remains despite external formalities and the new that comes in mixes with the old. In fact, with me the old one always remained more or less in control, but it wisely assumed a wait-and-see stance.

Several things happened. One was that my memory of the simple rural liturgy of my home church revived. I remembered the dignity and the quietness of that simple building on a Sunday morning. I remembered that the one thing that had obviously stayed with me from my childhood was the knowledge that something very important, something numinous, sublime, sacred, was taking place there and that silence was the proper response to the Presence. Thus my new consciousness of God was joined to the older half-forgotten one. Was it Mennonite? No, and yet again, yes. Or, rather, my experience transcended temporal barriers. The labels we use to identify ourselves, including the denominational ones, are like fig leaves that cover only part of us. They are totally insufficient to cover all that one is. They have their utility but they cannot pass for a suit of clothes.

By now the reader may be wondering why I went to Oxford. Was it to go to church and to develop a new and more satisfactory spirituality? Actually I went there for graduate studies, and specifically, for graduate studies in Anabaptism. If that seems odd, it was. Anyone who had some idea of what was happening in Anabaptist studies would have said that to do a degree in that field you go to Harvard, Zürich, Chicago, Heidelberg, or Amsterdam. One could say, therefore, that going to Oxford was not a very carefully considered plan.

Three factors determined the choice: I wanted to study abroad, I did not want to work in the highly structured setting of an American graduate school, and I had Baptist connections to Oxford. But, "all things worked together for good," not always obviously because one loves God. One just cannot explain why something that should not have worked did. It turned out to be a right decision because I got a lot more than the degree I bargained for.

I studied Anabaptism on the suggestion of my church history professor at McMaster Divinity School. It probably would not have occurred to me independently. And so I plunged into a controversial field. The first book I read there was—would you believe it?— Hershberger's *The Recovery of the Anabaptist Vision* which had newly appeared in print. In a way that book set the tone for my own subjectivity; for as I began to read the primary sources I turned quickly into a passionate apologist for the Anabaptists along the lines of the "Bender school." I was profoundly conscious that I was studying my own story, and I was grappling it to my "soul with hoops of steel." I was suddenly, again, a member of a minority group, not of the Mennonite church, but of a heroic group of Christian witnesses, many of whose views I shared.

I was impressed by the variety and dynamic of this movement. And while I was in some respects part of the "Bender school" of interpretation, I found that I did not like the suspicion in which people like Hans Denck and Balthasar Hubmaier were held by some Mennonite scholars. After having learned about Hans Hut, for example, I knew that Harold Bender had protested too much in his article "The Zwickau Prophets, Thomas Müntzer, and the Anabaptists" (*MQR*, Jan. 1953). The distinctions between these seemed to me not to be as clear as he made them appear.

There seemed to be too much special pleading there.

When I began my study of Anabaptism I did not know any major scholar of Anabaptism personally. I had not been in touch with Mennonites at all. The people who supervised me apart from my tutor (and whose counsel I sought) were those in England who were acquainted with Anabaptism—the Baptists Ernest Payne and Morris West and the Methodist Gordon Rupp. I also spent a term at the University of Zürich under the tutorship of Fritz Blanke. All of this resulted in somewhat idiosyncratic conclusions about Anabaptism.

Besides, I was not attempting to defend the orthodoxy or super-Protestantism of the Mennonite churches which I believed some Mennonite scholars were inclined to do. I was engaged in a very personal search and discovery mission.

What eventually came out of that study was much less important than the process itself. I was thrilled with the dramatic character of my ancestral tradition. I was overwhelmed by its ethical earnestness and its heroism. I was impressed with the internal coherence of the Anabaptist vision. It had defended the priesthood of all Christians, liberty of conscience, confession of faith and baptism in maturity, and a disciplined church. But these were all part of the Baptist story as well. I had, however, learned that discipleship and the renunciation of violence were integral parts of Anabaptism, and I concluded that they were not incompatible with the Baptist view of things. I concluded also that the rejection by Anabaptists (and Baptists) of much of the old church liturgical tradition was understandable at that time, but did not have to be perpetuated in the present.

My immediate goal when I returned from Oxford to Canada was to go into the Baptist pastoral ministry. But it was not to be. In spite of efforts to carry out what I considered to be a commitment, there seemed no place for me to serve. Instead, I became interim pastor of Westminster United Church in Medicine Hat, Alberta. Meanwhile I received an invitation to teach Bible at Bethel College in Newton, Kansas. This happened because of conspiracy for the good of the church in which my father, the Mennonite Primate of Canada, J. J. Thiessen, and Dr. Cornelius Krahn of Bethel College were involved. Letters had been exchanged, plans laid and put into operation, all unknown to me. I learned of this twenty-five years later when the correspondence came into my hands. It worked and that is why I am not quite able to say that my return to Mennonite circles was providential. I can say with absolute honesty that I thoroughly enjoyed the joy and satisfaction my decision provided for my father. There were again things to talk about.

When, on numerous occasions I was asked why I returned to the Mennonites I had to say that it was not because they were the ideal church or the closest to the truth. That is something one can never know simply because no absolute standard is accessible to us by which we can make such a claim. It was really not a plan of mine at all. Had this not been planned by others I should not have taken initiatives in that direction myself. Certainly I did not return with the idea that Mennonite churches were Anabaptist churches, because they were not. Nor was I sure that this was a permanent return. Some of the answers I gave were—and they were honest enough—that Bethel was the only institution that had offered me a chance to teach and I had always believed that I had a gift for teaching. I also said that I thought I could probably do a better job of teaching in a Mennonite school because I had a lot of a prior knowledge of the students. And I did enjoy my new association. Here was a Mennonite community where I could speak openly about my views on the Bible without being suspected of disloyalty. I could also safely disagree with Harold Bender without being admonished! I continued to work further on Anabaptism and began to publish articles, first in the *Baptist Quarterly* and the *Canadian Journal of Theology,* and then also in the *Mennonite Quarterly Review.*

It was in Kansas that I first realized how strongly ethnic Mennonites are. Part of that discovery was the strong ethnic component in the Mennonite Historical Library. Another was the annual Mennonite Folk Festival that took place on the campus. But I began to notice these things mainly because the girl I had married during my student years was not a Mennonite. Before long she was saying to me: "I'm afraid that if being a Mennonite means to share in this ethnicity, I won't make it in." What can you do with a maiden name like Strange among Friesens, Goerings, Epps, and Schrags? Mennonites are often quite unaware of how exclusive they can be without intending to be so. It also quickly occurred to me how un-Anabaptist this was, for Anabaptists had argued against all and sundry in the sixteenth century that nothing but faith in Christ and the readiness to follow him qualified a person to be a member of the church. This unrelenting preoccupation with Mennonite ethnicity was at least odd if not ironic.

The same thing was repeated when we moved to Waterloo in 1964. Frequently when Ruth told inquirers what her maiden name was an embarrassed silence followed. It put an abrupt end to the Mennonite game. That silence invariably implied: "If you don't have one of our names there's nothing further to talk about." In-group conversations immediately created an out-group of one. And how can one be a part of a conversation from which one is decisively if unintentionally excluded?

I learned long ago that there is no Christian faith that does not have its cultural setting. It is impossible to disentangle faith from culture. Cultural differences have always tended to be divisive, but surely they are part of "the wall of division" which, according to Paul, has been broken down by Christ on the cross. As long as folkways and ethnic traditions continue to throw up barriers to people, those traditions remain unredeemed and unliberated. Wherever they are celebrated as the human cultural coat of many colors and serve to unify people from diverse traditions, they serve their proper function. To be sure, over the course of our twenty-six years of living and working in Mennonite communities, Ruth has very occasionally been asked to share the ethnicity that is hidden in the name Strange, or Le Strange, as it was still written two generations ago. Moreover, during those years Ruth has unstintingly worked with me and supported me in my many tasks in the colleges and churches of the Mennonite conferences. We were full members of a Mennonite church for several years.

The more ready acceptance of people with other ethnicities into Mennonite fellowships is growing. We have experienced a lot of love and acceptance and our friendships are virtually all with Mennonites. Even now, when we no longer live in Waterloo, my work is related primarily to the Mennonite world, and will probably continue to be inasmuch as my study of and writing about Anabaptism is a service to that world and shows no sign of abating.

Not only that, but I enjoy it and have no desire to abandon it. For Mennonites and their history and life are a slice of human history that merits attention as much as any other. I also believe that having this tradition in my blood, as it were, gives me an understanding of it that I would otherwise not have. But I also believe that the other part of my life outside the Mennonite orbit, gave me some tools to look at that tradition with a greater degree of objectivity than I might otherwise have been capable of.

Of my sixty years I have been a Mennonite for only nine years if measured in terms of formal church affiliation. I was formally a Baptist for fifteen years. We have been "associate members" of Mennonite churches and full members of an interfaith house church for fourteen years. I am not now, formally, a member of any church. What does all of that make me?

Denominational and ethnic labels are temporary and have limited value for me. When I am asked for my religious affiliation I say that I am a Christian. When I am asked what my denomination is, I say Mennonite. I am not ashamed of the old nickname. After all, Methodist, Presbyterian, Baptist, Alliance, Lutheran are all similar nicknames. But my tradition is no longer limited to the Mennonite one. Before my ancestors were Anabaptists and Mennonites, they were Catholics for perhaps 800 years and before that Nordic pagans back to the ice ages. This last tradition has almost disappeared from our collective memory; only some Christmas and Easter customs and the names of the weekdays are left of it. The Catholic part of my tradition was fiercely rejected by my sixteenth-century ancestors; they became separated from it through corruption, protest, persecution, and suffering. But I've learned to go to St. Peter's Cathedral in Rome and accept it as part of the faith of my fathers. And Pope John Paul II is my bishop too.

Sometimes I feel that I've developed into a kind of ecclesiastical gypsy, having become familiar with at least four different church traditions and free in myself to work in any one of them. I also know that each one has its weaknesses and blind spots. Still, when all is said and done, I have to be honest and say that in the church of Christ I sit in the Mennonite section. I am, as I said at the beginning of these ramblings, a Mennonite because my parents were. To that fact, about which I had no choice, I have added and continue to add my own decisions to be there even though I might actually be affiliated and work elsewhere.

When I therefore confess that I am still a Mennonite, all the rest of my activity notwithstanding, I do not mean that in an institutional sense. For the church is people and peoplehood transcends institutions. I simply cannot muster much enthusiasm for institution building by which I mean primarily all the frantic programmatic and organizational hubbub that passes nowadays for Christian work. Mennonites seem to be especially afflicted with this disease; it is built into our tradition. I say this even though I still live and work in institutions. I am deeply troubled with our enormous investment of energy and means in church institutions because so much of it is a surrogate for faith in God. However, I've made my own extensive contributions to that activity and am likely to continue to do so. I intensely dislike the sectarian mentality that afflicts Christians everywhere, accompanied by blinkered vision and a cramped charity toward co-believers.

I see a world today torn by its many ethnicities, divided by innumerable walls that separate, and across which people fight and kill each other. The church itself is rent, the body of the Christ despised by its own members because their own cultural peculiarities are more important to them than that charity that begins to look for new ways of affirming Christian unity. The church, above all, needs to provide leadership in dismantling dividing walls, and that is a task which Mennonites too should undertake with much more vigor than heretofore. I believe that the denominational structure of the church belongs to its adolescence and that it is time we seriously begin working at alternatives. I have no clear vision of what will succeed the present system, but I'm anxious to do my bit to move the changes along. That's why I don't want to give my energies to confirming Mennonite separateness. I would like us to open up and be ready for the new world that is emerging. I would like to be at the front and not at the rear of the process.

To sum it all up, therefore, I am a Mennonite and I will remain one. But I hope and pray that the time will come soon when we can say a profound thank you! to Menno and promote him to his proper place alongside of all the other Reformers of the church, and that he will be placed there not only by Mennonites—we've always done that—but by all the rest of God's people as well. He will become the father of a lot of Christians who before did not know him, and Mennonites will gain progenitors who were once their enemies.

14

A Joyous Service Among the Children of Peace

William Klassen

William Klassen, the son of a Mennonite minister, taught Religion for many years at the University of Manitoba. His numerous published articles and books deal with Anabaptists and such Anabaptist leaders as Michael Sattler and Pilgram Marpeck. He has been a president of the Canadian Society for Biblical Studies and a Danforth Fellow in Religion and Psychiatry at the Menninger Foundation. For several years he was Dean of the Inter-Faith Peace Academy in Jerusalem, Israel. At present he lives in Toronto, with his wife, Dona Harvey.

I grew up in a Mennonite minister's home, so the fact that I joined the Mennonite church by baptism at age seventeen was not wholly unexpected. At the same time a number of my siblings did not do so and to this day have no connection with the church like many other preachers' kids who do not join the church at all, or if they do, leave it as soon as they can.

My father urged me to delay joining the church until I was at least seventeen years old. Like most people of that age I had little notion of what it meant to belong to a church, although I do recall that even at that early age it made me feel good that older people in the congregation affirmed me and welcomed me into the church. When as a teenager I followed the harvest from Texas to Manitoba in the summers, it impressed me that I was to be able to stop in a church on a Sunday morning and worship with the people and share the Lord's Supper with them. I learned then that wherever I was in the world, God's people were there too and I could feel at home. During college and seminary days I did not participate very much in a local congregation. Visits to jails and to congregations, however, with a singing group helped me to express my faith in ways that confirmed my commitment to the church. I saw education as preparation for church work, especially after a year spent up north where I saw firsthand the needs of our native peoples and the métis and the potential of the church to do something to improve their lot.

I was fortunate upon completing my residence for the doctorate to be invited to teach at our denominational seminary, the Mennonite Biblical Seminary in Elkhart. Most of the time from 1958-1969 was spent there.

Since leaving the seminary in 1969 there have been many occasions when the question has come up: Do you still attend church? Are you still a Mennonite? Some colleagues at the University of Manitoba were obviously irritated that church attendance made it impossible for me to play on their hockey team or to have a tenure committee meeting on a Sunday morning. Strange that no one ever suggested that we hold a meeting at a time when our Jewish colleagues could not come. For some reason it is often assumed that Christians are free to meet on Sundays. On such occasions I made it clear that I was indeed free in the sense of being able to make a free choice. I preferred to be in church with my family on a Sunday morning rather than in a university committee meeting or playing hockey. If that branded me as strange or queer, so be it.

Later on, working in British Columbia in the context of a thoroughly secular university, people treated me with some bemusement: . . . "Still going to church?" they asked with a note of surprise. I had to admit that once they shared with me their perceptions of the church, I could understand why they wondered. Such a church I could not, and would not, have attended either.

For me attending a church over the years has been no burden; it has been for the most part a joy and in any case something which is so close to the essence of my being that I cannot visualize life without the church or indeed my own existence without the joy and the challenge which the church as a community of dedicated believers has brought to me.

Once I suggested that we define a Mennonite simply as someone who takes a local congregation seriously as the context in which discipleship or following Christ takes place. I have had a rich variety of service opportunities on national and international boards of the church and enjoyed every one of them. But for me these do not constitute the cutting edge of the church. The church which keeps me is the local congregation in which we wrestle with such issues as what to do with the surplus in our budget (always a critical test on what it means to be the church), what to do with a sinner who is eager to confess or perhaps not eager to do so, or how to respond to a brother or sister when she asks for the guidance of the community in making a specific decision. I am impressed at the way in which certain theologians like Gordon Kaufman and Stanley Hauerwas pay tribute to the church and what specifically the local congregation has meant to them. I know other famous theologians and church leaders who have no time for the local congregation.

There have been three principal congregations in my life: Hively Avenue Mennonite Church in Elkhart, Indiana (1958-59); Charleswood Mennonite Church in Winnipeg, Manitoba (1970-81); and Langley Mennonite Fellowship in Langley, British Columbia (1982-1984). In addition I had very meaningful experiences at the first church where I was baptized and ordained: Homewood Bergthaler Mennonite Church and East Goshen (Old) Mennonite Church, where Marilyn and I began our married life during the years I was at Goshen College and Seminary. I would also have to mention the churches which put up with my attempts to lead them as pastor: Silver Street Mennonite Church in Goshen, Germantown Mennonite Church, and Calvary Mennonite Church in Washington, Illinois. To all of them I owe very much, for they helped to mold my ministry and to provide a focus to my teaching and writing which would otherwise not have been there.

The Hively Avenue Mennonite Church, 1958-69

When the Mennonite Biblical Seminary relocated from Chicago to Elkhart (1956-59), it was clear that a General Conference Mennonite church would need to be organized. Along with others who joined the seminary staff, and those who came to be a part of Oaklawn Psychiatric Center's staff, we had the privilege of starting a new congregation. Fortunately, there were also a significant number of people who were neither Oaklawn nor seminary-related so that we had from the start a congregation made up of farmers, construction workers, teachers and physicians, and the like.

We spent much time discussing such matters as financing a new building and outreach. I have always felt privileged to have been able to begin our family and my teaching career at the same time that a new congregation came into being. We resisted the building of a church building as long as we could. When we did build our own structure it was so modest and so austere no one could accuse us of an edifice complex. We had some very conservative people in that group, e.g., people who resisted Eisenhower's invitation to Khrushchev to visit America, but I am grateful to them for the willingness they had to discuss the issues and to work toward consensus.

It was hard to keep the congregation from being dominated by the seminarians or by the Oaklawn people, but overall I think that goal was reached.

My relationship to the Hively people became very meaningful and profound particularly during the years of 1965-66 when I was privileged to serve as coordinator of ministries for that congregation, and in that capacity to enter into the hurts and the joys of the members in a way which otherwise would not have been possible. In this congregation our children had their first experiences of coping with tragedy (a growth process aided by the church over the years). They had good teaching there by instructors who were deeply committed to the church. I, too, was privileged to teach there in a context different from the seminary but one that I found enriching in every respect.

Hively made it possible and indeed necessary for me to explain complex theological ideas to people who were not educated. It also gave me a context in which to participate in other people's suffering at a very deep level. Through those experiences my perception of the church as a covenanted community in which we all bear one another's burdens took on a deeper meaning.

Within that congregation there was also a caring group: people who were able to bear our own secret burden of a failing marriage and to assist us in finding resources for living through our own dark days of depression and disillusionment. It was for me a binding and a loosing community—a people who confronted me with my responsibilities but also pointed me to the forgiveness and strengthening of God when I faltered and fell. The Sunday our family took farewell from that congregation will long stand in my memory, and the dear friends we left behind will never be forgotten. That congregation, built in the late fifties and early sixties is today the home congregation for Tyler, our oldest son and his wife, Mary.

Charleswood Mennonite Church, 1970-81

In the decade before moving to Winnipeg I had found both the local and the wider involvement with the church very gratifying. I enjoyed writing Sunday school materials and also my participation in publishing a new hymnal as well as membership on the education committee of the conference. Most gratifying was the work with

Mennonite Mental Health Services which I was asked to chair for a short while. My assignment at the seminary entailed considerable public speaking throughout the USA and Canada; and I was privileged to serve as Bible lecturer for most of the district conferences as well as almost all of our colleges and seminaries.

With the public disclosure of the failure of our marriage in 1970 and our subsequent divorce in 1971, all invitations to preach and teach in congregations stopped or were withdrawn if pending. A meeting with our Conference Committee on the Ministry in the spring of 1971 resulted in a statement from them in which the congregations were encouraged to reaffirm my teaching ministry and to avail themselves of my services as they could. But the statement had no noticeable effect although my teaching ministry increased in non-Mennonite circles.

The Charleswood congregation which warmly welcomed me treated me as a wounded person and gave me much support and encouragement. I sang in the choir, taught some Bible classes, and in many ways they embraced me and allowed me to feel at home among them, even though it was clear that no one was supportive of the particular action of divorce or remarriage. When the second marriage, foolishly built on the ruins of the first, also disintegrated, even then they continued to accept me and assisted me in allowing myself the time I needed to get myself together before I considered another relationship that might lead to marriage.

During these ensuing years, the expert pastoral care of Ron Hunsicker, Cornie Rempel, Larry Kehler, and Dan and Esther Epp-Thiessen meant much to me. But there was above all the care that people in the congregation showed me by, e.g., inviting me to test my skills at cooking—for as a single parent, I was struggling to take care of my children in the kitchen, at least! This must not have been easy for the people in that church and it stands as a great tribute to them that they were able to minister to my needs in the very sensitive way they did. Generally, divorced males do not continue to attend church. Charleswood on at least one or two occasions even invited me to preach.

Five years later I met Dona and in 1977 we shared in church our desire to be married. There was encouragement for that step and the church council even gave permission to use the church building, which had been newly renovated and an addition built. Very quickly, however, it became clear that there was strong resistance in the congregation to our using the new sanctuary for our wedding.

Dona and I then invited those people who desired to meet with us one afternoon. There were about fourteen that did so, mainly women. It was not an easy meeting, but I would designate it as one of the most important meetings I have ever attended in church. The participants were divided into two groups: those who welcomed the opportunity to meet with us and ventilate their feelings about what had been going on in my life for the past five years, and those who were there to support us or just to listen. It could have been simply an exercise in dagger throwing, but it was not. Some of them spoke of themselves as failures as parents—although I felt, and said, they were not; others were frightened at what might happen to their children if someone like me would not be condemned by the church. Others spoke with passionate anger about the failures in my life and wondered at my audacity to attend church, even to continue on as a preacher or teacher of the gospel.

All of this one can understand—indeed, in earlier years I was exactly where those people were. I was comfortable at one time on the outside of a circle condemning the woman caught in adultery cowering on the inside of the circle. Now I was a sinner condemned by the church. Several people spoke on my behalf. They suggested that I be treated as a sinner; as one who had failed in marriage, but as one who also had the courage to try again and who wanted to start on a new footing. The meeting resolved nothing and I felt pained that no one could speak a word of hope to my condition and I was not able to communicate my repentance to them or the pain I had endured through marriage failure.

Shortly thereafter, the congregation met and passed a motion rescinding the church board's decision to allow us to use the church and urged that our marriage be delayed. By a majority vote they withheld their blessing from our marriage. This transpired at a meeting at the church on November 13, less than two weeks before the announced wedding was to take place and after the invitations had been printed. At a meeting on November 20 at the church, both Dona and I were allowed to present written statements in which we expressed regret that the church could not join with us in our joyous celebration and also indicating that we would proceed with the wedding in spite of the admonition from the church to delay. I was most stung by the refusal to give their blessing, since, as I put it, we come from a group of people which has taught for 400 years that we bless even our enemies. How could they withhold their blessings from our marriage?

Before the wedding took place on November 26, the church held a meeting on November 23 which resulted in a statement sent to us the following day which brought me to tears as I read it. For the congregation had been able to work out the matter and spoke some words of remorse to itself and to us individually which was pure gospel. It spoke of what had offended them, laid out the differences between us, but also affirmed that our relationship was able to transcend those differences. My father-in-law, never a great believer in the church, was deeply moved by the evidence that Charleswood as a congregation could make a confession and could go beyond that in the way that they did.

Throughout those weeks a number of colleagues and graduate students and others learned of the difficulties we were having. Some wondered why I bothered to stay in such a church. Was I some kind of masochist? The fact is that community matters to me; and I was not prepared to give up the profound community we had experienced at Charleswood simply because I had betrayed that community and some people were not able to receive my apology for that betrayal. The easiest way out might have been to walk away from it all. But even though there would be pain in trying the path of reconciliation, it was the only path we could take and we have never regretted it. Better to stay and work it out than to run away from a broken relationship. And that we did.

The congregation decided by a vote of 32-30 on January 29, 1978, to ask me "to refrain from all public ministry and teaching in the congregation until the next annual meeting in January 1979" and that "all of us seek through prayer and personal commitment and dialogue to bring healing to this hurting relationship." On March 18, 1979, that restriction was fully lifted. I continued to enjoy my work at Charleswood until January 1981, when we left Winnipeg and moved to Vancouver.

It might be worthwhile sometime to review that action and from the standpoint of the congregation deal with such questions as: What impact, if any, did it have on the young people in the church? Did it serve a useful issue of divorce? Would the sociologists and others in the congregation see it as a painful episode setting back the growth of the congregation or did it have some growth dimensions? What can be learned from it?

To some extent for me that entire decade was a period of stumbling and falling. I needed to lean on the church for help. I emerged out of that period a stronger and healthier person and the church was one factor in that growth. Another important factor was a Roman Catholic priest who was my counselor during my most difficult days and whose support gave me the courage to turn away from pathological behavior patterns and made it possible for me to embrace life more fully. The most important single factor was, however, the joy and strength I found in my relationship with Dona, whose joyous celebration of the good news that God loves you even when you do things that are hurtful comes to the heart of the gospel. Living with that reality helped me to recover confidence in my ability to be a husband.

The Langley Mennonite Fellowship

When we moved to British Columbia in January 1981, we were not prepared for the difficult time we would have in finding a church which had the correct balance between social concerns and personal renewal, between celebration and cerebration. It took us a year to discover a small fellowship meeting in an old church building just outside Langley. The building was always frightfully crowded, the worship service very often lacked organization and liturgical finesse and the pastor often forgot the offering! But the people were a rich mix of professionals and nonprofessionals, the poor as well as the rich, the emotionally fragile with the strong.

Above all, these people were able to receive us without reference to our past. They allowed us to work among them, to rejoice with them, and to weep with us. They rejoiced in our opportunities and we were able to share in some of the burdens they bore. After a year they elected me to be their chairperson and we moved through the difficult decision-making process of whether we should build a new building or buy another or what we should do.

The lower mainland of British Columbia is not noted for the

churches which take the gospel seriously along the lines of our foreparents, the Anabaptists. Yet this congregation spent more time keeping offenders out of jail by assuring that true reconciliation took place between offenders and victims than they did on their knees trying to get others to confess Jesus as Lord. In the deepest and most profound sense that congregation seeks the salvation of people, and because it invests so much of its time in that, it has a radiant joy that is hard to find in many churches these days.

Much of that is due to superb pastoral leadership from the team of Peggy and David Gustafson and the superb church musicianship of Marvin Regier and Alf Krause. But it is unfair to mention names—for what is remarkable about that church is that farmers and housewives, carpenters and airline pilots, all stand together with professors, editors, social workers, and medical doctors.

There really is no class distinction in that church. When I spoke to individuals at Simon Fraser University about this church, it was clear that they were coming from a different world. Theirs was the world of liturgical exactitude and precision and, as they said, of boredom in church; ours the world of celebrating what God had done in past aeons, the past week, and above all dipping into the resources of the Christian community to see what resources might be available the coming week.

We left British Columbia in 1984 to move to Jerusalem, where we were privileged to work and live during the past two years. Surrounded as we were by some of the most beautiful religious architecture of the world, soothed by the most beautiful liturgical statements of history, when we received letters from Langley telling us about the events of the church life at home, there were times we could not help but weep in homesickness.

What it all boils down to for me is that I view the church as people. What has kept me in the Mennonite church over the years has been the people, pained by their unfaithfulness to Christ, as I too have been unfaithful, struggling to find the path of God. We are a people on the move, looking for a better way, searching for a city whose Builder and Maker is God. Perhaps we move too often and too impetuously. Clearly we are too narrow in our outlook and we should be full members of the Canadian Council of Churches and of the World Council. Our voices deserve to be heard there on such issues as peace in the Middle East—indeed on peace in general. We speak in the councils of the universities and colleges of our land, in the parliaments, in the medical colleges and on the city councils. Why do we not speak in the church councils?

I am a member, by God's grace, of his church. It is an organization dedicated to change and to growth. It is open to self-criticism and indeed thrives on it. Because in my humble judgment the Mennonite church continues to be committed to responsible membership in a community where people really do care for each other, and to a community which reaches out beyond itself to all people as our neighbors and above all as children of God, and because we have something to say on the very critical issue of peace and war, I continue to rejoice in my belonging to that people. As can be seen from the above, such membership is to a large extent selfish. I belong to this people because of what I get out of it, but I hope by God's grace also to contribute to it and its witness in the world.

15

Mennonite Identity in Creative Tension

*Hedy
Leonora Martens*

Hedy Leonora Martens was born into a General Conference Mennonite home in Saskatchewan. She received her high school training in a Mennonite school, was baptized into Altona Bergthaler Church, and fell in love with a man of Mennonite Brethren background. For months she struggled with her conscience about whether to submit to a second baptism, required by the strict M.B. Church. She is interested in the role of women in the church and has written articles on this issue.

*N*ever *to have been asked to imagine the suffering servant stalking the hills carrying a machine gun; never to have been asked to see him aflame with the blinding fires of nationalism; never to have been asked to see him sitting at some upper-room oak table planning self-righteous strategies for the destruction of some enemy's military installation with its surrounding houses sheltering wives and widows and children and fathers and oh—so—young soldier boys fearfully clinging to their sisters ...*

... thoughts so poignant with gratitude I can taste the tears of them, here, in this Remembrance Day Service, surrounded by clean uniforms, the stirring tribute of the martial band fading away into the richly intoned words of Jesus, while minds struggle, surely struggle, with the dichotomy of those words of peace and these silently laid wreaths of war. Sad wreaths, sad flags, for all their pageantry, motionless kaleidoscope of color, held by motionless hands. Old hands. Remembering hands.

And I remember, too.

In earth-wrinkled hands; clothes, soap, and a toy, towel-wrapped and pinned with a safety pin.

In a Pennsylvania storehouse, barrels of food mutely waiting for earth's next disaster.

In a Winnipeg home, Vietnamese refugees adopting their sponsors, calling them Mom and Dad, Grandma and Grandpa, sharing their Christmas turkey, their gifts under the tree, and finally their faith.

In a Mennonite high school, Paul Schaefer and Gerhard Ens speaking to their "Kinder," recalling the bloody price our spiritual forefathers and foremothers paid for present freedoms, always without the shedding of any blood but their own.

The images multiply.

Frank H. Epp, unobtrusively guiding our young people's committee, no one recognizing, then, the inestimable privilege, the subtle influence, of this humble but consistent striving toward the creation of a just world.

Young Mennonite men and women bringing their bandages and healing witness simultaneously into the warring territories of north and south, winning their simultaneous trust.

A soft-spoken American Mennonite minister quietly but stubbornly fighting American draft boards to gain equal conscientious-objector status and so freedom from jail for young draft-resisters of non-Mennonite denominations.

A victim of assault in a Winnipeg Mediation office, shaking the hand of his assailant, fear and bitterness somehow draining away in the mystery of forgiveness.

While I watch, silently but deeply moved . . .

Images making the words of Jesus credible, my heritage of faith believable.

And I know why I am Mennonite.

In 1923, my parents, fleeing the aftermath of the Bolshevik revolution, emigrated to the Canadian prairies. So I was born into a General Conference Mennonite home on a Saskatchewan farm instead of into a Mennonite home in a Ukrainian village. During childhood, my existence was so insulated that I do not recall ever meeting a Mennonite who could not, like myself, trace his or her roots back to some Mennonite village in the Ukraine. To be Mennonite implied that common heritage. I do not know if I had any sense of differentiation, then, between my ethnic origins and my religious origins.

In my teenage years we moved to Manitoba, where I attended Mennonite Collegiate Institute in Gretna. It was probably here, through the study of Mennonite history, that I first began to form an articulated separation between my ethnic identity and my religious identity, and where I began to become more fully aware of the distinctive of the Mennonite (Anabaptist) way of interpreting and living Scripture. Also, while still in Gretna, I experienced the kind of Damascus Road conversion which is supposed to come only to those who have not grown up in a Christian home, or to those who have left it to lead a prodigal son/daughter existence. I fit neither category, but God, having a will of his own, chose to meet me in this way.

After being baptized in the Altona Bergthaler Church, life could have progressed quite simply if I had not fallen in love with a man of Mennonite Brethren background. For months I struggled with my conscience, trying to discern if it would be wrong to marry into a church which, from my perspective, was so bound by legalistic form that it would not accept me as a member unless I was rebaptized according to its specifications. This, again from my perspective, was asking me to deny my own experience and my own conscience. It was asking me to go on record as saying that my first baptism had not testified to a valid conversion.

In the end I concluded that it was unrealistic to expect that I would ever find a church which would agree with everything I considered right or wrong. So I decided that I could marry this Mennonite Brethren man (now my husband for 29 years). At the same time, I decided that I had to live by my own conscience, so I was not rebaptized. As a result, I was not on any church membership roll for about six years, at which time the Mennonite Brethren church reached the historically and theologically profound, courageous, and conciliatory decision to drop a large measure of its emphasis on form, allowing me to become a member without a betrayal of my own conscience.

That experience taught me much about membership in earthly denominations. I experienced in a minor measure the revolutionary security discovered by early Anabaptists, when they realized that they were not part of an earthly kingdom but of a heavenly one, and so what really counted was whether their names were entered in the "Lamb's book of life." No earthly body could exclude them from that.

There is a sense in which I could have belonged to any Christian denomination after this experience. Over the years I have lived in places where no Mennonite churches existed, and have learned much from Christians in other denominations which I had missed in my own. But I could never quite get myself to become a member of one of those churches. Their stance on war and all that grows out of that stance seemed too central a contradiction to the interpretation of Christ's teaching and life which had integrated my understanding of Scripture and had made Christianity credible for me.

Of course, had I been born into a Presbyterian family, for example, I might have remained a Presbyterian, even if I had become a nonresistant one—enough conscientious objectors of other religious persuasions have braved American draft boards in this past century as testimony to that possibility. After all, I do not agree with all tenets of my own church as it now stands either (some positions on the role of women in the church, for example, which I have written about in Mennonite Brethren publications; see *Directions,* Jan. 1976), but I have not on that account left this body of believers.

So in part I am a Mennonite because I was born into a Mennonite family and subsequently, upon encountering Christ, was baptized within that particular denomination. There is a covenantal sense, perhaps, to such a baptism, which is tied not only to the Christian church universal, but to a sense of loyalty to the particular church which brought one into contact with the living Christ, particularly when it also guided one into a correspondingly integrated lifestyle.

I do not, however, draw my ethnic identity from my identity as a Mennonite. Until I encounter further research to the contrary, I shall consider myself to be Flemish-Frisian in ethnic origin. A reading of Anabaptist history has served, for me at least, to separate those two identities. We have, after all, distant cousins scattered throughout Europe, who are not and never have been Mennonite; and we have thousands of Mennonite spiritual brothers and sisters who are ethnically, and even racially, unrelated to us. In other words, my "birth" into a Mennonite family makes me Mennonite only in the same way as my birth into a Reformed Church would make me Reformed, even though in both cases most of the original North American church members of these denominations also shared a common ethnic origin. So though I have surely become a Mennonite partly because of the providence of birth, I remain a Mennonite by conviction and choice; in fact, I am proud to be a Mennonite.

I am proud of belonging to a denomination which centuries ago bought with its own blood the freedom of religious choice which all Western Christians now take for granted, yet which never gained this by shedding the blood of others. I owe that heritage my respect and gratitude. I am proud of coming from and choosing to remain with a denomination which throughout its history has had nothing to do with persecuting Jewish or other minorities. It has preferred rather to pay the price of remaining a persecuted minority itself. I remain a Mennonite because I am a woman who believes that the grace of life was purchased through Christ's blood for women as for men, and the priesthood of all believers, such an important tenet of the Mennonite understanding of New Testament revelation, is for me the theology most consistent with that belief.

It is perhaps because of this tenet that Mennonite women, unlike most other women during the persecutions of the Reformation period, argued and died side by side with men in defense of their faith, and in defense of their right to choose it and to proclaim it. By belonging to the Mennonite denomination I have been given through these spiritual giants a spiritual heritage that makes me proud to be a Christian woman.

Unfortunately, even many of those who were born into Mennonite homes do not know about this heritage. Recently, I have spoken to a number of social workers in Mennonite communities who reported a high incidence of depression among Mennonite women due mainly to a low sense of self-esteem and a poor sense of self-identity. They linked this to a repressive theology regarding the role and status of women. I link it also to an inadequate knowledge of their own history. Although humility and simplicity in lifestyle have certainly always been important aspects of the Mennonite understanding of Scripture, this has been so for both men and women. These women seem to have lost the balancing interpretations of Scripture which lifted their Anabaptist ancestors to positions of equality quite unusual in their time. And they seem to have lost the sense of history which could give them a sense of pride and identity through such a heritage.

Even more disturbing are the rising reports on wife and daughter abuse particularly prevalent in homes which are highly patriarchal in structure. Again, a significant loss of the place of equality and respect often accorded early Mennonite women seems to have been lost to these people.

So we need to study our Mennonite heritage in order to rediscover and retain those distinctives worth retaining (remembering that our forefathers and foremothers died by the thousands to testify to their importance) and to maintain a healthy sense of identity; however, we also need to study our Mennonite heritage in order to learn how to become more inclusive and less exclusive—because that in itself is part of the original distinctive we have almost lost. Our heritage is really a Christian heritage, a part of the continuum of Christian history which has been lost to so many people of other denominations, but which really belongs to them all. We have owed the sharing of it for far too long.

Several years ago my husband and I spent a year in Britain. While there, we attended the London Mennonite Fellowship meetings, and came to know many members of that community, about half of whom had never been in a Mennonite Church, and most of whom had never heard of one before they encountered this one. Yet this small Mennonite fellowship was making a significant impact on the established religious climate of the British Isles. It had helped move the influential Anglican author, John Stott, to an anti-nuclear war stance. It was involved with helping Irish Christians find more peaceful solutions to their age-old conflicts; and it had provided serious Christian seekers with a theology and a history they embraced with intense relief, as though they had finally come home. Before we left, I had the privilege of interviewing quite a number of them, and their stories lifted my head permanently regarding my own heritage.

In fact their stories were to me the strongest endorsement of my Mennonite religious heritage and of its distinctives I had yet encountered. They were an endorsement based on the evangelical imperative to preach the good news to every nation and to every age. They labeled our way of interpreting and living Scripture as viable, as essentially Christian, as a part of the ongoing continuum and true expression of what the early church began when the Holy Spirit came upon them in order to give them power to live and to speak both the life and the teachings of Jesus. Because of these British Mennonites, I shall always remain an advocate of the Mennonite Christian distinctive—by whatever name it eventually appears.

That this distinctive happens to carry a denominational name that coincides with the ethnic label used by those Mennonite Christians who became a separated people through their centuries of flight from the Netherlands to Prussia to the Ukraine to Canada is perhaps unfortunate, in that it has the capacity to blind those of us who are members of that particular Christian pilgrimage. It may keep us from seeing the universal aspect of our particular understanding of Scripture. It may keep us from seeing the black and Oriental Mennonites as our denominational brothers and sisters, sharing with us a common root in Anabaptist (Mennonite) history. For me, however, it has also provided countless opportunities to share this part of the Christian heritage with the people who ask the inevitable question, "What is a Mennonite?"

Perhaps, then, our dilemma will be solved most effectively if enough of us, corporately and individually, simply apply the apostle Peter's answer to questions regarding our own spiritual (as well as cultural) roots: "Always be prepared to make a defense to anyone who calls you to account for the hope that is in you, yet do it with gentleness and reverence" (1 Peter 3:15).

Hopefully, this defense will also include creative ways of accommodating those Mennonites from the Ukraine who have not (yet) chosen the Mennonite faith, but who wish to keep, and have the right to keep, the cultural and ethnic roots which they believed were encompassed under the name Mennonite. We cannot in the telling of our stories deny them the right to these roots just because they have not chosen the religious aspect of them. To do so would surely not be Christian.

And hopefully, those of us who share these roots, and who have chosen to remain in the Mennonite faith, will also recognize that the need to investigate and to appreciate our own *cultural* roots is a healthy human need, deserving our support whether we are directly involved in it or not. It will do the cause of Christ no good if we as Mennonite churches are seen as opposing healthy attempts to maintain our particular cultural heritage. Rather, we should encourage the cultural endeavors of all ethnic groups within our denomination and within our community, so that we can truly become salt in those communities, encouraging the good, the beautiful and the true, even in secular culture. Much as we might like to reduce our dilemma to a simple either/or solution, we cannot do so with integrity. We will simply have to continue living with this tension between our religious and ethnic identity, always aware that to lose either would be a significant and irreplaceable loss.

However, we must learn to live with this tension in a creative, sensitive, and much more informed and inclusive way. More and more people of other denominational and/or cultural backgrounds are entering our churches through personal interest, through intermarriage, or through intentional evangelistic outreach. Far too often we have given them a Mennonite version of Baptist theology regarding the necessity of the new birth, as though that were the lowest common denominator of information we share with all people, while keeping the rest of our *faith* heritage to ourselves, as though it applied only to our particular *ethnic* background. This, in my opinion, is selfish, unreasonable, insensitive, unwise, and even insulting. We fear we will scare these people away by letting them in on our distinctives. On the contrary, however, I believe that many of these people come to us specifically because of these distinctives, only to discover to their disappointment that they could just as well have attended a Baptist or any other evangelical church.

This is not intended as a reflection on the evangelical churches. They are a part of the Christian continuum, too, and so have their own valid distinctives to value and to pass on. We have learned from theirs. We ought also to allow them to learn from ours. They have a right to be disappointed. We are denying them access to our spiritual roots, which could well become theirs. We are not allowing them to be fully grafted into the tree.

16

Mennonite—
I Think

Carol A. N. Martin

Carol A. N. Martin lives with her husband, Dennis, at Elkhart, Indiana, where they attend the Belmont Mennonite Church. She was an administrative assistant with the Institute of Mennonite Studies, spending most of her time on The Mennonite Encyclopedia *revision project. She has done some translation work for the Mennonite World Conference Newsletter. Carol is at present enrolled in graduate studies in English at the University of Notre Dame in South Bend, Indiana.*

I was not born into a Mennonite family, as is the case for a growing number of Mennonites. When I was accepted into membership in a Mennonite congregation about five years ago, I had a fairly clear idea of what it meant to be Mennonite. In the past five years, I have had extensive opportunities to observe and converse with a broad selection of Mennonite leaders and laypeople, and my definition has undergone considerable adaptation and questioning. I find little in the way of an objective definition of "Mennonite" among Mennonites to help me.

When I requested membership, I did so because of the emphasis Mennonites themselves put on the deliberate, ceremonial aspect of joining a congregation; as far as I was concerned, I was already de facto a member, whether official or not. I seemed to fit best with that local congregation, and the formal step of becoming a member brought no changes for me. The responsible committee was gracious enough to accept me into membership on those terms.

Becoming a member made no difference to me because I already brought what seemed to be required with me. I grew up in a conservative evangelical congregation (Plymouth Brethren, the "open" variety), and there learned to love and know Scripture and God's people. Radical discipleship and radical obedience to God's Word (including the assumption that obedience might well incur persecution) were taught as a way of life, as was nonconformity to the world. My mother was well versed in Foxe's *Book of Martyrs*, and although she did not read the stories aloud to me, she did retell many of them. At the age of three or four I made a clear decision as to which side I would be on. Among Mennonites, this seems to be viewed as too young an age to make a responsible decision, but it is indeed the point to which my later reaffirmations of faith have always returned. I was baptized at the age of twelve. I absorbed suffering servant ethics from our weekly meditative communion services centered on the crucifixion of Jesus, and from Peter, Paul, and Mary records, particularly the albums that consisted mostly of spirituals. The trio's participation in the March on Washington with Martin Luther King, Jr., was my first object lesson in nonviolent resistance to social injustice.

The first Mennonites I met were fellow students at Taylor University (Upland, Indiana). They were the first people I knew who integrated peace teachings into their faith commitment, as an ethical imperative requiring obedience. Since moving to Elkhart, I have occasionally heard Taylor semi-vilified as a sort of arch-rival to Goshen College, usually coupled with a plea to Mennonite parents to send their children to Mennonite institutions; for my part, I am quite glad that some Mennonites chose to attend Taylor.

At the time I first joined a Mennonite congregation, personal conversion (not necessarily of the revival meeting variety) coupled with radical faithfulness—living both inward and outward peace— would have been my basic definition of what it means to be Mennonite. It was a primarily theological definition, in which I was encouraged by ethnic Mennonites who wanted to grow beyond their own culture and to be able to speak to people outside of that tradition. That particular definition now seems quite incomplete, if for no other reason than that I doubt whether Mennonites can be defined in theological terms. Described, perhaps, but not defined. We have, for instance, a very broad tolerance in theological categories, some of which the congregation in which I grew up might not be recognized as "theological" at all.

The categories of conversion and discipleship, which I saw as basic to being Mennonite, are defined in different ways among Mennonites and shared with other traditions as well. The emphasis given to peace teaching seems to be the major factor distinguishing the Mennonite tradition from other groups, although Mennonites cannot claim even this as unique territory and differ considerably among the different groups as to the proper expression of that teaching.

It does not disturb me that the denomination I have associated myself with has or had a strong cultural identity. I had lived outside of North America for eight years, and it was already plain to me that one learns a great deal from associating with and identifying with a "foreign" culture. While it is true that the act of joining the church meant little more to me than accommodation to Mennonite practice, it is equally true that I was hoping to learn something very specific from Mennonites: I had already learned something about grace from living among Lutherans; I was hoping now to learn something about serenity from Mennonites. I had grown up in New Jersey, in an area where there were no Mennonites, but Mennonites were only a state away, and we were not ignorant of who they were or what they stood for. They were spoken of with respect as people of integrity. The Amish and Old Order Mennonites were the most easily distinguished; it was not, however, their dress or living style that most impressed me but what appeared to be an extraordinarily kindly and tranquil spirit, in both men and women.

Once safely within the Mennonite fold, it did not take too long to discover that the ideal of tranquil Mennonite womanhood was following prayer caps to the back corners of dark closets, while Mennonites of both genders were grappling to forge a new identity in the midst of major changes in the churches. After confiding to a few people what lesson I was hoping to learn, I kept it to myself; some people had been amused, others vented frustration at my expectations. The latter interpreted serenity as submission and repression, qualities and habits they were eager to shed. The virtue I was hoping would rub off by association had come into ill repute and seemed generally to be considered, at best, an ideal which had only been an impossible ideal.

It seems to me that, perhaps by default, we are defining ourselves in social terms, which raises its own set of implications and barriers. Many external cultural characteristics and activities of Mennonites I share: I know German well enough to speak fluent Hochdeutsch and Swabian well enough to understand Pennsylvania German quite well; I am an enthusiastic quilter and gardener; a healthy diet and simple lifestyle were important to me long before I saw my first copy of the *More-with-Less Cookbook;* and I have an equally virulent work ethic. These have made my entry into Mennonite communities easier. But ethnic Mennonites are socialized differently than I am, maybe as a result of being raised to be nonviolent. My energy level seems a bit stronger, I laugh a little louder, and I fairly often feel as though I have committed a minor solecism.

There are unspoken rules of behavior and nonverbal means of communication which I occasionally do not catch, and there are times when I know that a signal has been sent but am at a loss to interpret it. Or I discuss a little beyond the toleration limits of my partner: I believe that there are good ideas and bad ideas, or good ideas and better ideas, and that discussion, or even good, hammer-and-tongs argument, is an appropriate way to sort them out; but I see that assumption quite frequently translated as "conflict," which needs to be either avoided or "resolved." It would be quite easy to develop a reputation for fractiousness. The "Mennonite Game," in which I am not a player because I have no pedigree, does not help integration. I do occasionally take an interest in it as an exercise in understanding the cultural group of which I am trying to become a part, but I know very few of the people, and the social implications of each piece of information are lost on me. When I listen to an extended session of The Game, it is usually because there is a good storyteller in the group.

To push this theme a bit deeper: I have serious questions about our primarily social definition of community and the presence of God in that community. To be sure, God often acts through people, but to expect immanence almost to the exclusion of transcendence is surely to limit our perception of God's presence and work. Moreover, if we do not expect grace to be extended except in the phenomenon of community, what have we to say to the socially marginal or maladjusted, or even to people who simply do not like us—or even to people we do not like? It seems to me that we run a risk of wrongfully withholding God's grace.

I notice that I have been inclined to use the word "Mennonite" as an adjective, not as a noun. The choice is not coincidental; I do not think in terms of "Mennonite" being the final end in itself but as being a descriptive modifier to "Christian," or "follower of Christ." This reflects a concern that denominational expression be kept secondary to the primary concern of following Christ and that it be relativized by the awareness that there are many other groups and denominations who are as earnest as we are in their desire to be faithful followers of Christ, who have chosen different expressions for that desire, and who may have better solutions to some of faith's questions than we do. It is my view that, in such situations, Mennonite views or practices must yield to wider Christian views; the Mennonite solution should not be retained on the grounds that it is traditionally Mennonite or Anabaptist. It is conceivable that there could be conflict between "Mennonite" and "Christian."

Quite frankly, I do not love the Mennonite church and tradition in the same way that many Mennonites do. It would not cause me grave pain or guilt to go to a different church, if circumstances so dictated, nor do I view ex-Mennonites who have joined a Congregational, Methodist, or Roman Catholic church as deserters, or as having "gone worldly," but rather as fellow pilgrims who are toiling on a different stretch of the same narrow way. This is not an attitude expected—and on occasion, not tolerated—in a "convert"; it is much preferred that a convert be enthusiastic and wholehearted. I have heard, "If you don't like it here, can't you go somewhere where you do like it?" That sounds fairly close to the old slogan, "Love it or leave it." There is some sense in this; after all, why take the trouble and effort to "convert" unless there are solid convictions? However, I am neither a convert nor someone born within the tradition.

My way of loving the Mennonite church may not always sound like love, but it is comparable to the way I love my family and my husband, and even myself. Family, husband, self, and church are people who have been given to me, and I to them, to love not as ideals but as they are, which means knowing strengths and weaknesses, sins and virtues, not seeing only the stylized role or ideal of what we think we are or were or ought to be. It involves more than passive seeing; there are responsibilities to work toward mutual growth, bear one another's burdens, and, on occasion, share one another's guilt. If we have been given to one another at least as much by God as by our own choice, we cannot simply walk away when the situation does not suit; there is as much responsibility involved as privilege or preference. We may not have a right to quit.

Am I Mennonite? There are times when I identify strongly with the wider Mennonite church and culture, and there are times when I do not. I sometimes get badly tangled between "we" and "they." In desperation, I base my claim to be Mennonite on the objective fact that my membership is still in a Mennonite congregation; and I suppose it will continue there until my congregation decides that I am no longer sufficiently Mennonite. Then it will be up to the congregation to define what "Mennonite" means.

17

Ethics, Aesthetics, and Mennonites

John S. Oyer

John S. Oyer is a historian at Goshen College, Indiana, and since 1966 the editor of The Mennonite Quarterly Review. *His numerous publications deal generally with Reformation issues and more specifically with Luther and the Anabaptists. His book,* Lutheran Reformers Against Anabaptists, *was groundbreaking in scholars' attempts to understand the reasons for the persecution of Anabaptists.*

*I*n retrospect it seems to me that there has never been a time in my life when I was not a Christian in some sense of the word, and even more particularly a Mennonite; but there were frequent and long periods of time when I thought and felt otherwise. At some times in my life I have been deeply unsure about whether or not I was Christian; and I have been certain that I did not want to be Mennonite. Much of my religious awakening has been in fact some form of return—to God, but also to patterns of life I learned as a child and youth, and to Mennonitism. Christianity and Mennonitism have been coterminous for much of my life, even when I broke away and found some of my deepest levels of religious satisfaction in other religious traditions. To recount my way into Mennonitism is primarily to give an account of my foundational religious life.

I began life as a "good" boy. All hands admit it! Even my oldest sister, who has the most fabulous memory in our family, admits it. She thought that I was disgustingly good. I was guilty of a few peccadilloes but no grave sins. This goodness was a kind of scrupulousness. I was scrupulous about everything—errand-running, proper politeness to the neighbors, formal bedtime prayers, keeping my fingernails clean, and polishing my shoes on Saturday night. Without understanding it, I was maintaining a centuries-old Amish-Mennonite attitude about obeying *Ordnung* until that maintenance had turned into legalism, a serious blockade to genuine faith. Unknowingly I was acting out our traditional form of faith, saturated with petty works. Later I came to realize the seriousness of my Christian problem: how can a "good boy" become a Christian? I began to understand the shape of the problem when I studied the teachings of Paul, its size when I studied the insights of Luther.

When I was a boy Christianity meant my congregation and sometimes only slightly more—the (Old) Mennonite Church. I reacted
negatively to that church of the 1930s largely because it was con-
vulsed by a political struggle over *Ordnung,* something I came to
understand only much later in life. The church could not fully make
up its mind on the particular forms of its separation from the world—
though it knew well enough that it had to be separated. It had fallen
into the rut of uniformity of dress and similar simplistic resolutions of
the centuries-old problem for those who espouse a two-kingdom
theology, a resolution not unlike that made by some medieval
monastic orders. Our church would have been horrified to learn of its
own similarity to those earnest monks and nuns. Here was both an asceticism that denied beauty completely—we should clothe ourselves
uniformly in grays and blacks and ignore the bright reds and greens
and blues of God's good creation—and also a legalistic turn of mind
that could only accentuate scrupulosity and turn it into heavy guilt.

Legalism and exaggerated asceticism. My third problem with the
Mennonitism of my childhood and youth was its sectarianism, a problem focused most sharply by World War II and my sincere albeit
naive registration as a conscientious objector. Three years of alternative service in Civilian Public Service (CPS) camps relieved me of any
illusions about Mennonite perfection. But it also convinced me that
there were earnest Christians who hated war, dreaded participation in
it, but saw no alternative to the excessive evil of fascism; they entered
the army reluctantly. Later in graduate school I studied both the
resistance movement to Hitler, including that of both Lutherans and
Catholics, and also the Nazi attempts to emasculate both churches
with the organizational *Gleichschaltung* and the creation of a new
"German Christian" church. I have never been able to understand
some of my best Mennonite friends who think that nonmilitary alternatives to Hitler's intentions were viable. Many politically
dominant humans have indeed thrown down the gauntlet, demanding that they be dealt with through exclusively military means; only a
sound military thrashing will dissuade them, even when the cost must
be reckoned in thousands or even millions of lives. So it was with
Hitler, Napoleon, Alexander the Great, Louis XIV, Julius Caesar,
Sweden's Charles XII, etc., *ad infinitum.*

Sectarianism meant that we were both small and also insignificant; and its sting would not vanish even when we regaled ourselves with stale jokes about that special enceinte in heaven occupied exclusively by Mennonites.

In recent decades sectarianism has come to me as a pervasive ethnicism, one that makes evangelism difficult, in some places impossible. It is fun to play the Mennonite game. Even when one can provide a justifiable historical reason for ethnicity—the pervasive persecution followed by centuries of discrimination, driving people together and remaining unattractive to new blood—it remains a serious handicap. Mennonitism per se can hardly be an attractive form of Christianity when its majority is composed of people who are distant blood relatives, within certain regional-ethnic pools.

In my youth I was at best a compliant, but not a convinced, Mennonite Christian. My plight was intensified by my inability to appropriate the means of grace most prominently available to us in those bleak years: revivalism. Our congregation held evangelistic meetings annually. Those meetings made me feel guilty because I had no overwhelming spiritual experience that radically altered my life. I thought that God worked in humans only through some dramatic Pauline experience. A friend of recent years told me that he responded to twenty-seven altar calls. I responded meekly to one only, and that by self-consciously—almost in shame—standing at my seat. I dutifully joined the church through baptism at about twelve years of age. But I felt a vacuity of soul because God did not overpower me with some "spiritual" encounter. It took me decades to learn that God did indeed speak to me in a multitude of ways, and that I needed to learn how to listen patiently, and then to respond. But I have learned through bitter experience the falseness of cheap faith peddled by itinerant preachers who suggest, even when they make the point indirectly, that their particular way to God is the only one. That is not much different from the worst form of Roman Catholicism which makes the same type of claim: the exclusive grace of God is available only in those humanly shaped forms that they possess and administer. How blasphemous can humans get?

In both instances I do not mean to belittle forms of God's grace that many devout Christians have found deeply satisfying. Of course God works in them through those forms. It is only the human propensity for generalizing and making uniform their own particular appropriation of God's good grace that strikes me as monstrous. They should praise the Lord for coming to them as he does, but permit him to visit others in his own, sometimes strange but certainly different, ways.

God administered his turnaround to me only gradually, over a six-year period of time, from CPS years through relief work in Europe with the Mennonite Central Committee. I was drafted at the end of my freshman year of college, and spent three years as a registered conscientious objector in four CPS camps, followed by another three years of relief work in Europe. Did we merely sit out the war in CPS? People said we did. In the Shenandoah Valley of Virginia, whenever we drove through the small town of Grottoes, there was always some-one on the sidewalk, or even sitting on his porch, who would yell out "COs," or more pungently "yellow bellies." So that even in 1979-80 I could not adjust to the use of yellow as the color symbolizing release of hostages, a good color, during the Iranian hostage crisis. Even though I love its bright beauty as a color, it has always meant cowardice. In those days we were fourth-class citizens, or something thereabouts. Since that time I have come to blame the American government for not giving us the opportunity of working at some-thing more significant than soil conservation or forestry projects, or even mental hospital work. We were not permitted to enter foreign relief work, where there might have been physical danger. Selective Service was interested in drafting men for war service and they ob-viously did not wish to popularize the CO position. I learned in CPS that many Mennonites—and also Methodists and Baptists and Catholics—were intensely sincere and earnest about their faith, and that they possessed uncommon courage. There I also felt the love and support of Eastern Mennonites whose dress code had alienated me. I yearned for a more tight-knit fellowship, but at the same time one that would include my General Conference Mennonite brothers from Kansas.

I was shocked to move from the relative ignominy and disgrace of CPS to relief work in Germany after the war. Lutheran pastors, who could not have anticipated our attendance at their particular churches, told their congregations that these North American Men-nonites, by their active demonstration of Christian love, were the best contemporary examples of genuine Christianity. We felt like museum artifacts as people turned in their pews to gaze at us. But I also felt a strange uplift of spirit: this despised religion of my ancestors, now visited upon and grudgingly accepted by me, had some strange vitality, some Christlike character that I had not understood in my feckless youth. In the years 1941-45 in the United States Mennonites were lowly, ignoble creatures, hardly even worthy of citizenship. In 1947 in Germany they were paragons of Christian virtue. The contrast was heady but also humbling; neither extreme could be fully true. More than a decade later I was still filled with awe at how much the people of Kiel, a city of 350,000 inhabitants, remembered and respected Mennonites. One illustration only: In the summer of 1959 after a year of study at a German university, I wanted to sell a used Volkswagen. I advertised in several Kiel newspapers, and I remember vividly my conversation with a prospective buyer. He asked me where I had learned German. When I told him that I had worked for two years in Kiel with the Mennonite Central Committee, his face lit up immediately. From that time on he was willing to believe anything I told him about the car, showing an innocent childlike trust in the complete integrity of a man he could not have known personally.

In relief work I also learned to marvel at the power of God working through men and women whose inadequacies as Christians seemed to me more glaring and obvious than any Christian spirit. Our MCC units were composed of people who quarreled over petty issues and were overly concerned with status. Yet some people found Christ through us.

Take Heinrich as an example. During the winter semester of 1948-49 he left the University of Leipzig in the Soviet zone for the University of Hamburg in the British zone of occupation. As one of twelve members of the Student Council at Leipzig, he refused to kowtow to increasing pressure from the Soviet authorities. He left his family in the Soviet zone, painfully conscious of their exposure to increased pressure because of his flight. In the course of time he visited our center with other students. Many Germans came to our center largely because we had food and clothing to distribute. We quickly learned how to detect those who came for material gifts only. Heinrich was not one of them.

I asked him why he returned to us so frequently. Surely it could not have been our intellectual attainments that drew him to us. In a gathering of German students we always felt culturally inferior, because we were. Heinrich replied that he came because he found in us a light that he had never seen anywhere in his life. Really! How could the light of Christ emanate from us with all of our bickering? I was astounded to learn how God works with power through the very inadequate human resources at his disposal.

Another example. Willy was a German prisoner of war who worked for the MCC in France in 1946. While he lived with us at our center in Burgundy, his wife deserted him for the American soldier by whom she had become pregnant. He had lost all his material property in Germany. Now the only human tie that mattered to him had been callously broken. He was a shattered man. But he found faith through us, in a long and painful struggle. Again I was deeply moved by the power of God to work through Christians whose contentious lives seemed inadequate for the task of attracting people to Christ.

Back home in 1949, in college again at Goshen, I learned how God spoke more directly to me. First of all, through the Bible. In Bible courses and in our annual Bible lectures, there was a divine voice of power and love, utterly convincing, completely disarming. The Word of God was intensely personal, breaking through time and again to address my particular condition; it could be neither mistaken nor resisted. That quiet but insistent voice or spirit, articulated in whatever supersensory manner, burned within me. It came with conviction through the biblical messages of John and Paul, made vital by the teaching of Howard Charles and Paul Mininger and by the preaching of Paul Erb and J. D. Graber.

But the spirit came with joy in certain hymns, a joy that stabbed and burned but also cleansed and freshened, something like a spring breeze that bore the scent of flowers. It was not some mere lilt of spirit, evanescent; but deep and penetrating beyond any resistance I might try to offer. Gradually I began to realize that it was a joy that I had encountered in my earliest youth, primarily in music but sometimes in poetry, neither explicitly Christian. I remembered my first encounter with Bach. Our junior high school orchestra learned to scrape and blow its way through one of his most simple compositions, "Come, Sweet Death." We mangled the piece, but its pristine beauty transcended our horrible rendition of it, a brilliance of musical spirit that has always remained with me. The effect on me was breathtaking, haunting me with a joy that was both sweet and hard. The element of death in the piece was utterly lost on me.

There were later encounters with joy, in both music and dance. At twenty I heard for the first time Beethoven's "Violin Concerto," played by Yehudi Menuhin in Carnegie Hall when we made one of our periodic visits to New York City from our Poughkeepsie CPS base. The utter delight was beyond words; I was transported beyond my normal sensory level of existence. For weeks I could not drive from my memory the beauty of melodic line of each major theme; and I could recall instantly to mind every supporting orchestral part as well as each cadenza. Under the same circumstances I saw ballet for the first time: a performance of Stravinsky's "Fire Bird Suite," along with "Swan Lake" and other dances. Stravinsky was present, called to the stage for applause; I had never seen a man capable of such an ear-splitting grin or so delighted to be honored. I have loved him ever since, despite anything I have read since about his life.

Much later in life I came to realize how powerfully God had spoken to me through beauty, especially music. But the strangest part was this: I always returned from my most dramatic encounters with beauty fully resolved to live a moral life, a life of complete goodness and service. I have never been able to account for that feeling, nor have I ever cared to search for a theology to explain it. It has been enough to accept these encounters as God-ordained and let the matter rest, even when I learned of the awesome paganism and/or egoism of a Beethoven or a Mozart. To me those and other composers have remained instruments in the hands of God, a testimony to his power and love. And C. S. Lewis' *Surprised by Joy*, read long after these earlier encounters with joy through music, gave unsought explanation. Plato supplied some theoretical undergirding for the relation between musical mode and ethics. Surely my earlier ascetic Mennonite background made the forms and expressions of beauty more appealing to my spirit.

If the Bible and beauty led me to God, what led me to the Mennonites as the most acceptable body of Christians?

In reality I only came back. After all I was born and raised a Mennonite. This is both glory and shame to many of us—glory if we discover its deepest message and its biblicism, shame when we revel in its mere ethnicity. Perhaps I should abandon recounting personal experience, as if it were the only medium, and move on to analysis.

1. I returned to Mennonitism because of its moral emphasis, one that seemed to me to reflect the most accurately of any church I knew the emphases of both Old and New Testaments. We live in a morally wrong-headed world where some of the best moral virtues are twisted to savagely immoral purposes. The human capacity for courage is turned by the terrorists into killing both selectively and wantonly in support of their ideals. The human drive toward persistent systematic hard work is turned entirely toward material gain, or toward enhanced social status. The natural instinct toward parenthood is turned into mere lust. Even a natural instinct toward some form of self-preservation is turned into a vicious and stupid arms race of proportions beyond the comprehension of any human. Something has gone badly wrong, whatever analysis one wishes to follow. And that wrongness is deep—not merely a wrong turn at an unmarked crossing of two roads, a turn that makes us retrace our way and resolve quietly not to make that particular mistake again.

Put another way, Mennonite Christianity has not emphasized systematic theology heavily, in sharp contrast to many other Christian traditions. We are not a creedal church, even though we find no difficulty accepting most of the standard creedal formulations of the early church. Sometimes we have erred by turning anti-theological inclinations into opposition to any kind of rational inquiry touching religion, denying thereby one of God's good gifts to us, our minds. More frequently we have acted out Anselm's formulation unself-consciously: "I believe in order to understand"; rather than living within Abelard's dictum that one needs to understand theologically—thoroughly—before one can believe. There is nothing inherently wrong about Christians in other traditions insisting on a more rigorously theological approach to their faith. The theological inquiries that they pursue are necessary and useful. But we have emphasized obedience to what seem to us to be clear and compelling scriptural commands, especially those of Jesus, rather than a rational search for complete and thorough understanding of a problem such as, for example, the nature(s) of Jesus Christ. That seems to me an accurate biblicism, compelling and attractive in its own way.

But what or which morality? All Christians believe in living moral lives. Anabaptists and Mennonites have deliberately emphasized some balance between personal and social ethics. Personal purity of life, while trying to follow Jesus as example, was one of the Anabaptists' most attractive evangelistic emphases in Luther lands. And more recently we have been conscious of this emphasis in the early church, and of its attractiveness to seekers after truth who had not yet chosen the Jesus way. But we have wanted also an ethic that embraced a broader social pattern: refusal to participate in war, for instance. This is an integral part of a complete ethical emphasis. That Anabaptist-Mennonite refusal to bear arms in any war, even the just war, has been commonly misunderstood by other Christians. That balance between personal and social ethics I have found attractive in Mennonitism, deriving from a biblicism that is sound and accurate. From time to time the balance has come undone; but generally, Mennonites have worked to restore it.

2. Ethics leads immediately to Christology. Although theologically and historically one ought to put it the other way around—Christology leads to ethics—I am writing about my own encounters with these issues, in the order in which they occurred. Mennonites have seen Christ as both savior and example. Cast theologically one could write about the theology of the cross and the theology of the kingdom. As in ethics it is the balance that matters. If Müntzer and the Anabaptists after him could complain of Luther's sweet Christ, one who did not demand anything of them, not even faith (which his Father granted as gift), they could also speak of the bitter Christ, whose painful cross they bore in several ways but especially in persecution. These paradoxes have always intrigued me, but even more so, compelled me to believe in them by their biblical accuracy, by their deep truthfulness that will not let me go.

Christ saves me by his death and resurrection, a mystery that defies rational explanation but one that penetrates more deeply within me that other truths, than other shapes of (or realities about) truth. But Christ also lives as example for me to follow in loving obedience, even if that obedience means death for me as it did for him. More commonly, of course, that obedience does not lead to my death in our present sheltered existence, but to certain forms of discrimination against me, or to humiliation. Even if Mennonites and Amish happen to be praised uncritically at the moment, the mood of our respective fellow citizens can change suddenly, and almost certainly will. We will be shaken, and those among us who cannot bear the shame will find other religious alternatives. Even early church Christians were not persecuted all of the time.

When our churches undo the Christological balance, emphasizing one Christ or the other but not both—such is our present condition—then we have to act to restore that balance.

3. Community, fellowship of the believers: a condition and attitude I learned only gradually to see, respect and finally love, above and beyond its sectarian appearance. When I was a small child, our family finances were straitened far beyond my understanding, owing to the premature death of my father early in the depression years. Our local congregation literally fed us and brought us through. I realized this fact only later in life, but I never quite got the point well enough in hand to thank those who had rescued us. For instance, I vividly remember my mother's surprise, and then her sudden tears, when a formerly bitter critic of my father, from one of the neighboring Mennonite congregations, brought us a sack of potatoes a few months after his death. He could not say much, except for a few rather gruff words about potatoes being useful now. I have since learned that members of our congregation literally saved others also. The pattern was repeated throughout many of our congregations.

The forms of community in our heritage have included community of goods, with no, or only a little, private property. When I had begun to appreciate and examine my own religious tradition, I gravitated toward a position of a fuller communal existence, even when I recognized that an intentional Christian community made up of late twentieth-century individualistic Mennonites had little chance of genuine success.

I despair of adequately treating this topic. I returned to, and have remained, a Mennonite in part because of the attractive biblicism of this emphasis. It leads to another dimension that we never mention: sainthood. We remain biblical enough to recognize each other as saints, including some of our leaders. And we can recognize the spiritual greatness of some among us who are the most humble—that their love of Christ and the believers greatly transcends the few who try to achieve some status within Mennonite society. We have among us some "Sarah Smiths of Golders Green" of C. S. Lewis' *The Great*

Divorce; more important, we even quietly recognize their superior sainthood.

4. Mennonites do practice their own form of ecumenicity, even when it is not unlike that of some other Christian groups in the past. It does offset our sectarianism. Many of us recognize other Christian ways or paths, not the same as our own, each with its biblical and Christ-ordained validity. During the past fifteen or twenty years we have developed a spiritual kinship with Reformed, Lutherans, Catholic monks and nuns and layfolk, all of whom share with us their own biblical insights. Or more commonly, we have learned to work together with Christians of other traditions in relief and disaster conditions, without particular regard to obvious differences in spirituality or doctrine. That is an ecumenicity that transcends mere organizational union.

Ethics, Christology, community, and ecumenism—these are ways of describing why I came back to, and remain within, Mennonitism. When they are put analytically they can distort the ways in which they unfold within our lives. Or worse, they sound like a lecture in Anabaptist thought. The reality of my own religious quest and of God hounding me until I yielded is better described in experiential patterns: that is the way it all unfolded. Yet the analytical description remains accurate in its own way; it describes those particular clusters of religious thought and behavior, notably not others, within which my soul and mind developed. If they seem arid, the reality was otherwise. The pools of water from which I drank were rich and vital, and I thank God for them.

18

Operation Cataract, 1964

Peter Penner

Peter Penner, who teaches history at Mount Allison University in Sackville, New Brunswick, was born in Siberia, Soviet Union. With the second wave of Russian-Mennonite immigrants (1920s) he came with his parents to Canada. He attended various Bible schools, including Prairie Bible Institute in Three Hills, Alberta. During World War II he served as a conscientious objector in British Columbia and Ontario. He earned degrees at the University of Western Ontario and at McMaster University in Hamilton, Ontario.

*I*t was the year 1964. I had decided to enter a doctoral program in history at McMaster University. This meant in all likelihood that I would be leaving full-time ministry in the Mennonite Brethren (MB) church and joining some university as a history teacher. I was also in the midst of preparing a series of articles for MB "Student Services." Among these was "Reclaiming Marginal Men" (*Mennonite Brethren Herald*, March 13, 1964), first given as a talk at MBBC in February 1964, about which some asked: "Is it autobiographical?"

All of this reflected some ambivalence about my vocation as a minister and about my church. In a word, an earlier vision had clouded over. What was needed to correct the blurred vision was a new prescription or an implant to remove the cataracts, so to speak.

It was my good fortune, therefore, to be permitted, at age thirty-nine, to attend the Mennonite Graduate Seminar arranged by William Klassen. Present at Elkhart to give papers to a select group of graduate students were John Howard Yoder and Victor Adrian, to name several. They focused on our Anabaptist/Mennonite history and heritage in a manner most meaningful, almost revelatory to me. Adrian, representing the MB church, gave the premier presentation of his thesis, "The MB Church: Born of Anabaptism and Pietism" (*MBH* insert, March 26, 1965). His provocative paper was more than matched by Yoder's, entitled "The Recovery of the Anabaptist Vision." This was a brilliant encapsulation of Guy F. Hershberger's 1957 collection of essays elicited by the challenge of H. S. Bender's seminal paper entitled "The Anabaptist Vision" (1943). Yoder concluded:

> The historical meaning of Anabaptism, which is Biblically justified, is not identical with but in serious conflict with contemporary Mennonitism. We thus must choose between a profound repentance and renewal, recommitting ourselves to that vision, being judged by it and thereby being justified by it in spite of our cultural inferiority and our separateness; or we must face the difference between that vision and our present existence and conclude that out of faithfulness to the Anabaptist vision the Mennonite denomination should cease to exist.

Rightly or wrongly, I left Elkhart reflecting on the injustice done to my generation of MBs (the 1950s), not least at Mennonite Brethren Bible College (MBBC), where we never heard about Bender's paper. Though I realized I had to share the blame for remaining ignorant of it, nevertheless I remained somewhat pessimistic about recovering anything as meaningful as our Anabaptist history and heritage within a church which was then intent on articulating a new theological formula as a series of "distinctives." Adrian's paper, though it turned over a new furrow or two, nevertheless could do little to broaden the MB focus beyond a return to 1860. As a matter of fact, anyone who gave a "pre-1860" interpretation was suspect, until the mid-seventies. (For the debate sparked by a J. A. Toews' paper, see *MBH*, March 10, 1972, to June 2, 1972.)

The publication in 1965 of Delbert Wiens' scintillating study of the MB church, *New Wineskins for Old Wine*, only made me ask in my review of it: "Has the time arrived when some will choose between being side-tracked [on the one hand] in a comparatively sterile evangelicalism and an alignment [on the other] with those desirous of recovering the Anabaptist vision?" Had I not been told as a home missions pastor serving in Toronto that I should not waste time on inter-Mennonite fellowship and dialogue? (*MBH*, April 15, 1966, 6-7.) Though "brotherhood" was one of the MB distinctives, it was apparently meant to apply, in some minds, to a MB brotherhood only.

All in all, 1964 provided a new plateau from which to evaluate my first forty years, while it placed on me a new burden of knowledge about my spiritual heritage. Actually, that year saw the final resolution, fortunately, of my sometimes painful disorientation from fundamentalism. The metamorphosis was triggered at MBBC. I was astounded in 1952 to hear that E. C. Manning (politician, radio preacher, and pastor) had publicly burned in his church a copy of the new Revised Standard Version of the Bible. I was even more astonished that some sectors of my church wanted MBBC faculty to take a strong stand against what McCarthy-era Christian anticommunists called the pink-tinged Bible. Fortunately, in ways I cannot remember, a little booklet by Bender, Lind, and Lehman fell into my hands. Their 1953 publication for the Mennonite Church entitled *The RSV: An Examination and Evaluation* confirmed my own view that the RSV was the product of honest, competent biblical scholarship and which had given us Scriptures which were a vast improvement over the seventeenth-century King James Version.

More than ever, I realized at MBBC that I had been shinnying up the wrong theological tree, especially since 1945. While working among conscientious objectors in British Columbia forestry camps from December 1943 to April 1944, I was told about Prairie Bible Institute, Three Hills, Alberta. What a missionary school it was, my new friends claimed, and what a significant Bible teacher L. E. Maxwell was! As a result, I attended there for two years (1945-47). During those years I also gravitated toward the Associated Gospel Church. I had also been influenced by the early ministry of Charles Templeton, just when he was rebuilding a burnt-out Avenue Road church in Toronto as his launching pad to a flamboyant career as an evangelist. You see, as a conscientious objector I had had to go from the relatively sublime task of planting trees in British Columbia to a ridiculous job in the hide cellars of Canada Packers in Toronto. Fortunately, during the winter of 1944-45, to compensate for our daytime miseries, several friends and I assigned to this "Red Cross" work made friends in Banfield Memorial Church (Mennonite Brethren in Christ, later Missionary Church), and found excitement in attending Templeton's Sunday evening rallies. (Templeton, *An Anecdotal Memoir*, 1983.)

While Maxwell's disciplined environment and Kesick-like Bible teaching gave me a solid footing in the Bible, it was while at PBI that I was directed toward study and service within my church. It was a fatherly letter from a man I greatly respected then, J. K. Janzen, which helped to steer me away from taking a path into some other church. He was the father of some of my Vineland friends, lived in

Grimsby, but served in those years as principal of Virgil Bible School. Freely translated from the German, he wrote:

> I felt sorry about you; did I not see in you numerous talents given by God; and my prayer was: Ach! would that Peter Penner would not leave us. Why, I thought, does he not attend our schools? We recognize the strength of the Three Hills school, but have observed that most young people who go there bring back changed attitudes toward our church. [JKJ to Penner (November 26, 1946).]

Encouraged by such concern I steered a course toward preparation for leadership in the MB church. At age twenty-two I went back to high school, at first to Virgil (later called Eden), and at twenty-five to MBBC, Winnipeg.

Janzen's letter prompted me to revaluate positively the path along which I had been led. I recalled that Henry H. Janzen and others had persuaded my grandparents (Peter Wiebes, and he an ordained minister of the so-called "Kirchliche") and my parents to be rebaptized by immersion in 1936. Also, had not my spiritual pilgrimage been fostered in the Vineland MB church (on Victoria Avenue, where I was baptized at age sixteen)? Had not the brethren there guided me into taking a conscientious-objector stance? Though in retrospect I lamented the breaking up during the mid-thirties of the UM/MB fellowship in Vineland (typified in my mind by the recollection of my father's working shoulder-to-shoulder for several years at Chris Fretz Farms with John [later Bishop] Wichert), nevertheless, I was always grateful for the freedom-in-fellowship Vineland young people enjoyed and for the opportunities for learning through *Bibelbesprechungen* and of service and activity in that church.

From my perspective twenty years later, MBBC in the 1950s was not such a great school *academically*. But what more could I then have asked than to have three years of teaching by men of the stature of A. H. Unruh and John A. Toews? Most happily, even though I was not a music student, we had Ben Horch as the leader of an impressive music program. We took our *Kernlieder* (hymns of Mennonite faith) as we traveled conference-wide as *a cappella* choirs and male quartets. We heard Unruh, cherished by many Mennonite groups, give his stirring sermon: "Das Durchbrechen der ueberlieferten Ordnungen" (The breach in the transmitted ordinances of the MB church). And Toews warned against interdenominationalism (yesterday's para-church). (See *Voice*, July 1, August 1953, and May/June 1954, respectively.)

Having identified myself with these brethren and their colleagues, and having taken the popular route from MBBC to the old Waterloo College, ordination followed in the Kitchener MB church. During nine years, interrupted only by two years for a Master's degree in history, I served in the MB conference. Four years were spent as a home missions pastor, first at Lindal, Manitoba, and later in Toronto.

During three years as a teacher in British Columbia, I also became involved in provincial conference work. During that time there was always another wholesome influence in my life, preparing me for an inter-Mennonite role, making me in attitude more like Harvey Taves, an ecu-Mennonite. At least so it appears now. In his inimitable way, the late Frank H. Epp drew me into a longtime association (since 1956) with the *Canadian Mennonite* and then the *Mennonite Reporter* as a contributor of news, and sometimes of opinion. Without a peer, at least for me, he exemplified in his life and books what it meant to be Anabaptist/Mennonite in an age of enveloping American fundamentalism, with all of its extremist manifestations from the early fifties to well into the seventies. In a word, he helped me, rather unwittingly, become prepared for Operation Cataract, 1964, and then to do something positive with it.

My earlier decision to take on the burden of a more perfect knowledge of my Anabaptist/Mennonite heritage was strongly reinforced when I arrived in 1965, at age forty, at Mount Allison University, a United Church-related school. Laurie Cragg, the president then, well read, an active United Church layman, went out of his way to welcome me as a representative of that background. A paraphrase of what he said was this: "You will likely be alone here as an Anabaptist/Mennonite. Therefore you must take every opportunity to contribute to university and church life from 'the left wing of the Reformation.' " How glad I was then that I had also read in the field of Reformation history at McMaster, not as a bread-and-butter course, but just for myself. (My primary fields were British Imperialism, Modern Britain, and Confederation Canada.)

Also, once we were far removed from the Mennonite epicenters and living in New Brunswick, going on sabbatical in the United

Kingdom, or traveling in West Germany, it was marvelous how often questions about our cultural background led to an opportunity to tell of our faith. Our peculiar story of a migrating people who had come to Canada from Russia, yet had retained in varying degrees the burden of Reformation and Russian history and the Anabaptist/Mennonite heritage led to many questions. Both my wife, Justina, and I have had the following scenario repeated dozens of times. Oh, but you were born in Canada. Your English is virtually accent-free. No, we were both born in the Soviet Union, and were brought by our parents to Canada when we were still in infancy (1926). But you say you speak German rather than Russian, and yet have never lived in Germany! How is that? Well, German was our mother tongue because we lived in villages (in the Ukraine or Siberia) where we had the privilege of maintaining our Mennonite culture (which included the German language and Anabaptist faith).

The fact is, of course, I could have taken the road of many others into a new identity, or another religious affiliation, such as a Baptist church. I recognized the strength of some temptations to give up the Mennonite identity. Many (because of their advanced assimilation to the prevailing uniculture) have been embarrassed by the "bonnets and buggies" imagery conveyed by the media. Yet I have discovered that those of our people who have resisted modernization and welfare benefits on grounds of other-worldliness and self-reliance are often more admired and respected by thinking people than those of us who unthinkingly compromised our position on all fronts.

I told the Sackville clergy in 1978 about those compromises which continued to embarrass me. The following have little in common with the essence of the Anabaptist/Mennonite way. To allow ourselves to be transformed into North American fundamentalists by talking right-wing positions on matters of war and peace has been contrary to the injunction in Romans 12:1-2. This became all too evident in the Vietnam War and the Arab-Israeli conflict. Many Mennonites unthinkingly became caught up in the Christian anticommunism of the "Far Right" and have given support for the free-enterprise system which maintains the status quo in the world, where 20 percent consume 80 percent of the world's resources. Ron Sider has since spoken to that issue in his *Rich Christians in an Age of Hunger*.

None of these attitudes are surprising, of course, if it is true, as a

British Columbia Mennonite told me in 1960: We have taught our young people to make money, as quickly, as easily, and as much as possible (*so schnell, so leicht, und so viel wie moeglich!* were his very words). We have weakened the Anabaptist/Mennonite thrust with our personal aggrandizement. Having become wealthy and assimilated, is it any wonder we felt uncomfortable with those Mennonites who resisted modernization. Is it any wonder that some wanted to change the name and to form Bible fellowships rather than being Anabaptist/Mennonites with a mission to the whole person?

Much more significant has been the personal question, however: Can I be a Christian without being Anabaptist/Mennonite? For others this may be a wrong equation. For me it became the primary one. Was there something so foundational to Christianity in Anabaptism that *I* could not be a whole Christian without being Anabaptist/Mennonite? For me the onus—the burden—is the knowledge of which I wrote earlier. If I know the intricacies of a position for which men have died, I can hardly be nonchalant about it. And if I became persuaded that I could not have defended the Lutheran, or Zwinglian, conception of the church in practice (as manifested between 1517 and 1531), or the Calvinist church as set up after 1541 (though in many ways I admire the Elizabethan Settlement in England after 1561), then there is all the more reason for looking to the alternative view of the church and Christian lifestyle represented by the Swiss Brethren and Menno.

What, then, is there about my heritage without which I can hardly be a Christian? Jesus' answer was: "How can you call me Lord, Lord, and not do the things I say?" Or, as Hans Denck put it, "No man is a Christian who does not follow Christ in life!" The easiest of the key principles is, of course, the voluntary free church based on believer's baptism. This was truly revolutionary then and has continued to be so wherever Anabaptism is fully recovered. The more challenging principle is *Nachfolge* (discipleship, Luke 14); redemptive fellowship, following the "rule of Christ" (Matthew 18); a reasonable but nonconforming service (Romans 12); and the rejection of the glorification of saints, nations, war heroes, and racism. As John Howard Yoder put it in his article for the MB *Christian Leader* (July 5, 1966), the Mennonite fellowship must be "borderless"; or as others have said: You cannot enter into the kingdom of God without your brother! (cf. *Mennonite Reporter*, February 3, 1986, 8.)

If this statement of faith, which is neither fundamentalist nor se-cular/humanist, has validity, then the onus of persuasion must be laid on others as well: on the merely ethnic Mennonites living scattered, as well as those who are anxious to change the name for all the wrong reasons. Also, the work of acting as a corrective on reformed doctrine since the sixteenth century must go on! My wife, Justina, and I, however, have never felt it was our duty to plant a Mennonite church. Rather, we would be ourselves, as illustrated above, and interject Anabaptist/Mennonite ideas, and even culture, whenever and wherever possible or necessary. In our case, though we joined the Sackville United Church (NB) in 1967, we made a decision, though quite alone here, to maintain our Mennonite identity. The United Church of Canada (UCC), perhaps more than any other, permitted us just that. It is not doctrinaire in a fundamentalist way. Too often, as critics have pointed out, the UCC has allowed the world to set the agenda. Nevertheless, the UCC provided us freedom to be ourselves.

Utilizing the principle of penetration, as suggested by President Cragg, I have "taken Menno to the Mount" by giving guest lectures on the essence and history of Anabaptism in a variety of settings. Reflections on my position as an Anabaptist Christian teacher at a university led me to research the subject of Mennonites in the At-lantic Provinces (MAP): professionals like myself, MB Christian Service and the Dartmouth MB church, MCC/VS in Newfoundland, the story of the Siegfried Janzens and the John Esaus. Articles followed in the *Mennonite Reporter* in 1974 and 1975. This led to the calling into being of a loosely organized community known as MAP. On Thanksgiving 1985, MAP celebrated its tenth anniversary. Its main purpose has always been to insure that our common heritage and its outworking in real life are held before us.

Now in the 1980s, my life has come full circle, in one respect. After two decades here I had the opportunity of writing a history of the very church from whose ministry I withdrew myself. It deals solely with the country-wide *church planting* of the Mennonite Brethren church since 1883, under the title *No Longer at Arm's Length*. Though I could not be entirely uncritical, the research and writing was, in many ways, a labor of love, and gave me many rewards, not least, the reestablishment of many meaningful contacts within the MB church.

19

Why I Am Still a Mennonite

Calvin Redekop

Calvin Redekop, trained in sociology and anthropology, has studied religious minorities, including the Arminians, Hutterites, Old Colony Mennonites, and numerous communal groups. He is the author of numerous articles and books. His book, Strangers Become Neighbors, *deals with the Mennonites and Indians in Paraguay. Redekop is a professor of sociology at Conrad Grebel College, University of Waterloo. He and his wife, Freda, are the parents of three sons.*

My family had come through the Great Depression in the northeastern Montana area of Wolf Point with little more than its pride and support of a struggling community of fellow pioneers. By 1937 my parents had decided that hope "was gone," and in good Okie style moved to the West Coast to start life over again. We moved into a rundown house standing by itself on a lonely rise, and began to work in the prune, cherry, and hop fields. I developed a sense of awareness that we were poor. Yet there was also something that I could sense in my extended family, most of whom also moved to the West Coast, and the religious community in which we lived (Dallas, Oregon) that told me we were part of something important which gave me some sense of security.

Wanting to be accepted and part of the larger world, however, continued to tug at my heart. The grade school era was relatively benign, but when the fall freshman initiation party rolled around during my first year of high school, I wanted to go and be a part of the gang. My parents, of course, did not approve and did not want to take me to the celebration. When a senior student, also a basketball star and hence a BMOC, invited me to go along with him, I did not know the full reasons for his invitation, but I suspect he was suspicious that there was something unusual about "that Mennonite." What is more, I think he liked me. I gladly accepted.

The evening began jovially enough, but took a turn for the worse when I was forced to go through the hazing of the "belt line." I will never forget the extreme pain I felt as several of the older students gave me some especially hard straps on the rump as I crawled between the legs of the line of boys, one of the strappings hitting me in my groin, and I thought I would die. I knew several of the fellows were bullies and they persisted in teasing me and making fun of my background. Because I did not fight back they got an extraordinary pleasure.

The evening became even more alienating for me when my "gracious" host put me in the backseat with his sister, and with his girlfriend in the front seat, drove to a tavern for a few beers (I had never had one in my life), and then drove to a secluded lane for some "heavy necking." The sister was attractive enough but I just could not understand what was the meaning of all this, when I hardly knew her and had no interest in "sinful" physical contact. (Lest anyone be offended that I did not respond to the normal opportunities of sexual intimacies, however benign, let me comfort them by assuring them that I had and have the normal sexual urges and am attracted to females.) But my upbringing (super ego to the cynical Freud) was overwhelmingly strong and still is, for which I am and will ever be thankful to my parents and church community.

It was a great relief to be let off at the ramshackle home much after midnight, though with the feeling that I had been "raped," that I had been forcefully dumped in filthy water. All night long my mind tormented me and raged in confusion. But it began to form some type of focus for the tumult with the phrase that kept coming back to me: "You are different from them; you don't belong in that crowd." A fifteen-year-old cannot understand very much about the meaning of history, the subtleties that create uniquenesses and centers of consciousness, but I knew I was different. I remembered the tense battle my older sister had gone through two years earlier in getting permission to go to high school. She was the first in my community to go, and although she was very bright, in retrospect it seems to me she had two counts against her: our people did not see any use in going to high school; and even worse, she was a female and what would a female do with a high school education?

Through later years the awareness of being different became to be an accepted fact. I did not question it. I simply accepted it as not discussable and felt secure in my inner world of being a part of a separated world where my extended family was pretty much the social and cultural world in which I moved, and in which my grandfathers on both sides (both ministers) served as spiritual legitimizers of my religious world. The authentication of a world through hearing the mellifluous sermons of my grandfathers Sunday after Sunday, where at least half the congregation were members of my extended blood family and married in-relatives, can only be experienced, not expressed.

But the high school initiation described above, which intruded to my experience along with many other similar events, increased my anxiety and ambivalences. My friends in church and neighborhood were Mennonite, but in high school I was drawn toward others, because I felt the world provided the opportunities for personal achievement, including engineering as an occupation, which to me at that point seemed to be the ultimate in creativity and achievement.

The we/they mentality became a "slough of despond" for me with the onset of the draft of World War II. I was caught between two conflicting forces: The pull of mass culture and peer groups beckoning me to become a part of the "real world" by signing up as a regular for the army; and the call of my church and the wishes of my extended family, especially parents, who followed the nonresistant faith of my grandfathers. As is the case in most of life, the decision as to which way to go, was made most undramatically: I was designated a 4F—not physically fit for the military because of my deafness.

The subsequent years of my development necessitated a long struggle in coming to grips with the question or problem to identify with an "in-group" which had offered all the security of the full life, i.e., family security, friendship, and religious tradition which had all the dimensions of a past, present, and future. The uneasy feeling that this was somehow inauthentic, irrelevant, and even wrong, came to me from various quarters, but above all from my peer group, persons who had been influenced by the fundamentalist evangelical movement that was making inroads into some of the more susceptible groups, such as the Evangelical Mennonite Brethren (my childhood church) and the Mennonite Brethren (in which most of the rest of my relatives and friends lived and moved).

While many of my friends in my peer group and the larger circle of religious community succumbed to the rejection of the mediated heritage and tradition, there were two reasons why I clung doggedly to remaining a Mennonite: my subconscious somehow has intuitively always valued the validity and beauty of history, tradition, and the commonplace, so that I have always deeply enjoyed the life in the local community and congregation; and my intellectual pilgrimage in which I made the astounding discovery slowly, though ever more permanent, that every person grows up in an "in-group," a plausibility structure which for him or her forms the sole locus of reality, and that no one can live without it.

Thus I came to the realization that I had been led to believe that it had always been all right for Jews to claim a tradition and to be proud of it, but it was wrong for Mennonites and other people, that it was a perversion of human and religious history. But which I slowly discovered was contrary to all we knew about human history. Why should Christians deny for themselves a sense of history, heritage, and substantive meaning in order to be in God's plan, yet revere the Jews as a people who had the tradition that nurtured the man-God we worshiped? I began to realize that God's story was told through the history of peoples as any reading of the Old Testament will attest. That it was a curious truncation of salvation history to say that peoplehood stopped with the nativity and that only Jews counted. Of course, the question of *which* tribe or people *carried on the* holy history continued to rear its ugly head, and for many years the overreaction that the Mennonites were the true bearers of the holy people after the Reformation was tempting for me. I am afraid I argued that position often, knowing it was not rational, but did not understand the subconscious conflict.

In the light of emotional study, dialogue, and intense living, I came to the conclusion that the Anabaptist-Mennonite heritage was God's gift to me, and to reject it was merely replaying Esau's selling of his heritage for a shot at the adulterations and abominations of the middle class. Not that the Anabaptist-Mennonite heritage was the fulfillment of Christianity and that "extra Anabapticus nula salus." True, the Son of God had already been produced in a people, but many more sons of God needed to be raised up and my heritage was one of the channels by which this could possibly be done. This would have been enough to keep me in the Anabaptist-Mennonite fold, but the clincher for me has been the continuingly necessary gratification to discover that my heritage is being considered by other traditions as having been a special medium of grace for some of the "hard sayings" of Christ.

The idea of the narrow gate, the few that will enter therein, and the seriousness of obeying Christ's commands have seemed to catch the essence of the revelation of the Creator God, or so it has appeared to me. I, along with other human beings, am the product and beneficiary of a specific and local transmission of people in relationship. To lust after the gods of another tribe simply ignores the irrational motive of such a choice. To allow others the authenticity of a heritage such as the Jews or Lutherans, but to deny it for myself was not only illogical but contrary to the way God made us.

To ask the question "Why am I a Mennonite?" may therefore be the wrong question or even a false way of asking it. For as individuals we are what we were created. One can therefore probably only ask, "Why do I *remain* a Mennonite?" This is a more reasonable and remarkable question and I have already actually answered the question in the above. For the same reasons can be given to the former question, but the latter question makes the answer make more sense. To ask me *why* I am a Mennonite is to ask the question sociologically. To ask me why I *remain* a Mennonite is to ask the existential and theological question.

For every plausible structure it is important to have an authoritative mythology which legitimizes the whole system. I remain an Anabaptist-Mennonite because the "mythology" of the heritage is germane to humankind and what I know about how God relates to it. Unless I question the validity of everything, I must accept the external authority of the Christian tradition. According to that tradition, my Anabaptist-Mennonite heritage is so centrally located that I can't think of a soup so good that it would tempt me to try it and forsake mine. My many Quaker, Jewish, Catholic, and other religious tradition friends have great heritages as well, and I have greatly benefited from relating to theirs. I remain in mine, however, as I have said, because I am stubborn, and because I have become convinced of the reality of a pluralistic universe and for the rightness of it, and because I have enjoyed my particular window on life.

The human church where all people will have one king and think one way is simply not in harmony with the way the world has been created. And even though from a theological perspective the one God created the heaven and the earth in harmonious functioning fashion, it soon lost that, and what is more, the message of his only begotten Son was of a divided and splintered world which he said would remain divided into at least several factions, for did he not say, "Straight is the road and narrow the gate . . . and few there are who enter therein"?

The Old and New Testaments give us few indications that before paradise has been fully instituted all the sheep from time immemorial will have one shepherd. No clues are given as to who would be the surrogate shepherd in Christ's absence. A "corpus Christianum" attempted by the early Roman Church leaves a bad taste in our mouths. But this is not to say that pluralism expressed in hopelessly splintered groups, each thinking it is the truth, is the logical conclusion to the matter. I *remain* an Anabaptist-Mennonite because of the vision that the paradoxical unity will not come by the suppression of pluralism by the state or the institutional church, but by those who respect the inherent normalcy of pluralism. The vision is to achieve the unity in the spirit from below, through the goal of generating a center of reality and meaning which is voluntarily achieved and which works from the center of consensus and mutual humanity and sinfulness toward a cosmological vision of being one even as "my Father and I are one."

Throughout my life, I have been plagued with the ultimate solipsist question: "Why am I me? Am I sure I exist?" My membership in a "family" where there is a long string of ancestors, of sad and painful events, as well as happy and humorous dimensions in all of them, has helped me to solve that question—"I am a part of a larger picture, and I *fit!*" I decided that a Jewish boy had the same solipsist problem, and solved it the same way: Ergo, praise God for a sacred canopy, under which I could stand.

I remain in the Mennonite canopy precisely for the same reasons, though it is raised to a higher level of abstraction. "Why is the Mennonite tradition?" can be answered in the same way—"because it is an authentic and real part of the larger family of God's flock, and without it, something would be missing." We, as a Mennonite family, and I, as one of many who make it up, are a part with others of the families in the kingdom of heaven.

20

More Than Ethnic: Redefining Mennonite Identity

John H. Redekop

John H. Redekop, who received his early education in British Columbia, teaches political science at Wilfrid Laurier University in Waterloo, Ontario. He is active in the Mennonite Brethren Church and has been the moderator of the M. B. Conference of Canada for several years. His many popular and scholarly articles and books deal with such issues as nationalism, labor problems, Christian ethics, and the Christian in politics.

All people are ethnic. We all belong to some racial group or blending of groups from which we learn customs, language, social views, and often also religion. Our roots in our ethno-racial groups, whether minority or socially dominant, provide us with much of our identity, values, and reference points. Because all racial and ethnic groups are of equal intrinsic value and because our ethnicity plays such a major part in our lives, we should affirm who we are and be grateful for it.

It was not always thus with me. Raised in a sheltered Saskatchewan community my earliest recollections, understandably, included the notion that Mennonites, especially Mennonite Brethren, ranked high. The fact that Mennonites dominated that rural community and that the local Mennonite Brethren congregation included most of the local notables doubtless affected my perception. To be a Mennonite in that smallish world was to belong.

The situation changed. In grade 7, in a large British Columbia public school, I began to feel embarrassed, almost ashamed, about being a Mennonite. Numerous times I tried to hide that fact. (Using German as a church and home language in 1945-46, just when the veterans were returning, didn't help the situation any!) Simultaneously, I compensated for my growing inferiority complex by excelling as much as I could in my schoolwork as well as in extracurricular activities. I was determined to prove that I was no second-rate person just because I was a Mennonite.

A few years later, while attending the Mennonite Educational Institute at Clearbrook, British Columbia, my understanding of Mennonitism began to move beyond the mainly linguistic and cultural. My first systematic instruction about the sixteenth-century founders, particularly the martyrs, affected me deeply. During my five years at the M.E.I., I gradually developed first a grudging, and then an unqualified, respect for those forebears. Admiration followed.

Strange as it may seem, at that time I did not seriously relate the beliefs of those radically biblical Reformers to my own personal or corporate Christian experience. The explanation may lie in the fact that I believed much of the later Mennonite experience in Russia to be unworthy of emulation. I remember thinking, "What's particularly Christian about developing new agricultural crops and breeding first-rate cattle?" It seemed to me that improving the economy, developing new strains of hogs, or even bringing about significant educational reforms, as Johann Cornies and others had done, was basically unrelated to the fundamental concerns of Conrad Grebel, Menno Simons, and their courageous brothers and sisters in the faith.

By the time I completed high school my commitment to the biblical rediscoveries of the sixteenth-century radical Reformers was firm, even though my thinking about Mennonites was confused. As a result of some research projects I had even clarified my thinking on the peace issue and was beginning to affirm it publicly, even though I thought of it mainly in terms of avoiding military activity. Peace conferences during the Korean War, 1950-1953, reinforced that focus.

The subsequent years spent attending several universities produced serious cross-pressures. On the one hand I became more and more convinced that theologically the Mennonite position, especially as proclaimed in the early years, was sound. On the other hand I sometimes hid my Mennonite identity. Some of the criticisms and jokes I heard about Mennonites seemed to be valid and they rekindled earlier feelings of inferiority and embarrassment. Frequently I was troubled by this ambivalence. During weekends in Fraser Valley, I derived both social fulfillment and spiritual blessing from my Mennonite milieu but during the week I tried to blend in with the crowd, which included non-Mennonite Christians. This dualistic existence bothered me and I thought much about it but I did not know how to resolve my dilemma.

During my U.B.C. years I also began to understand the biblical basis and the Christian significance of the Mennonite Central Committee. Already in high school I had eagerly listened to vivid accounts of relief and of refugee movements. The colorful reports by C. F.

Klassen and others in the crowded M.E.I. auditorium had been highlights for me even though I did not really make the connection to Anabaptist ethics and servanthood. That came later. As I interacted at university with some fellow Mennonites who had completed a term with MCC, I began to see how servanthood motivated them, at least most of them. Accordingly, when I spent a year studying in Germany, I made it an item of high priority to visit the grave of C. F. Klassen, who had recently passed away in Germany. Together with another Canadian Mennonite studying in Germany, I also undertook several trips to Mennonite heritage sites in The Netherlands, Germany, Switzerland, and Austria. The faith of the founders had become my faith.

When I returned to Canada in 1956 to get married and begin what I assumed would be a lifelong career teaching high school, I rapidly built a Mennonite/Anabaptist library. When my wife asked me what I would like to have as a gift for our first Christmas together, I requested *The Complete Writings of Menno Simons*, which had just been published. It remains a valued volume. I also committed myself to spread the good word to others, especially young people. As a member of our B.C. Conference Youth Committee I prepared a study guide, *A Study Outline of Christian Nonresistance*, to be used in all of our B.C. churches. I also expanded my writing in various periodicals, especially Frank Epp's *The Canadian Mennonite*, where I had become an editorial committee member and columnist.

Even as I drank deeply from the heady Mennonite ethos of the Lower Fraser Valley, as well as the Canadian Mennonite community generally, I was still troubled about my own identity and by what it meant to be a Mennonite. In particular, I didn't know how to come to terms with the fact that substantial numbers of people who considered themselves to be Mennonite and who were accepted as Mennonites, both by non-Mennonites and other Mennonites, obviously were not Christians! These people were Mennonites by birth. Whether they ever made any profession of faith was quite another matter. The ethnic reality was fully clear—and for me disconcerting.

Gradually, during my four years as a high school teacher, 1956-60, in that B.C. heartland of "Menno country," at least a few questions were answered. Opportunities to interact with George Brunk, Harold Bender, and several other prominent "Old Mennonites" helped broaden my understanding of the wider Mennonite community and of vibrant Mennonite servanthood. I visited various types of Mennonite communities. Extensive reading and research in ethnology helped me to understand the complex reality. Reluctantly I concluded that at least the Russian, the South American, and the North American Mennonite immigrant groups had acquired a dual identity. They had "evolved" from sixteenth-century Christian communities to nineteenth- and twentieth-century ethno-religious peoples with the ethnic aspects often being dominant. I cannot say that I was particularly pleased with my new understanding (it was new for me!), but at least I could now make some sense of the fact that the town drunk was known by everyone as a Mennonite while new Christians with British or French backgrounds, who joined our local church, were not described as being Mennonites.

Since the mid-1960s, following graduate studies, my thinking may have matured but it has not changed much in this area. The dual and therefore confusing meaning of the term "Mennonite" has been illustrated countless times. I am committed to help redefine Mennonitism and to promote particularly the biblical doctrines and lifestyle which the sixteenth-century radical Reformers rediscovered.

Globally, the Mennonite situation is complex. Partly because in so many countries, especially in The Netherlands, Germany, Switzerland, France, and many of the developing countries where mission activity has been done, Mennonites have not been transformed into ethnic groups, we must be careful not to generalize unduly. The term Mennonite means various things in various countries. In most countries the problem of the dual meaning does not exist. My experience and investigation points to a problem found mainly in Canada, the U.S., the Soviet Union, and part of Latin America, and thus my analysis and prescription are not presented as globally applicable or necessary.

Any study of the widespread confusion about what the designation "Mennonite" represents must rest on actualities, rather than on hope or earlier history. Let us not try to deny the obvious facts. Accordingly, we must acknowledge that whatever the word Mennonite may mean for those of us who are Mennonite by birth as well as rebirth, in our time and in our society it has become primarily an ethnic designation. Aside from the shelves of sociological literature substantiating that fact, we have empirical data.

In a 1985 national Canadian survey, which I supervised, involving 1,670 respondents, about two-thirds of whom were of Mennonite "background" (a common code word for ethnicity), the responses came in as follows. Only about 4 percent of the mainly non-Mennonite university student respondents (345 from six campuses in Alberta, Manitoba, and Ontario) perceived Mennonites as only ethnic, but 64 percent saw them as being both an ethnic and a religious group. Thus 68 percent said that Mennonites are ethnic. Only 30 percent of the students agreed with the statement that "the word Mennonite refers to a religious group." Significantly, Mennonite Brethren congregational respondents, some 320 leaders and 230 lay members from across Canada, gave very similar responses. About 3 percent said that "Mennonite" refers to an ethnic group, 60 percent said that it refers to both a religious group and an ethnic group. Less than 34 percent of these 600 MB church members (about 50 did not indicate if they were clergy or laity) agreed with the statement that "the word Mennonite refers to a religious group." The summary figure of about two-thirds of the respondents seeing Mennonites as ethnic or ethnic-religious and one-third as primarily religious held virtually constant across the country. It held constant for all Mennonite and non-Mennonite groups and for MBs with Mennonite parents as well as those who were first-generation Mennonite Brethren.

In light of the above it is not surprising that only 17 percent of the non-Mennonite response group indicated that becoming a Mennonite is determined "by personal choice." No less than 19 percent checked "by birth into a Mennonite family," and 59 percent opted for "a combination of birth into a Mennonite family and personal choice." Thus 78 percent said that a person becomes a Mennonite by being born a Mennonite. Despite their earlier 63 percent assertion that the word "Mennonite" refers to ethnic or ethno-religious identity, the Mennonite Brethren respondents were not willing to acknowledge the consequences of such a situation. A full 53 percent agreed with a view that "becoming a Mennonite is determined by personal choice," 7 percent opted for "by birth into a Mennonite family," and 38 percent checked "by a combination of birth into a Mennonite family and personal choice." Apparently many Mennonite Brethren who acknowledge Mennonites as ethnic, nevertheless want to believe that ethnic reality can somehow be ignored.

Invited statements from numerous academic and public experts unanimously agree with the overall survey findings. My letter asked, does "your agency consider Mennonites to be part of a larger German ethnic group, a separate ethnic group, or not an ethnic group?" (Sometimes the options appeared in altered sequence and sometimes the grammatical structure was slightly different.)

Responding for the Department of the Secretary of State of Canada, Adrian Papanek, Program Officer for Canadian Ethnic Studies, wrote, "Mennonite projects are funded and listed as Mennonite projects and not as German projects or as a sub-group under the heading of German projects. Mennonites are definitely considered to be an ethnic group" (Personal letters, February 3, 1986).

A. W. Rasporich, coeditor, *Canadian Ethnic Studies*, wrote, "The editors of *Canadian Ethnic Studies* consider the Mennonites to be a separate ethnic group" (December 23, 1985).

W. R. Petryshyn, Director, Cultural Heritage Division, Government of Alberta, wrote, "Our practise is to allow community groups to decide for themselves whether they are an ethnic group. The Mennonites of Alberta have chosen to accept this self-definition and to participate on our advisory body—the Alberta Cultural Heritage Council—where they have played an active role" (December 10, 1985).

On occasion the responses varied, but not much. Chuck Sutyla, Director, Arts and Multicultural Branch, Department of Culture and Recreation, Government of Saskatchewan, wrote, "The department provides funding for the Menno Van, a travelling exhibit across Canada explaining the history of the Mennonite community in Canada from 1786-1986. . . . The Saskatchewan German Council is an umbrella organization which represents all German speaking people throughout the province, including the Mennonite community. Generally speaking, however, the Mennonites are regarded as a separate ethnic group based primarily on their religion and their cultural history" (December 2, 1985).

Robert F. Harney, Academic Director of The Multicultural History Society of Ontario and past president of the Canadian Ethnic Studies Association, provided an exceptionally insightful comment: "I believe that the Mennonites of Canada are best understood as an ethnic group. When we use the ethnonym Mennonite here, we mean the evolving ethnoculture and sense of peoplehood which has grown up over time among early Mennonite immigrants of Germanic descent as well as the infusion of Russlander Mennonite culture in the last ninety years or so." Noting that there are "more Mennonites in Zaire or Taiwan than in Ontario," he recognizes a conceptual dilemma. "Ethnic groups don't proselytize, but I persist in my view that there is by ethnogenesis a North American ethnic group called Mennonite, no matter how religiously inspired the original peoplehood was, or what divisions exist between Russlander and earlier people" (January 10, 1986).

The Hon. Eugene Kostyra, Minister of Culture, Heritage and Recreation, Government of Manitoba, wrote as follows. "We in this province have accepted the principle that ethnocultural communities have the right to determine how they wish to be identified. The Mennonite community has chosen to be identified as a separate ethnocultural group from the German community and participates as such in various intercultural endeavors. . . .

"The Mennonite community has for the most part availed itself of the Linguistic Support program and have (sic) received in 1983-84 $7,640.00; 1984-85 $14,060.00; 1985-86 $25,000.00 for a special grant for Mennovan . . ." (December 17, 1985).

Michael Goeres, Executive Secretary, Manitoba Intercultural Council, writes, "Mennonites are registered with the Manitoba Intercultural Council as a separate ethnocultural community" (December 27, 1985).

The sequence of responses could be lengthened, but surely the crucial point has already been proven. Whatever else they may be, the Mennonites of Canada, *partly* because of their own conscious decisions and actions are generally seen as an ethnic group.

Such a situation leaves me with a fundamental problem. What do I mean when I say, "I am a Mennonite"? Am I referring to the theological rediscovery of the sixteenth-century radical Reformers or am I referring to the Mennonite ethnocultural transformation and self-definition, corroborated by the assessment of experts as documented above? Or am I referring to both, thus blurring important distinctions and utterly confusing the issue?

Maybe we can clarify our thinking, at least partially, by describing three broad categories of North American Mennonites, or at least three usages of the term.

Ethnic Mennonites

This type is found across the continent. The distinguishing trait of this group is that while its members have abandoned—or have never had—any religious commitment, they are still seen as Mennonites by themselves and others because of their ethnic traits. They have traditional Mennonite names, traditional Mennonite foods, usually at least some remnants of Low German or the Pennsylvania Dutch dialect, and various remnants of Mennonite lifestyle. Often there is a preoccupation with Mennonite writing, painting, history, handcrafts, and Mennonite performers ranging all the way from professional hockey to the opera. (What ethnic Mennonite's interest has not been suddenly aroused when he recognizes an obviously Mennonite name on television or in a headline?) Although this group has no religious emphasis, let alone Anabaptist distinctives, it fits nicely under "Mennonite," one of the twenty-eight major cultures of Canada cited in *Cultures in Canada*, by Jack Bavington and others, Toronto, 1976. Indicative of the self-image of this group is the 1980 comment by a restaurant manager in St. Jacobs, Ontario, "We don't pass ourselves off as being a religious organization. We are Mennonites" (*Kitchener-Waterloo Record*, October 11, 1980).

Ethnic-Religious Mennonites

This group consists of people who generally share the ethnic traits and interests of those in the first category but they are also religious. They combine common traits of "birth" with those of Christian "rebirth" or at least religiosity. They come in two main subcategories which cut across conference and denominational lines.

(a) *Ethnicity dominant*

This subgroup consists of those who tend to be closed towards non-Mennonites. Some are inward and backward oriented. They often cling to the old ways. However, their religion is authentic. Some drive buggies; others drive cars and live in middle-class suburbia.

(b) *Religion dominant*

This group, thoroughly Mennonite in background and ethnicity, tries to minimize, and sometimes hide, any distinctive culture. Often the name "Mennonite" is dropped in church designations. Theologically, this group ranges from fundamentalist to liberal. Some stress Anabaptist theological values, most don't. We find this type by the thousands not only in the various Mennonite conference, but in Baptist, Christian and Missionary Alliance, Evangelical Free, United, Anglican, etc. Many have obviously dropped their Mennonite church connections but generally their ethnic ties persist.

In both subcategories the dominant emphasis tends to become even more dominant with the passage of time although the lesser component has an amazing resilience.

Religious Mennonites

For this group Christianity, specifically Anabaptist Christianity, is the uniting glue. This was, of course, originally the only category of Mennonite. In the early decades of the renewal there was no distinctive culture, no ethnic peculiarity. There were no Mennonite names. Nowadays this category includes not only the "ethnics" but also a few converts and some "transfer" members, that is, Christians having a non-Mennonite ethnic identity but belonging to a Mennonite Church. Sometimes these "non-ethnics" feel like outsiders. One such person, a deacon in a Mennonite Brethren church, told me, "I am a member of a Mennonite Brethren church but I am not a Mennonite." Members of this "Religious Mennonite" category try to overcome the "problem" of Mennonite ethnicity by emphasizing evangelism, discipleship, and community identification. Various ethnic values may be seen as significant but only as secondary to the evangelical Anabaptist religious belief system.

Where do I see myself fitting into this scheme? I categorize myself as a "Religious Mennonite," at least in intention. But I still have a problem. I want to affirm both my faith and my ethnicity. Up to a point, but only up to a point, I can convince myself that for me personally there is no problem. I simply say that I am a Mennonite and that I am grateful for it. Since "Mennonite" covers both concepts, ethnic and religious, and since the two are thoroughly fused in my experience and identity, that's presumably adequate and accurate.

Logically, of course, the situation is not that simple. If I call my faith "Mennonite" and also call my ethnicity "Mennonite," as many of us do, and if I acknowledge the fact that faith and ethnicity are not synonymous, then what shall the person call himself who shares my Anabaptist/Mennonite faith, but has Italian parents and culture? Can he be a Mennonite in the full sense of the term, the double usage of the term, the way I can? Of course not. He already has his own different ethnicity. Therein lies the inescapable dilemma, a contradiction which integrity requires us to acknowledge and to address.

What, then, are the options? In general, I see four. First, those of us with Mennonite ethnicity and who are committed to Mennonite/Anabaptist theology can fuse the two. Adopting such a stance means that if a person with a non-Mennonite ethnicity wishes to join our Mennonite church, he must try somehow to adopt some Mennonite ethnicity, both frustrating and virtually impossible in the short term, or he can become only a partial Mennonite. A slight variation of this first option involves separating the idea of Christian peoplehood from the idea of ethnic peoplehood but still calling both of them Mennonite. This variation solves nothing, although it may ease one's conscience. At times my feelings and desires tug in that direction; fortunately, the logic and ethic of my faith prevent me from settling for that easy, widespread, but intrinsically un-Anabaptist option.

Second, we can deny that there is a Mennonite ethnicity and strive to defend and practice Mennonitism as a religion only. I took this stance briefly but found it untenable. It was untenable because it was inaccurate. It forced me to deny an important part of my heritage and identity and to ignore social reality. Integrity soon compelled me to abandon this option. Besides, why should anyone have to deny his ethnicity?

Third, we can accept the historical Russian North and South American fusion of Mennonite ethnicity with Mennonite/Anabaptist theology and then, motivated by a desire to be faithful to the great commission and the New Testament mandate for the church, reject both, at least publicly, and especially in church settings. Such an attempt to eliminate ethnic barriers from the church results in an unfortunate and unnecessary denial of the great Anabaptist rediscoveries of the full biblical gospel. At one time I briefly toyed with this option but rejected it precisely because it required me to reject both my Anabaptist emphases and my ethnic identity. Sadly, from my perspective, many young "Mennonite" leaders and numerous "Mennonite" congregations are choosing this option. They argue, or at least assume, that if they are forced to deal with Anabaptist theology as part of a larger Mennonite ethnoreligious package, then, because the Christian gospel requires them to build bridges to people from many ethnic backgrounds, they must reject the entire unified Mennonite package. They argue that if Anabaptist theology is fused with one particular ethnic group, then they have no other choice. There are also some people, of course, who reject Mennonite/Anabaptist theology because they don't like its uncompromising tenets, especially the peace emphasis and the discipleship lifestyle, but use the ethnic packaging as a convenient scapegoat.

Fourth, we can accept the fact of Mennonite ethnicity and the propriety (desirability) of Mennonite/Anabaptist theology. We then assert that we want to affirm both. Given the fact that our ethnicity is known throughout society as Mennonite, as well as the fact that our theology demands a multi-ethnic orientation, we then decide not to label the theology as Mennonite but as Anabaptist or something else to which other ethnic groups can have equal access and with which they can identify fully. That's biblical!

This last option describes the nature of my commitment to both Mennonite ethnicity and Anabaptist theology. I derive my identity from both, because for me they are very closely intertwined, and I can strongly and unashamedly affirm both. But I can do so only by separating the two phenomena conceptually and publicly and giving them different names. While my church and denomination might still be dominated by Mennonite ethnics, if my suggestion were adopted the church structure would not be officially labeled "Mennonite" and that would eliminate a formal hurdle for those who want the Anabaptist gospel but possess a non-Mennonite ethnicity. Where a sense of Mennonite ethnic exclusivity is still a problem, attitudinal revision is also required; such an acceptance of Anabaptism expressed through various cultures would enhance and maximize the significance of the formal change. But note, neither a church name change nor an attitudinal change by itself is sufficient. Both are necessary and together they make realistically possible the achievement of the desired end—obedience to God's Word—at least concerning what the church of Jesus Christ is and how it should function.

Lest I be misunderstood, let me emphasize that the reason for my suggestion that the Anabaptist theology and Anabaptist church (in some parts of the world) should not be called Mennonite does not arise from the fact that some Mennonites are not Christian. After all, some people who call themselves Christian are not Christian! It arises, as stated, from a desire to avoid confusion and distortion. One is born into an ethnic group; one is born again into the church. A true religion is open to all; an ethnic group is not. The two phenomena are profoundly different and that difference should be reflected in the names. Concerning the one name we have no choice and need none; some of us are Mennonites and will always be Mennonites. Concerning the other one, the theological or church designation, we do need a change and should make it.

Let me clarify my reasoning fully. I argue for a "religious" name change not because of any rejection of what Mennonitism meant in the sixteenth century, but precisely because I want that great rediscovery to be clarified and reemphasized and retained. I am prepared, indeed eager, to separate Mennonitism from Anabaptism so that Anabaptism can be proclaimed for what it is and thus salvaged.

I am deeply grateful for my ethnic heritage. Indeed, it provides increasing satisfaction. Mennonite culture is deeply ingrained within me. I value it more and more as I get older. Mennonite foods are more delicious than ever and, more importantly, traditional Mennonite values and family ties more valued. But I am even more grateful for my Anabaptist Christian faith. Its inclusive emphasis on the atonement, the new life, baptism on confession of faith, discipleship, community, mutual assistance, servanthood, the love/peace ethic, accountability, biblicism, missions, the separated life, and a willingness to put first things first, including evangelical Anabaptism itself, are vital. As I ponder them, my gratitude to God grows for the rewarding identity which he has graciously given me.

Why am I a Mennonite? I am a Mennonite because my parents were Mennonite—I was born into a Mennonite family. Why am I an Anabaptist Christian? I am an Anabaptist Christian because I became convinced that the Anabaptist faith to which I have been exposed since childhood constitutes authentic New Testament Christianity, an authentic Christianity that must be available to all.

21

Through the Mennonite Looking Glass

Magdalene Redekop

*Magdalene Redekop, who comes from southern Manitoba,
teaches English literature at the University of Toronto. She has
published articles on Canadian, American, and British literature,
as well as a biography of Ernest Thompson Seton. She is author of
the book,* Alice Munro and Our Mock Mothers: Reading the Signs
of Invasion, *(1988). The following chapter was written in the summer
of 1986. She is married and is the mother of two adopted children.
children.*

You won't find it in the basement of the church where I learned my Sunday School lessons when I was a child. Once, not long after I had "flown the coop," I returned there in a nightmare. The dank classrooms (where we used to sing "Heavenly Sunshine") were prison cells. Through the small, grimy windows up at ground level I could see green grass and yellow sunshine and I could catch fleeting glimpses of children playing. The Sunday school world, by contrast, was a shadowy world of black and white. The superintendent (who did not look like anybody I had ever met) was the jailer. He stood near the large carcass of a slaughtered pig which was strung up from the ceiling. In exchange for giving him their offerings, the children received from him a slab of raw pork. In my nightmare, I fumbled my offering—the quarter given me by my father for this purpose— and it rolled out of sight into the dark corners of the cement floor. The jailer, however, offered me a different coin which I could then offer back to him—perhaps fumbling it too? With this suggestion of an endless cycle of pseudo-offerings, the nightmare faded. It has haunted me ever since.

If the reason is not to be found in that cellar, then why (you may well ask) do I still call myself a Mennonite—and I do. A glib way of looking at my life so far would be to see it as a flight from the claustrophobia of that nightmare world. How can the I—Magdalene Falk—of that nightmare be, in any sense, identical with the girl who was one of the singing "Falk Sisters" or with the I—Magdalene Redekop—who now teaches literature to university students? I do have frequent differences of opinion with earlier versions of myself, but I

227

also catch myself returning repeatedly to a point of sameness which I can account for only by calling it my Mennonite "identity." While teaching, I often find it necessary to account for my passion on certain issues by confessing to my students that I am a Mennonite. When you do this in Ontario, people are confused by a mental picture (reinforced at regular intervals by front-page photographs in the *Toronto Star*) of "horse-and-buggy Mennonites." Even urban Mennonites sometimes talk as if they believe that the genuine Mennonites are those who withdraw from the modern world. If pictures of horses and buggies help along the feeble imaginations of nostalgic Yuppies and Muppies who can no longer envision a life of simplicity, then that is good. I am under no illusions, however, about the intrinsic value of a way of life that deliberately denies the most redemptive feature of the human imagination: the ability to identify with *other* ways of living. All efforts to withdraw from the world lead, for me, to a point of reversal. At that turning point I realize that the one withdrawn from needs love, needs empathy—needs, in short, to be *identified* with.

I see "identity" as being in motion; not a noun, but a verb—as in "to identify with." This makes it difficult to come up, as I have been asked to do, with a thumbnail portrait of myself as a Mennonite. When I picked up my Mennonite looking glass, intending to record the image reflected in it, I found that it was blurred and fractured. Identity, I reminded myself, will be found only when the mirror becomes an open window. *Then* we will know as we are known; *now* we see through a glass darkly and know in part. Such knowledge as we do have comes from making the effort to imagine the other side of the looking glass. To go beyond the solitary reflection and to reach out to identify with the other is to aim at the fulfillment of a vision of communal identity where the church is one body. This goal defines, for me, the Anabaptist vision. Other religions have equally valid ways of envisioning it.

If this vision is a wish-fulfillment dream in which the self is integrated with a community, then the nightmare I described is an anxiety dream in which the self is alienated. In *The Educated Imagination*, Northrop Frye defines literature as "a wish-fulfilment dream and an anxiety dream, that are focussed together like a pair of glasses, and become a fully conscious vision" (Toronto, 1963, p. 43). I teach literature because of my conviction that such a full consciousness is necessary to life and growth. It is only if we recognize that the looking glass is divided in this way that we can see *through* it instead of gazing *at* it. In my search for this kind of focus, I was reminded of the stereoscope that my father gave me before he died. The stereoscope has "slides" divided into two pictures; both are two-dimensional and they are apparently identical, but they form a three-dimensional image for the viewer because the angle of vision is different.

As I sorted through my mental pictures of the past with the aim of using the stereoscopic method, I found a picture of the one-room school—Roseville—where I spent nine years learning about difference. Oh, don't get me wrong. The other children in the school shared my "Mennonite identity" in the sense that we did all have Mennonite parents. Identical, however, we were not. My sisters and I had to live according to the rules set by an exceptionally strict father. Being a Mennonite in the larger society of "Englaenders" paled before the immediate horror of the specific ways in which we were different from all the other girls. They wore pants; we wore skirts. They had their hair cut and curled; we were taught that this was sinful. They went on skating and baseball excursions; at such times we stayed behind in the empty schoolroom.

The response of the children to such peculiarities was to devise ever new forms of torment: sand in the eyes, a broom handle in the stomach, a lunch pail crashed down on an unsuspecting head, and (of course) taunting and name-calling. These may have been isolated episodes, but they were fuel for the fear that grew inside me like an ugly growth so that I felt nausea on the way to school each morning. By the time I reached the age where peer pressure is felt most intensely, my brothers and sisters had left (I being the youngest of twelve) and I was left to defend myself as best I could. My *Selbtstschutz* or self-defense consisted of smiling. Sound easy? Never underestimate the pain of smiling when all about you have curls and your hair is in severe braids.

"Thou shalt love thy neighbor as thyself," was the impossible rule I kept telling myself to follow, but I knew very well that my smile was false. Once, during one of the fifteen-minute recesses that I dreaded, a schoolmate came at me without warning, flailing her arms in my face and drawing blood. In a farcically literal reading of Scripture I turned the other cheek. How it must have infuriated her (alas, the thought still gives me a wicked pleasure), but what else was I to do? We were nonresistant, after all. I knew very well, however, that my gesture was as full of pride as hers.

I remember retreating to the cramped furnace room in which there was a small blurred mirror. After I had cleaned my face and willed myself to stop shaking, I practiced my smile. I have a vivid memory of being repelled by the ugliness of it. What I was suffering could not be dignified by association with those thousands of Anabaptists whose deaths are written up in the *Martyrs Mirror*. What I was suffering was simply the burden of my own separate self. I think of that smiling face when I read Gerard Manley Hopkins: "I am gall, I am heartburn. God's most deep decree/Bitter would have me taste: my taste was me." If you were lost and could go to hell for curling your hair, then it was my schoolmates who were outsiders and I who was the insider. But I knew that I was the one that was lost. "I see/The lost are like this, and their scourge to be/As I am mine, their sweating selves; but worse" (Hopkins, Penguin, 1953, p. 62). How I longed to be "found," to be like my classmates, to have curly hair, to wear jeans, to skate. I desired not to be myself more earnestly than they could ever have desired not to be me. I was the outsider and my difference made it possible for them to play at not being Mennonite. I am reminded of them whenever I meet people who are embarrassed by their ethnicity.

The result of my experience was that I was fascinated by outsiders in the community. They helped me to make my first efforts to move through the looking glass. I remember, for example, a Mexican Mennonite girl who briefly attended the same school. She too wore a dress and had her hair in braids but, in addition, she wore an apron (the subject of much hysterical mockery), and she could not speak English. I formed a reluctant alliance with this girl. I was never quite sure whether I despised her for being like me, whether I despised myself for being like her, or whether I despised our schoolmates for despising us both. I was aware of the poison in my friendship, of the betrayal that made me reject identification with her. Even as I struggled in a clumsy way to befriend her, it was my own face that kept reproaching me from the surface of that clouded looking glass.

I remember, also, a visit to a neighboring farm where my friend

Mary Penner lived. The Penners (I have changed the name to protect their privacy) were made outsiders by their poverty and this was signaled by the fact that there were no trees in their yard and there was no paint on their house. I have no memory of Mary's father (perhaps he had died), but her mother must have been a remarkable woman. Mary Penner's mother made flowers with tissue paper. Mary Penner's mother could turn a box of pink Kleenex into fragile carnations. With red crêpe paper Mary Penner's mother could produce astonishingly lifelike roses which she sold to be worn as decorations at weddings. On this particular visit there was hiding and shrieking and chasing and falling which all ended in humiliation for me. I fell, rolled, and got up to discover that I had rolled in what we called a cow pie (no money here for fences). My clothes, my arms, everything was smeared with cow shit. I can remember the gentle kindness and tact of Mary Penner's mother. I remember the overpowering smell of fresh cinnamon rolls and the fact that I could not eat them for thinking of cow pies. Since I cannot remember being tormented at school with the incident, my friend Mary—blessings on her, wherever she is—must have kept a loyal silence.

My memory, however, is not unmixed with shame and it is not because of the cow shit. I am still ashamed of myself when I remember that I hated to go home wearing my friend's clothes. I felt revulsion for the high-pitched, soapy smell of poverty that clung to them. My gratitude for her kindness was mixed with a painful sense of my own treachery. If I loved my neighbor as myself, I should surely not mind *being* her during the time that it took to walk up her long driveway and down the long driveway to my own home. But I did; oh yes, I did! Trying to be myself and yet trying on the clothes of an outsider: for me that is an apt image of what it means to try to be a Mennonite.

Notice that I said "try." It would go contrary to the very concept of Anabaptism to say that I was born a Mennonite. I think it was Kierkegaard who commented that we give birth to the fathers we deserve—and that goes for mothers too. The process of grieving since the death of my parents has involved such a birthing experience and in what follows I will be reflecting on those aspects of this process that have to do with defining a Mennonite identity. I learned my lessons in stereoscopic vision from both my parents, but it was my father whose example led me to give this the name "Mennonite."

My father—William H. Falk—had a twin brother and perhaps this taught him something about double vision. In pictures of them as youths, both men are seen striking jaunty poses and wearing their hats at a rakish angle but they were very far from being "identical" twins. One of the last gifts my father gave me was a photograph of himself with his twin, taken shortly before that brother's death. In this photograph, two elderly men confront the camera with sober faces that look like masks. There is very little to suggest the radical difference between them. That may be the reason why my father gave a copy of that picture to each of his twelve children. In reality, my uncle was an "outsider"; he was an alcoholic and he played the role of "town bum" with a certain flamboyance. As bishop or *Aeltester* of the church, my father played a very different role, but it was obvious that he longed for "identification" with his twin—"Venn nich hea, dann doa" ("If not here, then there"), as he would have said. I knew that my father's separation from his brothers (another brother had committed suicide) was a source of pain for him and that his yearning for identity determined the way he acted in the *Bruderschaft* of the church. There too, however, among his spiritual brothers, he experienced division.

Since my father was one of the founders of the Rudnerweider church (leading the split from the Sommerfelder church), I had an immediate experience of the schismatic nature of the Mennonite community and I saw this as a form of tolerance. My sisters and I sometimes joked that we could disagree with our father and start our own church since he had done so himself. I was impressed by my father's respect for other Mennonite churches. The groupings and regroupings of various factions seemed to me to argue for a flexibility that modified the insistence that there was only one way. Instead of feeding his ego, the task of leading such a split seemed, furthermore, to confirm my father's suspicion of individual pride. His ability to detect signs of conceit was unequaled and he applied his rigorous test to himself with the result that he refrained from wearing a tie, in contrast to all the other preachers in his own church.

The undertaker who prepared my father's body for the coffin was persuaded to omit the tie, but I noticed that he put one of those mock-handkerchiefs with jagged edges in the pocket of my father's jacket. *Spetze*, my father had called them (fairly spitting the word out), and had seen them too as a sign of conceit and affectation. Never mind—my father had the last word. The usual eulogy was replaced at his funeral, at his request, by the reading of a poem about the need to die to the ego and to give Jesus the glory. I knew that my father's pride was more profound than that of men who needed *Spetze*, but what was more important was that he was wary of his pride, always alert to stamp it out wherever it reared its ugly head, even after his death. We never do escape pride, of course, but his heroic efforts to do so are not easily forgotten. Nor did I ever lose sight of the fact that this was central to his identity as a Mennonite.

He was passionately committed to being a Mennonite. His belief in pacifism necessitated that each prospective son-in-law be quizzed rigorously on his knowledge of the historic peace witness. He handed out quantities of booklets entitled "Sollten Christen kriegen?" and the word *Krieg* was associated, in his sermons, with the horrifying image of *der boese Feind*. His belief in mutual aid meant that he shopped at the local co-op store even when the prices at the Red and White store were lower. His belief in the need for the separation of the church resulted in an insistence on the use of Low German in the home and High German in the church.

His passion on these issues, however, seemed different from his passionate preaching on damnation and the need to avoid it. We were taught, of course, that people who were not "saved" would go to hell. Did that mean that Billy Graham's wife would go to hell for wearing lipstick? I can remember the intensity of my fear for myself and for those millions and billions and trillions—beyond imagining numbers of others—all going to hell, helter-skelter, without so much as a hint that there was a way to avoid it. Cowering under the huge prairie sky, we sensed always the approaching end times. When my father burned the stubble fields, I could smell the acrid smoke of hell in my nostrils and I wondered who would be taken and who would be left. If I believed in a literal hell of that sort, the conclusion was inescapable: I had to be a missionary.

The annual "Missionsfest" was a glorious event. There was the big tent, flapping loudly in the warm wind. The choirs sang with a thrilling intensity. The congregation sang lustily of the day when we would all "come rejoicing, bringing in the sheaves." Then there were the missionaries, the people who had put their lives where their mouths were. Never mind that after they had stayed at our house all summer (on "furlough") eating *Schinkefleisch*, we ended up eating bologna in winter. Never mind that the American missionaries were sometimes patronizing. They were exotic emblems of self-sacrifice. The inglorious side to this glorious occasion, however, was the pleasure that came from the complacent knowledge (surrounded by comforting multitudes) that you were not one of those perishing and in need of rescue. Surely not. Surely not, at least, if the Lord would only come quickly *now*, just *now*, while you were eating your *klik* and lettuce sandwiches made on store-bought bread (such a treat after roast beef and homemade buns.)

The image of hell was hard to reconcile with the quiet pace of life in the community. I sensed in my father an aversion for the flaming rhetoric of the non-Mennonite evangelists who came around, implying that the Mennonites needed saving. The moment when the name of the church he had founded was changed from Rudnerweider Kirchengemeinde to Evangelical Mennonite Mission Conference (under new leadership)—that moment was definitely not a high point in my father's life. Why not, I asked myself? In the end, I learned less from my father's consistent preachings than from the inconsistencies apparent in the shape of his life.

My last memory of him is as an aged man, an outsider marginalized by the church he himself had founded. Few came to visit him, although he had spent his life working without a salary, fitting visitings, marryings, buryings, and comfortings in between seedtimes and harvest. He seemed content to be just another retired farmer. Perhaps he took this as a last lesson on pride, but I could not escape the impression that he felt he had failed. I had brought him, as a gift from Holland, a print of Rembrandt's "Jeremiah Weeping." He kept this picture in a prominent place and once told me that he identified with the image of Jeremiah. In his very failure, however, I saw his prophetic strength. His imagination was so powerful that no actual church *could* realize his vision.

I saw the redemptive qualities of that vision, also, in the way my father treated outsiders. In his sermons it was clear that Jews and Indians would go to hell unless saved by God's grace. When, however, members of these minority groups approached our farmhouse, my father did not appear to respond with an urgent evangelical approach. What he did do was to insist on providing clothes, food, and gasoline to the Indians (with the result that they returned to our house repeatedly). One elderly Indian man and his grandson were allowed to sleep in my father's *Staefche*—the quiet little study in which he prepared his sermons and which was out of bounds for us. There was a Jewish merchant who sometimes came around in a battered truck, selling fruit. I watched from the window of the house and was impatient for my father to bring in the box of overripe bananas— a rare treat. What took him so long? The length of the stay, the leisurely postures of the two men, the expression of benign friendliness and curiosity on my father's face, the fact that the man returned frequently—all these were surely not consistent with the idea that this man was being told he was going to hell. Different, he certainly was, and my father knew all about difference.

For my father, indeed, difference was a concept that was central to the very idea of religious identity. His insistence on the use of the German language had nothing to do with a celebration of Germany; on the contrary, it symbolized the separation of church and state. The wall of language created a space for religious freedom and he fought to keep that wall up, always insisting that he could not speak English. When outsiders came around, however, the wall vanished and my father suddenly, mysteriously turned into the gracious host speaking English. Paradoxically, he expressed a high admiration for scholars who spoke numerous languages and he encouraged me to learn as many as possible. His sensitivity to the power of language was extraordinary. He did not like us to say "Hi," for example, because it reminded him of *Heil*. Looking through his stereoscope, he saw that the affable "Hi" to the insider can be the other side of the horror of *Heil* (or hell) for the outsider. It all depended on that slight difference in angle of vision. "Daut haft uck noch *dei* Sied" (it has also *that* side), he used to say. Or was it my mother who said that?

Did I say that my father gave me the stereoscope? I was wrong. It was my mother who gave it to me after my father died. Come to think, there are a few other details I am not so sure of. Did I invent Mary Penner's mother? A telephone call to one of my sisters confirms that, yes, she did exist. My sister remembers, however, that it was raisin bread, not cinnamon rolls, and that she too had trouble eating, not because of the cow shit but because of the related problem of flies (no money here for screens). It is odd that I should have forgotten Mr. Penner, since another sister, when consulted, remembers that he always seemed to her frighteningly big when compared to Mrs. Penner, who was tiny. My sisters' memories, however, tend to confirm my idealization of Mrs. Penner. They remember, for example, a Christmas when we all admired the beautiful dresses that Mrs. Penner had made for her daughters—every stitch done by hand (no money here for a sewing machine).

Such a coming together of memories is reassuring. History, after all, is empirical truth. Or is it? If, for example, I asked my brothers, would Mrs. Penner still exist? If you knew my father, you may be protesting by now that this is not the man you knew, that I am writing what my father himself called "uetgedochte Geschichte" (thought-up stories). You are free, I say, to invent your own version. It is fitting that it should be my mother who gave me the stereoscope, because she would have understood or at least accepted my way of using it. My mother knew that a fact should get out of the way of a good fiction. She knew the difference between the truths of fiction and the facts of life. I once dreamed that some members of my family had formed a jury and that I had been sentenced to hang for not believing in the literal truth of the Bible. My mother was not on that jury.

Before she became Mrs. W. H. Falk, the bishop's wife, my mother was Elisabeth Schellenberg, a girl admired for her slender beauty and for the ease with which she composed poetry. Her awareness of her gift was buried deep in her past; her life gave evidence both of the talent and of the consequences of burying it. She was a high-spirited woman who loved my father, babies, muddy children, flowers, birds, strawberry ice cream, telling outrageous stories, laughing, and reading. She read and read and read. Like Alice, she was a good reader: she could leave her world behind, venturing through the looking glass or down the rabbit hole. Often we would climb up on my parents' big bed with her and sprawl around her, abandoning ourselves to the sheer pleasure of her storytelling. She would read from the latest installment of fiction in the *Rundschau*, translating the High German into Low German as she went and adding comic digressions of her own. When I experimented by writing an adolescent mystery story, my mother (I discovered later) read it secretly and was upset that I threw it out before finishing it; she wanted to know how it would turn out. When I began ordering parcels of books from the University Extension Library, she read them all immediately, claiming that she had to see if they were "good" ones. She didn't fool me.

I was conditioned to believe that what my mother was doing when she read fiction was running away from reality. This escapism could be tolerated by society, but not affirmed as something good in itself. Certainly it had nothing to do with being a Mennonite. "She has a good imagination" was a phrase that always seemed to me to be spoken in tones of damning faint praise that implied it was on a level with having a special but useless gift, such as naturally curly hair. The community regarded creativity as a marginal activity, perhaps even a suspicious one. My great-grandmother, one of the earliest Mennonite pioneers in Manitoba, wrote poetry and this always seemed to me a sign of her indomitable spirit. It was my uncles, however, not my aunts and not my mother, who dared to write poetry. If drinking alcohol made my father's brother an outsider, then writing poetry did much the same for my mother's brothers. Who knows what it would have done for the women in the family, doubtless no less talented.

My education in literature has taught me to respect the power of the human imagination, but it has been difficult for me to reconcile this with my identity as a Mennonite woman. I always took for granted that it had something to do with my mother. The more I studied, the more I came to see her love of fiction not as a secret addiction, but rather as "the secret of morals." In order to love (and how she loved us) we must "imagine intensely and comprehensively," we must put ourselves "in the place of another and of many others." The "great instrument of moral good is the imagination." The words were written by Shelley in "A Defence of Poetry" (1821), but it was my mother who brought them to life for me. Her life, however, also gave me a vivid picture of the tragic waste of those powers. A severe limit was placed on them partly by the nature of the books available to her and partly because her sphere of action was limited to her family.

The more powerful an imagination is, the more it demands discipline and the romances of Grace Livingston Hill could not offer the kind of disciplined release of power that comes, for example, from following King Lear's progress to the point where he achieves imaginative identification with Tom o' Bedlam. Unlike my father, my mother did not make the constant effort to identify with the Indians, for example. She probably thought of them as still more mouths to feed. Her imagination was focused, instead, inward into the family and was engaged in the constant effort to keep the family united.

Although this was sometimes a heroic achievement, my mother probably did not think that it had anything to do with her love of fiction. She had internalized the prevailing view that fiction has only a frivolous, ornamental relation to life. Since I saw a continuity with her on a deeper level, it came as a shock to discover that she did not see it. Once, during a visit to Toronto, a colleague spoke flatteringly about me to her in the way that people do when they think they know what a parent wants to hear. "Oh yes," she responded proudly, "her father was a great orator." There are at least two ways of looking at her statement. One is to see that she was being selfless. The other is to see that she saw herself as self-less, as being without self. Like the girl in my nightmare, she did not think she had any gift to offer; the offering is transferred by the girl from one man (the father) to another (the jailer), but she herself has nothing to offer. My mother seemed to think of her womb in this way, as a sort of conveyer belt for talent. When I pointed out to her that I made my living by reading and writing about fiction, she seemed intrigued but puzzled. It was hard for her to see any continuity between us in the area of my profession. The earthy vessel of her own body was her offering and it was here that she looked for continuity. Her gift to me was, in her view, not positive but negative: it consisted of not urging me to have a baby; it consisted of keeping her mouth shut.

I think it was because my mother was always working so hard to keep her mouth shut that her body was constantly betraying her. She lived with chronic illness. Having an imagination can be dangerous to a woman's health if she lives in a society that seeks to repress it. I am not, of course, speaking only of Mennonite society. My mother was in good company. Like Virginia Woolf and George Eliot, she suffered from severe headaches. Many of the novels she read reflected the nineteenth-century cult of the woman as invalid, of woman as a diseased mother in the constant act of dying. For a Mennonite woman who asks: "Mirror, mirror on the wall, who is the fairest of us all?" the mirror always answers in a deep, male voice: "Fairest Lord Jesus, Ruler of all nations."

The power of this Ruler is more devastating for a Mennonite woman than it is for a man. The man's imitation of Christ, after all, can take a practical form as he shapes the rules of his society in an approximation of the ideal rules. The more restricted the area of the woman's power, the more passive she is forced to become. The Word that "was in the beginning and that was God" also has different implications for a woman. The man, especially if he is a preacher, may work creatively to find words to intimate the power of that Word. Not so the woman (who is struggling to keep her mouth shut), as we are learning from feminist writers. Sandra Gilbert and Susan Gubar have probably never met a Mennonite mother, but they describe her in "The Queen's Looking Glass" (*The Madwoman in the Attic*, New Haven, 1979). When he was in good spirits, my father sometimes called my mother "Queen Elisabeth," but her reigning powers were restricted. If she doesn't wish to turn into the wicked stepmother in "Snow White and the Seven Dwarfs," the only alternative for a Mennonite "queen" may be to turn the glass into a martyr's mirror and to hope for better things in the next world.

The image reflected in my mother's looking glass was one of considerable beauty, but she was not happy with it. She particularly hated her mouth which, she once told me, was too small. She would clown with glee for her grandchildren by taking her dentures out and making herself truly ugly and unrecognizable. Her mouth may have been small, but she reproached herself constantly because it talked too much. She loved the song "I'll Have a New Body, Hallelujah!" as sung by Tennessee Ernie Ford. In her vision of heaven, she had a perfect, healthy body and, judging by the rollicking rhythm of the song, I know that body is dancing now. Is it, however, a body without a mouth?

This disturbing image captures the historical position of women in the Mennonite church. Women did not participate in the forging of the Anabaptist vision. It was not women who had to think about being conscientious objectors during the war. My father did not quiz prospective daughters-in-law on their attitudes to pacifism. In what sense, then, can a woman be a Mennonite? In my own case, it sometimes seems to me that my father chose me to carry on his Mennonite convictions. I was the youngest of twelve but there was a younger child, a boy called Menno, who had been born dead. Perhaps the hopes that had been pinned on him fell back on me. Whatever the reason, my father's expectations of me were unusual, to say the least: he wanted me to be the medical doctor that he had always yearned to be himself. If I had been born a boy, I might have been called Menno.

This was not, however, the message that came from the community. The women were Mennonite, not because they held passionate opinions, but because they made the quilts, they made the borscht, they made the varenike. It was my father who made the decision to offer hospitality to the Indians, but it was my mother, my sisters, and I who served the food and made the beds. While the *Bruderschaft* was making the important decisions in the main body of the church, the *Frauenverein* was in the basement, getting the food ready. They might be talking, but they did not have a voice. It was assumed that the woman had no offering to bring the "jailer" out of her own self. The only way she could be seen as making such an offering would be to work as an MCC worker or as a missionary, at a geographical distance from the Mennonite community itself.

Even within the community, a woman with a practical nature could still make a very significant contribution. But what about the woman with an exceptional creative talent? What about the woman who has the ability to envision an ideal church? What happens to that power if the woman is not allowed to give voice to it in ways that could change the real church? Such talent, turned inward, causes guilt and depression. The single most significant cause of neurosis in the Mennonite community is the stifling of the imagination.

Small wonder that my mother's visions, unlike my father's, were not consciously Anabaptist and that her imaginary ideal world was painfully remote. Her homesickness, her *Sehnsucht*, her *Heimweh*, was so estranging that it was accompanied by a sense of the *unheimlich* or the uncanny. The uncanny comes from a sense of simultaneous life and death and that is how, as a child, I saw my mother's otherworldliness. Even then I sensed that her reading of fiction was a way of surviving. Entering her wishfulfillment dreams (even when it was only Grace Livingston Hill) and seeing them *as* dreams, *as* fiction, saved her from the total despair of a literal homesickness for heaven. During the times of her greatest misery, however, she did not read. She listened to records about heaven. At such times my mother seemed already dead to me—an absence, like an estranged ghost. She listened, her eyes closed, when my sisters and I sang her favorite songs for her, but that was different. I knew very well that she didn't *really* want to be anywhere else—at least not yet, not until her beloved daughters had finished singing. Imagining her (after I had left home) listening to our record—"The Falk Sisters Sing unto the Lord"—was more painful because there was distance and absence.

My own *Heimweh*, the love for my absent mother, now stirs in me the painful memory of her yearnings when I was very young. She would listen to the Chuck Wagon Gang singing rousing gospel songs about another world, a glorious world in which I knew there would be better daughters than I could ever be. I felt it as an iron weight on my chest. I now realize that her pleasure in the rhythm, which was basically country and western, was far from being totally otherworldly and that it was no more sinister than my own pleasure in listening to "hurtin' songs" when I feel blue. At the time, however, the literal belief in heaven stood in the way of such comfort so that I was comfortless even as my mother was comforting herself.

As I grew older, my mother's *Heimweh* began to irritate me. No, it angered me (how hard it is to be honest). My arguments with my mother always returned to this point. I didn't dare argue with my father, but my mother was another story. It wasn't that I wanted her to be a different person; it was rather that I wanted her to be a person. If my father's modesty was a potential form of pride, moreover, my mother's powerlessness could also become a form of power. Power takes the form of passivity when it has been denied the right to take active forms. My father was a passionate preacher and he exercised his persuasive power in the pulpit, making occasional use of his large handkerchief when the tears flowed. After the service, during Sunday dinner, he always seemed to feel especially mellow and warm toward the world. He had had his say. My mother's role was to keep those handkerchiefs dazzlingly white (not to mention his shirt, since he refused to wear a tie), to fight like crazy to keep her mouth shut, and to make sure the dinner was ready when we came home from church. After the service, my mother usually had a headache.

Is it not ironic that a pacifist church continues to do violence to women in this way? The traditional Mennonite belief in the priest-

hood of all believers ought surely to remove the barriers to the acceptance of women in positions of responsibility. Why is it, then, that
Mennonite churches are not ahead of the Anglican and even the
Catholic churches in this area? Is it possible that the reason has to do
with the fact that the ethnic customs that define us as Mennonite (or
so we are told in articles written by men) could not exist without the
labors of women? Perhaps we need to begin by teaching more men to
cook. I know one Mennonite man who makes excellent varenike.
How many Mennonite women do you know who preach an excellent
sermon—or are allowed to do so?

I could go on to suggest that Mennonite identity, as defined up-
stairs by the men, may be built on the bodies of the women who offer
their labors in the basement. I could go still further and compare this
to the fashion in which Egyptian pyramids took shape, on the bodies
of the slaves that built them. If I did, you would accuse me of exag-
geration, to which I would respond, quoting William Blake: "The
road of excess leads to the palace of wisdom." By envisioning, in
excess, our full potential to make a horror, we energize ourselves to
construct a better world and to repudiate that horror. I believe, in
short, that we should not deny our consciousness of this violence, but
rather exaggerate it by using our imagination—the better to avoid it.
What we have tended to do in the past is the exact opposite: we seek
for ways of defusing the danger.

One safety valve, for Mennonites, is singing. My sisters and I sang
our hearts out and I remember the experience with intense joy. We
also had opinions, usually silent ones, on everything. I am glad that
my singing voice, as one of the "Falk Sisters," comforted my mother.
I was not willing, however, to let it go at that. Professor Redekop, the
Mennonite teacher, wrestled with her mother, saying in effect: "I will
not let you go, unless you bless me." I struggled to know my mother
as a person and to have her know me as a person, but being a Mennonite stood in the way.

We did make some headway, however. Perhaps my mother came
to see something of herself in the looking glass of my life. A far more
important catalyst for change, however, was the fact that both her
husband and her father died. Suddenly, my mother was no longer the
Mennonite bishop's wife but just another poor widow. Like many
other women in the same situation, my mother was forced to think

about who she was and what she had to offer. This was not an easy process. A preacher's wife, despite hard work, is almost invisible to the church during her husband's lifetime; when he dies she may drop out of existence completely.

After my father's death, my mother commented to me several times that she had loved him too much, that she had turned him into a god, and that her grieving process was the experience of learning this. To me it seems not that she loved him too much but rather that she had been conditioned to think that love for him meant sacrifice of herself as a person. Oddly enough, a Mennonite woman may have to become a feminist in order to be a Mennonite, if by this one assumes a radical Protestant stance that opposes idolatry and affirms the free choice of the individual.

During the time preceding her death, my mother became increasingly life-affirming. If she had her life to live over again, she told me, she would be more reckless, go barefoot more often. When I found that she had painted flowers on the cement floor of the basement, I gave her a set of oil paints and canvases. She painted one picture for me in bright, primary colors. Like a woman used to thinking she had nothing to offer, she asked me what else I would like her to paint. "Paint whatever *you* would like to paint," I replied. "You know what I would *really* like to paint?" she asked, in hushed, conspiratorial tones. My mind went blank. "*Flowers!*" she said. I should not have been surprised. Religion, for her, had always derived from a sense of wonder which could not be crushed. A trip to the Toronto Zoo with her was a religious experience. The skin of the giraffes seemed to her like velvet. The fluid swimming of the seals left her speechless until she thought to marvel at the fact that in heaven she too would be able to swim.

I gave her the usual argument, suggested she take swimming lessons, but my heart wasn't in it. I knew that she was ill. I also knew that what I respected in her was not the swimmer but her ability to *imagine* perfect swimming. In her imagination, the perfect place would be a place of total liberty—she would fly, she would swim, she would laugh, she would talk. She had always had this vision, but toward the end it seemed to me that she was devising ways of releasing its redemptive energies into the world around her. In the hospital, she expressed irritation with the people who came around singing just those songs that she had always loved. She now called them "Begraftnis Leida" (funeral songs). *"You have to want to live!"* she said to me, with a vehement stress on each syllable. She died a few days later. She was only sixty-six. At the funeral, the preacher (a man chosen by my mother because of his respect for my father) gave the eulogy to my father that had been left out of my father's funeral service. He had hardly a word to say about the woman whose body, so talkative in life, lay silently before him.

And what does all this have to do with my being a Mennonite? I'm still trying to find out. Maybe you can help me. Maybe you also had a Mennonite mother who had a lot of headaches. Are you really content to believe that she was delighted to spend all day over a hot oven baking for you and that this makes her a Mennonite? It would have been easy for me to do a portrait of myself as my father's Mennonite daughter, and then add: "By the way, I also had a wonderful mother." It may be more useful, if more wrenching, to respond to the silences of our mothers than to the sermons of our fathers. There is no alternative to using your imagination in the face of silence. My imagination was thus very active during the long night before my mother's death. Her mouth was plugged up with hospital machinery that breathed for her. Her eyes were closed. She could communicate only with her eyebrows. It was a vivid picture of what had been done to her in life.

One of my sisters ("she has a good imagination") feared that my mother would believe that God was punishing her in this way for having talked too much. We have not, however, been left with the image of a martyr. We celebrate the spirit in our mother which always won out over the temptation to acquiesce to disease, despair, and death. I cannot look at the skin of a giraffe, at a seal swimming, without remembering her and celebrating life. She never did have time to paint those flowers for me or to be a grandmother to my children, but the life she affirmed was plenty good enough for me. Should it have been good enough for the church though? I sit at my typewriter weeping, but it is not because my mother died as we all will because all flesh is as grass. If that were all, I would be content to weep into my borscht (if I could get my husband to make it). I weep in public because something in my mother was not allowed to live fully *before* she died that other death.

Do not ignore my tears and those of my Mennonite sisters as we begin to weep into our typewriters, lamenting the lost voices of our absent mothers. Do not be alarmed at the excess. Do not dismiss the weeping women from your church with the words: "She has a good imagination." If you do, you will only impoverish the church. You will, furthermore, be going contrary to what is best in the Anabaptist vision. It is because of my father that I weep into my typewriter rather than into my borscht. It is not that he did not himself exercise his authority to keep my mother from talking and laughing too much (it never worked; she was irrepressible). It is not that the Mennonites of the past have not exercised their authority to keep women silenced. It is the *power* to envision something better that we should emulate, more than the specific details of the past.

I am enough my father's daughter to hope that the Mennonite church can open itself up to the voices of women. We cannot do so, however, if we pretend that it is possible to separate memory from imagination or if we deny that we have anxiety dreams as well as wish-fulfillment dreams. The imagination of John, in the Bible, saw the church as a bride adorned to meet her husband. Mennonite historians sometimes remind me of an elderly bride who gazes into her mirror and says to herself, "I am the fairest of all churches." We are so busy admiring ourselves that we may not notice that the position of the husband has been usurped by an abusive tyrant. These historians have something to learn from elderly women who, being no longer pretty, keep in mind always that it is Jesus who is the "fairest of ten thousand."

To see Jesus as an abusive husband and the church as a geriatric bride is the image that results from the profound failure of the imagination among Mennonites. If the imagination is denied, all that is left to communicate religious vision is the feeble voice of reason. The best that it can come up with is a ridiculous tyrant in the sky. You know the one I mean. He's the man with the white beard wagging his finger at us all. He's the man who has a *reason* for everything he does. He's the man who arranges for trains and cars to come into collision so that young lives may be lost—for reasons known only to him. Blake called this product of reason "Nobodaddy" and viewed it as a form of idolatry. Why in the world Mennonites continue to bow to this idol when the Bible tells a powerful story of the incarnation is still baffling to me. A radical anti-idolatry stance seems consistent with what is best in my heritage. The early Anabaptist aversion for Catholic images cuts two ways. It can be taken as a sign of hostility to human creative power but it can also be taken as a repudiation of idolatry which affirms creative power on a different level. To insist, for example, that the wine does not literally turn into blood is not to say that the ritual has no power but rather to define the nature of its power as imaginative.

It must be clear, however, from what I have written so far, that I do not believe that unearthing the "faith of our fathers" and trying to adhere to it rigidly is going to get us liberated. I have been taking liberties with the details of my past because of my faith in the re-demptive power of human creativity. But how far, you may be ask-ing, can this liberty go? To get mixed up about raisin bread and cinammon rolls is one thing, but to be careless about whether or not your mother believed the Bible literally or your father was evangel-ical—now that's quite another thing. What is the nature of our responsibility to the past? In my view, the emphasis has to be on the affirmation of life, not death. The past should not be a dead hand reaching forward to kill the present joy. It should, rather, make the present more alive. If, in defiance, I conflate my mother's dying words: "You have to want to live" with Blake's "Everything that lives is holy," then who are you, you murdering literalist, to deny me that source of life? My mother may never have read Blake, but I am daily blessed by my conviction that she knew Jesus as someone who had the very best of imaginations: the ability to identify with another. It is the metaphor of the incarnation that is redemptive, not the twisted rationalization of Jesus as an abusive tyrant.

In my nightmare, my "self" is buried alive, entrapped in a dun-geon. I am not content with leaving her there. So far I have not allowed this autobiography to become fiction but you may have noticed that a story has been struggling to get out of my clutches. I have stayed (with an effort) on the jagged edge of the looking glass because it is a useful place to be if you want to dramatize some of the problems associated with being a Mennonite and working with litera-ture. In order, however, to get my "self" out of the dungeon, I have to make a leap. Running away is not an option in my view; we live, after all, with the reality of historical structures. One self-defined "happy ex-Mennonite" told me that being a Mennonite, like being a Jew, is a curse because you can never escape it. I agree that you cannot escape; indeed, you are probably more a prisoner of it if you think you have escaped than if you wrestle constantly with it. Is it a curse? Since the church in my nightmare can be taken as a kind of metaphor for an entrapping historical structure, my answer must depend on my interpretation of the nightmare.

Let me summon my courage and descend into that cellar again. Looking at it more closely, I find that what is most frightening is not the darkness or the pig but rather the kindness of the jailer. This is the peace that destroys. What is frightening is the circularity that traps the girl in an endless cycle of offerings that are not in fact hers to give and that therefore are not worth sacrificing. That is the reason for the slaughtered pig, a parody of the Lamb of God who *was* worthy to be slain and therefore has redeemed us.

One way of escape would be to tell myself that it is after all my dream and that I can just stop dreaming. Like the king in Alice's dream, however, the jailer might simply retort that I exist in *his* dream. Kenneth Burke tells the story of a woman who dreams of finding a brute in her room and says fearfully, "What are you going to do to me now?" whereupon the brute answers: "I don't know; it's your dream." The limitations of Burke's perspective derive from his apparent inability to see that the dream, in fact, is never just ours. I *was* dreaming my jailer's dream, in a sense; that, in fact, *is* the jail and it is the reason why the jailer appears kind. Our dreams reflect the power structures of the society we live in. It is true that we can recover the power we have projected into the kind brute in our nightmare, but our power is not absolute. We need help from each other.

Let me see if I can invoke a wave of my mother's laughter to carry me out of my dilemma. Laughter is a form of self-lessness which *is* good and which is related to something Bakhtin calls the "carnivalesque." A woman speaking Low German on the prairie may arrive, sooner than the man, at a place where all ranks and hierarchies are flattened, where being Mennonite has to do, not with an organized body of reasoned beliefs (understood only by the Mennonite bishop or by the theology professor) but rather with something disorderly and wild. She may realize that the only way to avoid the paralyzing masochism of the martyr's mirror is to embrace the condition. Take out your dentures and entertain the children. Imagination is redemptive not only because it helps us to construct enclosures and identities but also because it helps us to break out of them, accepting life as an exuberant disguise. As a child I was sometimes frightened when my mother transformed herself by removing her dentures and speaking in a strange voice. Now I realize that I would rather have a mother in disguise than a mother without a voice.

What I am suggesting is that the looking glass may become a window only if we are willing to appear ludicrous. One of my mother's favorite stories concerned an accident that involved a horse backing through the window of a bedroom and getting stuck there. She insisted that the story was true and it came complete with pieces of glass in the baby's cradle and horse buns on the floor. The punchline of the story was the housewife's instant response: "Geff me de Gaefel; eck vor em specke!" (Give me the kitchen fork; I will prick him.") In Low German, the word for the instrument used in the kitchen is *Gaefel* and the word for the one used in the barn is *Fork*. The radical disordering of worlds (male and female, barn and house) was represented in this ribald story by the word *Gaefel*. The fact that it was spoken in the manner of the Mennonites who lived *Jandsied* (on the other side) rather than in our own way (we would have said *Gaufel*) added further zest to the joke. I cannot remember whether the woman succeeded in dislodging the horse's ass. It didn't seem to matter. I suspect my mother was laughing both *at* the woman and *with* the woman in her story.

I have allowed the horse's ass into my portrait, stuck in the center of the frame, because I believe that the Mennonite church has something to learn from the housewife. The abject or the humiliating, when acknowledged as such, when embraced rather than denied, can be the source of renewal. Julia Kristeva says something like this but I didn't need her to teach me that; I had already learned it from my mother. A woman's weapons are whatever is ready to hand. My mother, however, would not have wished me to use a "Gaefel" against the kind jailer in my nightmare. He means well, after all. My mother would say: "Mutzt gescheidt senne, Maglena." ("Be good, Magdalene.") Let me, instead, take that broom which I see over there in the dark corner of the cellar. I remember that my mother once threatened to use it against a tramp that came around looking for a handout from my father. At the risk of turning this into a portrait of a Mennonite as a mad housewife, I will shoo the jailer up the stairs and out of the house. House, did I say? Why yes, the church has suddenly become a house and the time is the day of the annual pig-killing bee. That is why the children are playing happily. And over there, I see the neighborhood women who know exactly what to do with all those intestines. Shall we invite them into the basement? Here they come. Mary Penner's tiny mother is leading the way and my own mother is there to welcome them and to assign the tasks. In no time at all, the dark dungeon is transformed (as it was once a year) into a hive of bustling activity and, yes, the women are talking. Listen: my mother is telling a story.

You see how easy it was? You see, also, that I could not have done it alone and that the story is not finished. There are only women. Although I like men very much, I cannot seem to put them in the picture. Is it because I am not sure they would like my mother's stories? If the men could see their way to allowing the construction of a stairway from the basement to the main tabernacle, perhaps I could turn the house into a church again.

It may be that my inability to finish this story is related to the fact that I almost never go to church. I know a lot of Mennonites who think I ought to feel guilty or less Mennonite because of this, but I always hear my father (a radical Anabaptist, if ever there was one!) telling my mother, when she had a headache on Sunday morning, "Na, daut kaust due je uck tues downe." ("Well, you can do it at home too.")

To be a Mennonite is, for me, to work toward the subversion and renewal of the structures of society. If you look at it that way, then the institutionalized church, the actual buildings, the long lists of members—all may be worth no more than one powerful story by Rudy Wiebe.

Having said that, however, I must confess that I have a need to identify with the Mennonite people and to be associated (however loosely) with a specific Mennonite church. There is a powerful pull inward into identification with one's own people and an equally powerful pull outward to identification with the "other." Being a Mennonite, for me, has something to do with being both outside and inside and with using this tension as a source of life. MCC workers do this very well. Since my own talents lie in a specific area (I hope I have a good imagination), I express my Mennonite "identity" by taking students repeatedly through the discipline of venturing out of their skins to "identify with" another world. I do this in the hope that, when they return to their separate selves, they will be more alive and more likely to work toward life.

I see my job not only as a form of regular moral exercise, but also as the very breath of life. This breathing rhythm, however, is not something one can achieve alone. My association with the Mennonite community gives me strength because it allows me to tap the resources of a communal imagination. The fact that I can do this better by not attending church may say as much about the church as it says about me. I used to accept that what I did for a living put me on the periphery of the Mennonite tradition; I now believe that it puts me at the vital center.

In a society built on violence, to have a vision of a world at peace and to work toward that vision is a political act, an act of resistance. I think of difference and dissent in this way, not in terms of horses and buggies. If we are true to the traditional insistence on the separation of the church, we ought to nurture such a vision of difference. Nonresistance, at its best, is a resistance movement; at its worst, it is a means of acquiescing to the powers that be. The *Martyrs Mirror*, by helping along our imaginations, ought to prevent us from taking this option because to do so is to betray the vision of difference which was affirmed by the thousands of Anabaptists who were tortured and killed as subversives because they advocated the separation of church and state.

The power that lies behind the will to construct peace, however, derives from the ability of the imagination to envision war. It is here that the Mennonite imagination tends to flounder. We cannot challenge the flickering TV images of Star Wars ("twinkle, twinkle, little war") offered by a cardboard-cowboy president, unless we nurture a more profound vision. It is here, where you might expect a male prophet that I would remind you again of the Mennonite housewife. Had you forgotten her already? "Faith of our mothers, living still, in spite of dungeons...." We cannot imagine war and peace, heaven and hell on an impossibly vast scale. We cannot think the unthinkable. The imagination is more intimate: it loves what comes close to the bone. You may not be able to motivate yourself by imagining the blood spilt by the Anabaptist martyrs centuries ago, but it may help to see your own mother as a martyr.

I use the stereoscope my parents gave me because I believe that it is paralyzing to see evil and good as absolutes. What we need is a Mennonite marriage of heaven and hell which will make it possible to progress rather than to stand pat on history, gazing at ourselves in admiration in the looking glass. We need to domesticate hell and heaven. In laboring to give birth to my Mennonite parents, I try to do this. You may have noticed that experiencing the difference in angle of vision between my father and my mother has forced me to revise my portrait at every turn. These revisions are never-ending. Even as you read my writing, I may be erasing some of it. I cannot arrive at a final definition of my identity. I cannot pin myself wriggling to the wall, like a specimen of Mennonitism, and nail a list of firm beliefs under it. What we need is not so much a recovery of the Anabaptist vision, as a perpetual re-vision of it.

This revision could take many forms. Reconsidering our stance of withdrawal is an urgent concern in a world bent on self-destruction. I do not separate this, however, from what I have said about laughter. It is laughter alone that makes it possible to consider *any* re-vision. Notice that I have used Low German to help get myself moving again whenever my story wanted to stand still. My father often said, "Daut jeid aula met de Velt met" ("It goes all along with the world"), which I translate as the sensation that all things tend toward a devilish inertia. I affirm from my Mennonite past those parts that help me break out of stagnation. The *Muttasproek*, or mother tongue, helps because it is the language of domesticity and laughter.

My mother's story helps because it is not merely a diversion; it is a subversion. New life comes, oh yes it does, from the sun/Son; it also comes up from the subterranean depths. From deep down in those sub-sub-basements of our anxiety dreams where we keep the faith of our silenced mothers, comes not only the sound of weeping but also the outrageous laughter of the mad Mennonite housewife. She is beside herself. Her laughter, like that of Baudelaire, indicates a dualism in the human being: "the power of being oneself and someone else at one and the same time." (Quoted by Julia Kristeva in *Revolution in Poetic Language*, New York, p. 223.) No identity is worth having if you cannot imagine it erased.

As I write, I am myself and I am the translated voice of my mother's dying body, the body without a mouth. To forget, however, that she remains "someone else" would not only be presumptuous but would lead to paralyzing nostalgia and sentimentality. In an earlier version of this story, I concluded with the image of my mother and Mary Penner's mother dancing in heaven at the wedding feast of the Lamb. To do this, I had to violate the Mennonite prohibition against dancing and follow the imaginative desire for total identity. In the Bible this ultimate union is often seen in terms of a sexual metaphor, reminding one of the joke that Mennonites object to having intercourse standing up because it might lead to dancing. Erotic bliss may be a good metaphor for heaven (John seemed to think so), but life is in the awareness of difference—whether it be sexual difference or the difference between *Gaufel* and *Gaefel*.

This point was brought home to me (necessitating yet another revision) when I had the chance to ask one of my brothers about the Penner family. He remembered Mr. Penner and the older sons in the family. He did not remember my friend Mary at all and had no personal recollection of Mrs. Penner. He did, however, have a story to pass on. The story goes that Mrs. Penner's oldest son (who has since died himself) refused to dance at his own wedding because he had promised his mother, on her deathbed, that he would never dance.

This sobering clash of memories draws a brutal dividing line between the imaginary wedding in the New Jerusalem and those real weddings decorated with roses made by Mrs. Penner. My sense of having transgressed on somebody else's family history forced me to double back in my story and cross out the family's name, substituting a fictitious name. Should I also cross out my image of the mother dancing in heaven? Would you mind doing it for me? If you do, you will smell the past as an odor of death and decay.

As the letter of the law reaches out of the grave to kill the spirit of life, I experience, again, that sense of the uncanny, of the *unheim-lich*—and just when I thought I had invented such a nice homecoming. Seeking for what Wallace Stevens (in "The Idea of Order at Key West") calls the "ghostlier demarcations" of "ourselves and of our origins" leads to a confrontation with the ghosts of the past. It is only by responding to my mother's silence that I can counter this with an affirmation of the breath of the Holy Ghost, the spirit of eternal life. My mother's song is, in the words of Stevens, "like a body wholly body, fluttering/ Its empty sleeves." It is an emptiness requiring a perpetual translation which is always false, a mouthless body resulting in a diffusion of voices, a speaking in tongues in languages which I cannot always understand:

> Whose spirit is this? we said, because we knew
> It was the spirit that we sought and knew
> That we should ask this often as she sang.

22

Coming in
Out of
the Cold

Al Reimer

Al Reimer was born in Steinbach, Manitoba, a town which his Mennonite ancestors had helped to establish when they came from Russia in 1874. He tried a variety of jobs before settling down to an academic career. He studied at the University of Manitoba and Yale University. Since 1960 he has been teaching English at the University of Winnipeg. His numerous articles and books include translations, literary analyses, and a novel, My Harp Is Turned to Mourning, *published in 1985. Reimer is married and has three children.*

*I*n the beginning, of course, I didn't know I was one, and by the time I found out, I didn't want to be one. After boyhood dreams of hockey glory and other happy fantasies, I was overtaken by a nightmare of rebellious adolescence. Stumbling through my dark teens desperately, I wanted only to get away from the Mennonite community that held me in bondage. Growing up in a simon-pure Mennonite prairie town (Steinbach, Manitoba) was bad enough for someone who wanted to be an artist—any kind of artist at that stage; but I had the further misfortune of having my mad teens coincide with the infinitely greater madness of World War II. I still believe that cruel coincidence gave a slightly cynical warp to an otherwise blithe spirit.

One of the things war did even to Mennonites safely removed from it geographically, was to give them that old apocalyptic feeling that the end was near. In Steinbach that led to mass evangelical campaigns as precisely planned and executed as any military assault in Europe. In our community pulpit conversion became a dramatic fact of life reenacted season after season with stunning virtuosity by glamorous teams of evangelists from all over North America. Attending revival meetings was mandatory in our family, as it was in many others, and was expected to produce results where Sunday school, ordinary sermons, and stern parental admonishments had all failed. But terrified as I was by the fiery sermons and thundering altar calls, I resisted stubbornly, beyond all reason, including my carefully erected intellectual defenses. Those paltry straw houses were invariably blown away by the powerful blasts of pulpit oratory. I didn't stand a chance, and I knew it. And still I held out.

I knew I was risking eternal damnation by not submitting, but somehow the public shame of making that long guilty march to the front of a hangar-shaped "tabernacle" long enough to house a squadron of Spitfires, and baring my soul to the whole community was more frightening than eternal damnation. I quaked and cowered even more when I saw my cousins and schoolmates—sometimes even my buddies—doing it. At such moments I would not have been surprised if the fiery pit had opened at my feet and the cackling fiends had pulled me down forever. I knew it was what I deserved. And still I sat, irrevocably condemned, too terrified to make my move.

In between those tabernacle ordeals I was reading furiously, trying gamely to fortify my mind and soul against the next onslaught—the poetry of Keats and Shelley, the novels of Dostoyevsky and Turgenev, then Kant and Nietzsche and Schopenhauer. Most of these authors I found right in my father's well-stocked library. My father was a teacher and minister, an intellectual who loved books and ideas. He was proud of my intellectual curiosity and propensity for books and saw me following in his footsteps and even going beyond them in future, as long as I didn't leave Mennonite ground.

My mother, on the other hand, had almost no formal schooling; what she had instead were shrewd perceptions about people and a flamboyant way with the Low German (the only language she knew, really) that could tickle your ribs or pin you wriggling, depending on her mood. She regarded serious reading (Scripture excepted) as a black art that tended to corrupt people. When I came down from my room for dinner, she would take one look at my book-tired eyes and exclaim: "Jung, du kjitjst aul wada soo diesta ute Uage" ("Boy, you've got that dark [she meant sinful] look in your eyes again"). She guessed that my eager reading was changing me, and not for the better from her point of view. My father would reassure her and take my side. I knew instinctively that from my parents' perspective my father was wrong and my mother right. So I was forced to develop my intellectual self with furtive stealth, like adolescent boys developing their sexual selves.

By refusing to conform, by not submitting to the blunt tactics of family, school, and tabernacle, I was early branded a rebel at large, the "black spit of the chapel fold." And yet, most of the time I had trouble remembering that I was a sinner destined for the flames un-

less I changed my ways. I could not really believe that the voices singing in my soul, the ideas rioting in my mind, the sheer ache and throb
of my nameless desires were all inspired by Satan. And there was that
other voice, a quietly assured voice that I could hear whenever the ca-
cophony of guilt and terror subsided. "Dare to be yourself," it said,
"don't let them wear you down. You will walk out into the wide
world intact. You must." And then I would take heart and nurse my
silent contempt for those who were weaker, who were already meekly
tied to church and town.

Being a rebel with a cause is, of course, a great feeder of your
youthful ego. That I was destined for a spectacular career in the waiting non-Mennonite world seemed to me self-evident. If only I could
get out of this ethnic backwater into which I had fallen through no
fault of my own. In the meantime I had to suffer the double indignity
of existing in the midst of a queer, fanatical sect of people in a tiny,
backward town set in the middle of the culturally bleak Canadian
prairie. It was a cruel joke, but someday I would have the last laugh.

My father, who loved his Mennonite heritage with a passion born
of deep knowledge and even deeper commitment, tried to get me
interested in Mennonite history and culture. I remained loftily unim-
pressed, convinced that I was growing up in a historical and cultural
vacuum. The story of my ancestors I found utterly devoid of drama or
glamor. Coming to Manitoba as plodding pioneers in 1874, they
remained dim and pious nonentities who had, I was sure, seldom
smiled or done anything exciting, or even had sinful thoughts. True,
there was my great-great-grandfather, Klaas Reimer, the early church
reformer in Russia. He had been the founding leader of our church,
the Kleine Germeinde. But that didn't excite me either; I found our
church deadly dull. And there was no Mennonite literature or art that
I could relate to at all.

The one Mennonite topic that did interest me was the tragic recent
history of the Russian Mennonites. That distant world, so recently
lost, had been filled with enough violence and dramatic suffering to
have a romantic if somewhat macabre appeal. Most of my schoolboy
pals came from families which had immigrated during the 1920s, and
I enjoyed listening to their parents' stories of both the good and bad
times in Russia. The foreign-looking mementoes and souvenirs
cherished in these homes—the gray photos of splendidly moustached

young men in *Selbstschutz* uniforms, the Russian travel documents, the exotic-looking but utterly worthless ruble notes—fired my imagination and aroused envy. Here was Mennonite history worth considering. This was human drama worth talking about. But then it wasn't really mine and it was all irretrievably in the past anyway.

A man who came to symbolize that lost world of Mennonite Russia for me was the editor and writer Arnold Dyck, who lived in Steinbach during those years. I found myself mysteriously drawn to this dignified-looking man, although I'm sure he was scarcely aware of my existence. Occasionally I found myself sitting at the Sunday *Faspa* table with him at the home of one of my close friends, and observed him and listened to his casual comments with great attention. In some obscure way I sensed a kinship with him. He too was "different," an outsider who did not fit the Steinbach mold. He had a quiet sophistication of voice and manner that I could respect. He was, I suspected strongly, a clandestine intellectual who knew the world.

True, he was only a Low German writer whose humorous stories about "Koop enn Bua" my father read aloud with great relish. I knew, though, that no writer who lived in Steinbach could really be as good (or as funny) as this one appeared to be. But I had to admit that for a Mennonite this witty, urbane, obviously well-read man was pretty unusual. I could take pride in sharing a cultural heritage with him, no matter how humble it was. At least Arnold Dyck proved that it was possible for a Mennonite to write, even if only about his own people, and I nourished my own hopes on that.

I made my getaway from Steinbach with ill-concealed haste, and congratulated myself on having made a clean escape. I couldn't believe my new freedom. I kicked up my heels like a spring-sprung colt. How exhilarating to be able to pass for "white" in the world out there, to find that I wasn't carrying my Mennonitism around on my back like a telltale hump. During my years as a singing and acting student in Vancouver and later as a university student in Winnipeg and at Yale, I considered myself to be fully assimilated, my ethnic background fading behind me. I married a non-Mennonite wife and began raising a family in a non-Mennonite social and religious environment.

I even welcomed the opportunity to return to Winnipeg to accept a university teaching post. The move was not without risks, I realized.

In Winnipeg, with family and old friends nearby, Mennonite contacts would be frequent. I would be forced to work out some stance or accommodation toward the Mennonitism I thought I had left behind for good. Not that I was very worried. I felt secure enough in my new identity and confident that I could ignore or resist the old influences and pressures in a manner that would not alienate me from the Mennonite community completely.

To my surprised relief, I found that the Mennonite prison I had escaped from years earlier no longer existed, at least not in Winnipeg. Everywhere Mennonites were emerging from their traditional ghettos and boldly making their way in various professions and fields they had never entered before. The quiet in the land were clamoring for attention and being heard. Suddenly it was quite respectable to be a Mennonite—in Winnipeg it was becoming almost fashionable to be one. Rather than playing down or disguising their ethnic identity, even sophisticated Mennonites were taking a new pride in it.

At first I felt a little cheated by this turn of events. After all, I had devoted much time and effort to the meticulous unmaking of myself as a Mennonite because I was convinced that was the only way I could achieve the personal goals I had set for myself. Now young Mennonites were achieving similar goals without even leaving the fold. Nevertheless, I couldn't help taking a new interest and pride in Mennonite achievements. Almost in spite of myself, I was drawn to Mennonite ethnic culture and history, although I still regarded the church with cool aloofness. And the more interested I became in the Mennonite experience, the more aware I was that I was sharing that experience vicariously from a self-imposed distance, that I was flirting with a Mennonite identity I was not ready to assume fully. I can see now that I was actually a Mennonite ready to come in from the cold.

And when I did come in it was by an oddly circuitous route via the former homeland of my ancestors in Russia. I could never have anticipated that a brief trip to the Soviet Union, casually undertaken in the company of my father and a large group of Canadian-Mennonite tourists, would so profoundly change my life. I welcomed the opportunity to visit a country whose history and culture (its literature in particular) had always fascinated me, not to mention my long-standing interest in the Russian-Mennonite story. My plan was to keep a daily journal on the trip so that I could write some articles on the experience when I came back. My point of view would be that of an uncommitted, third-generation Canadian of Mennonite background with no personal or family connections in the land of his distant ancestors.

I soon discovered that it would not be easy to act as a detached, objective observer on this trip. Except for my father and my brother, the other forty or so members of our group had either been born and raised in Russia, or were the children of parents who had come from there in the twenties. Almost all were eagerly looking forward to reunions with blood relatives in places like Moscow, Riga, Zaporozhye, and Alma-Ata. This would be an emotional and nostalgic pilgrimage, I soon realized, and not the usual kind of bland group tour. The unpretentious, mostly elderly people in our group simply assumed I was one of them and treated me accordingly. They soon had me speaking *Plautdietsch* I thought I had forgotten long ago. And what Canadian Mennonite of my background and generation could resist the family intimacy fostered by the warm embrace of that mothering language?

By the time we reached the former Mennonite colonies in the vicinity of Zaporozhye I was no longer a spectator but an active participant as excited as everyone else at the prospect of visiting those ghostly places of the past. We had already experienced the bittersweet joy of meeting living Russian-Mennonite relatives, themselves forgotten relics of the past it seemed, and were to meet many more. The emotional highlights of the trip were already doing something to me that I had not expected. They had a direct, naked intensity that gripped me. I had never felt anything quite like it.

First there were the places—the graveyard museum of Russian-Mennonite life and culture before the Revolution. Images, vivid, unforgettable images and sights, etched themselves straight onto my mind and heart. I needed no camera to record them. The once-magnificent complex of schools in Khortitza-Rosental, the very heart and soul of the Old Colony: the tarnished elegance of the cream and red-brick *Mädchenschule*, its dainty facade violated by a gigantic portrait of Lenin over the front entrance, caught at my heartstrings. Across the street, in an even sadder state of decay, the venerable *Zentralschule*, and up the street the handsome Pedagogical Institute in which so many dedicated Mennonite teachers had been trained.

These slowly crumbling buildings stood in mute testimony to a once thriving, forward-looking Mennonite culture in this land. I felt a terrible personal loss, as though I had come back to Steinbach after many years and found it thus.

That aching sense of coming home after long absence grew even stronger the next morning when our tour bus reached the gently rolling plains of the Molochnaya. Here at last, I exulted, was the ancestral home that had lain buried within me all my life. My paternal grandparents had come from this settlement. And when we reached the village of Petershagen which, my father informed me, our ancestor, Klaas Reimer, had helped to establish in 1805, I greeted the spirit of the place as my own. Never had I felt more alive, more eager to explore an environment than I did on that daylong drive through the Molochnaya villages. I understood now what it meant to relive history—literally, passionately, inconsolably. Again the images of a moldering past transformed themselves into powerful symbols: unforgettable the battered stone corpse of the Schöensee church foundering in the weeds beside the road. Built shortly before World War I, its graceful, semi-Gothic style had made it, as the old photos attested, one of the handsomest churches in Mennonite Russia.

Shocking also was the dilapidated state of the once unique school for deaf-mute children at Tiege, our last stop. The building now housed the local soviet, and the brisk young secretary (mayor) received us affably in his second-floor office. As a gesture of hospitality, I suppose, he took a heap of loose photographs from his desk drawer and spread them out before us. They were Mennonite photos of the old days—school and family pictures and the like. I was flabbergasted. Why had these photos been preserved all these years? And why was this young official showing them to us now? Didn't he realize that these were sacred relics to these Mennonite tourists, anonymous reminders of a martyred people? As I gazed at the serenely posing faces I wondered what had happened to these people as individuals. Which ones had managed to escape, and which ones had been killed in the holocaust or dispersed to the desolate regions of the East? I wanted to shout: Give us back the people and never mind the pictures. But of course I left as quietly as the rest, the smiling secretary shaking hands all around after putting his precious Mennonite photos back in his drawer.

And in Alma-Ata, one of those remote cities of Mennonite exile, we met some of the dispersed survivors, refugees in their own country. It was as though the faded old photos in Tiege had come alive after all. Sun-burnt and smiling, they met us in the warm moist dawn at the airport. Thrusting huge bouquets of gorgeous flowers at us, they drew us all immediately into the orbit of their simple, loving natures. They were irresistible. One wrinkled, toothless *babushka* mistook me for her nephew from Winnipeg and beaming radiantly hugged and kissed me with the fierceness of joyous love. When I pointed out her error (in Low German) she laughed and said it made no difference. And it didn't. I embraced total strangers as though they were my relatives too. In spite of all cultural and linguistic barriers, enforced separation and long absence, a sense of Mennonite peoplehood was at work here that was wondrous to behold. Whatever else, these people had no trouble with their Mennonite identity. Their deprivations and sufferings had taught them to wear their ethnicity like a winter coat for warmth and comfort, not for style.

I came home from that trip with the feeling that somehow things would not be quite the same for me again. I wrote my articles for the *Mennonite Mirror* half hoping that would be the end of it. It wasn't. The ethnic vision that had come to me so unexpectedly in the Mennonite graveyard of Russia demanded something more of me. And if I did become a Mennonite again it would have to be a total commitment, not just a nostalgic ethnic ego trip, short-lived and ultimately irrelevant. I wanted to be more than a "Plumemoos enn Werenetje" Mennonite. For the first time in my life I felt a deep desire to become a Christian, a Christian Mennonite. It seemed like the logical, mature, spiritually fulfilling next step in my life. I had desperately resisted conversion as a youth, but now I found that there was no longer anything to resist. I could step into the communion of Mennonite believers without fear of any personal loss, indeed with everything to gain. A process that I had once regarded as an abject surrendering of personal integrity, I now saw as an entirely natural and inevitable surrender to the Will of God.

This spiritual metamorphosis did not take place overnight. In fact, it took several years during which I became ever more preoccupied with Mennonite history and culture. I realized after a while that I had not only found a new Mennonite identity but a new side-career in the rapidly developing field of Mennonite studies. My special area of interest is still the Russian-Mennonite story—its history, literature, and culture. During the years I was working on my Russian-Mennonite historical novel, *My Harp Is Turned to Mourning*, I made several more visits to the former Mennonite colonies in the Ukraine. Each of those visits intensified my sense of emotional and spiritual identification with the Mennonite past, and my feeling of urgency to depict in fiction the tragic curve of Russian-Mennonite experience. It is, after all, the tragic curve of all Mennonites.

The past fifteen years have without doubt been the richest and most rewarding of my life. Living as a Mennonite in Winnipeg at this time is particularly exhilarating. Never before has there been such a large and dynamic Mennonite urban community anywhere, a community that for the most part still has roots—or at least memories of roots—in the old Mennonite ethnic village. It is a rapidly assimilating Mennonite community confidently building for itself a solid social and cultural base within the larger society. There is not a profession—from politics to surgery—a vocation or career—from stockbrokerage to acting—that is not being followed with success and distinction by energetic and ambitious Mennonites. So far the ethnic cohesion is holding to a quite remarkable degree. Whether conscious of it or not, this generation of urban Mennonites is still drawing strength from inherited spiritual and ethnic values.

In my less optimistic moments, however, I wonder how much longer this ethnic vitality and stability can last in the urban setting. Can Mennonites who spend their working hours in mainstream society and generally follow the mainstream way of life expect to retain their ethnic identity for very long? For now that identity can still be claimed, although at a cost not always recognized by those who take pride in it. We may be taking our final ethnic fling, with the hangovers and self-examinations that usually follow final flings still to come. A late stage in ethnic self-consciousness (if not in ethnic disintegration) is an increased interest in ethnic art. In the Canadian-Mennonite setting, at least, there has never before been such a preoccupation with Mennonite history and ethnic culture, and particularly with the artistic achievements of "Mennonite" artists.

Predictably, much of our current interest in Mennonite culture and art is somewhat pretentious, undiscriminating, or shamelessly nostalgic. Let a concert or film in Winnipeg be advertised as "Mennonite" (no matter how tenuous the connection) and our Concert Hall overflows with Mennonites who otherwise seldom if ever set foot in it. We buy books on Mennonite subjects written by Mennonite authors, and even books on non-Mennonite subjects written by authors with "Mennonite" names, although we may never get around to reading them. We purchase kitschy paintings and crafts at Mennonite fairs and exhibitions because they were done by Mennonite artists. And we still proudly identify as "Mennonite" performing artists who have long since lost contact with the Mennonite community.

Meanwhile the few genuine creative artists we have, poets, novelists and artists who dare to prick our self-inflated, middle-class ethnic balloons, who challenge our comforting ethnic stereotypes and expose our cultural hypocrisy, are either ignored or contemptuously dismissed as being beyond the pale of Mennonite faith and respectability (all too often, alas, placed on the same level).

And yet, it is precisely at this stage of our identity crisis as a peoplehood that we most need artists of vision to define us, to tell us what we really are as ethnic groups, to test the validity of our ethnic claims. We can certainly be good Christians without remaining Mennonites, but we can't be good Christian Mennonites without a clear understanding of how our Anabaptist faith conjoins with our ethnic heritage and our cultural perceptions and values (and that is as true of Indonesian and African Mennonites as it is of Russian-Canadian Mennonites). We ignore the artist at our own risk, as the American-Mennonite poet Jeff Gundy reminds us in a recent article: " . . . as we seek to invent and imagine what it means to be Mennonite in these yeasty and perilous times, we can little afford to ignore anyone whose antennae may be more sensitive than our own."

Unfortunately, our better Mennonite artists face a serious dilemma. If they try to function as Mennonite artists within the Mennonite community, their art will tend to remain provincial and accommodating rather than critical and exploratory. If they leave the community to join mainstream artists, they will soon go beyond their Mennonite distinctives and risk losing touch with what nurtured them. Some disregard the risks and leave. Others stay, but may become schizophrenics who are never certain as to whether their Mennonite identity helps or hinders their art.

As one vitally interested in Mennonite culture and art, I empathize keenly with the artist of Mennonite background who feels that being a Mennonite in the full sense of the word is incompatible with his role as a creative artist trying to break new ground. But perhaps the plight of the Mennonite is not unique after all. There is a sense in which all true artists function as subversive schizophrenics who follow the biblical injunction of not ever letting the left hand know what the right hand is doing. It seems reasonable to suppose that for at least some talented and ambitious Mennonite artists the painful war within them over their ethnic identity and loyalties is a necessary pre-condition as well as the immediate cause of their art. Rudy Wiebe, for example, has made an international reputation as a visionary novelist of great power by exploiting his own experience as a Christian Mennonite and his Mennonite tradition.

What I came to see during my years in the wilderness was that rejecting my Mennonite identity did not automatically liberate my artistic sensibility and get my creative juices flowing. On the contrary, it exhausted me psychically for a time, seeming to enervate whatever creative powers I possessed. What I lacked during that time, I realize now, was exactly that creative tension that comes when a deeply felt and asserted ethnic experience—one that is bred in the bone—is pitted against the much wider and more complex perspectives of a larger, more sophisticated society. I no longer had any prison bars to rattle, no motives for dreaming up escape routes.

Now that I'm back in I also know that the bars and the escape routes are still there, but they are within me now. There are times when I feel that being a safe, secure, reasonably successful middle-class Mennonite fully assimilated to a non-Mennonite urban society is a far cry from what our Anabaptist ancestors were all about. While I believe deeply and fundamentally in such Anabaptist-Christian tenets and practices as discipleship, peoplehood, nonresistance, peace, and love, I find it difficult, if not impossible, to live them consistently in the often confusing welter of daily existence. And I know that believers of other faiths and cultural backgrounds can easily put me on the defensive with deeper, stronger, and more honest manifestations of faith and conduct than I can muster much of the time. And occasionally I get enraged or very despondent over the hypocritical, shallow, and uncaring ways of fellow Mennonites.

But there are also times when I am profoundly grateful that God (or merely an accident of birth) has allowed me the privilege of being a Mennonite of my particular tradition. Theological hair-splitting has never been a hobby of mine, and I have already expressed my aversion to the strident "conversion" imperative borrowed first from European pietistical sources and reinforced more recently by American mass evangelicalism. Instead, I love what I regard as the central Anabaptist-Mennonite tradition (and I am aware there is more than one authentic strand in that tradition). I am drawn powerfully to the collective religious and social identity of my people—to their "covenant-conviction," to borrow John L. Ruth's term, to their emergence and continued existence as a searching, fearless-of-consequences group of people who desire to carry out the will of God, as they perceive it, in an atmosphere of discipleship and practical love.

For me being a Mennonite means first and foremost expressing my humanity—much of what I think and feel—in what I regard as Mennonite "forms," that is, my church, my Mennonite community with its receding ethnic content, and whatever Mennonite art and culture I can help to define, affirm, and render meaningful to others. I want to express my Mennonite identity and convictions by helping to celebrate and preserve those things in our heritage that are historically authentic, inspirational, noble, courageous, or merely colorful and unique. I also want to be free to expose and criticize that which is ignoble, hypocritical, ethnically meretricious, and crassly parochial. I do not want to support or contribute to a factitious, self-glorifying, smugly idealized Mennonite art and ethnic culture. A complacent Mennonite bourgeoisie is no better than any other bourgeoisie—worse if one considers Anabaptist-Mennonite origins.

I believe that I can best express my Mennonite identity and help others understand and express theirs through my work as a writer, translator, editor, and commentator. However modestly, we Mennonites are beginning to assemble our own unique collection of literary and other creative myths—stories, myths, and other artistic icons that will in the end tell us more—and more vividly—about our own individual and collective identities as Mennonites than anything else can. For, as John L. Ruth has warned eloquently in *Mennonite Identity and Literary Art*, (p. 53):

If the artist's work of a vivid representation of the holy meaning of our identity is not done, the sociologist stands ready to dissolve that meaning by his tables and his graphs, the ecumenical preacher to find rhetoric to make it appear selfish in its particularity, and its only remaining defenders, the parochial obscurantists, to reduce it to the level of tribal ethnocentrism.

The "holy meaning of our identity" is not an idle phrase for me. I am a Mennonite because I want to devote what remains of my life to finding out what that means.

23

How I Became a Mennonite Brethren

F. J. Ross

Frederick J. Ross, a practicing physician living in Winnipeg, is a Mennonite by choice, that is, one who was not born into a Mennonite family. For some ten years he was very much involved in a Baptist church, "but for the past few years," he writes, "I have attended a Mennonite Brethren church and this is the denomination with which I most closely identify." While Mennonite culture was quite attractive to him, it is the doctrines of the Mennonites which are the strengths of his adopted church. Ross is married to Helga Martens.

H aving grown up in an evangelical fundamentalist church in Manitoba, it was only inevitable that someday I should cross paths with Mennonites. However, I think I was, at least in a theological sense, a Mennonite before I had even known who Mennonites were. That is to say, I was taught from early childhood by Christian parents the basic tenets of Anabaptist doctrines which Mennonites died for hundreds of years ago. Such distinctives as adult baptism, the Lord's Supper as having symbolic and commemorative meaning only, the doctrine of nonresistance, and the idea of a pure church separate from the state were taken for granted. All this coupled with a deep sin-consciousness characterized my upbringing and even my beliefs and thoughts today. So it is in this sense that I am first of all a Mennonite, belonging to the Anabaptist tradition.

Nevertheless, over the years and through the influences of many people in my life I have become enamoured with the Mennonite peoples themselves—their culture, traditions, and ways. I have put my foot firmly across any ethno-cultural barriers that might exist and have identified strongly with Mennonites, coming to love them dearly as I have other Christian people of other backgrounds.

My own religious background is somewhat eclectic: my mother is from a Brethren Assemblies upbringing, my father was raised a Presbyterian. For a while as a child I attended a United Church Sunday school but most of my early years were spent in an evangelical interdenominational church. For ten years I was heavily involved in a Baptist church but for the past few years I have attended a Mennonite Brethren church and this is the denomination with which I most closely identify.

My first encounter with Mennonites occurred in high school when I became involved in an Inter-School Christian Fellowship (ISCF) group. Each year this organization would have out-of-town weekend meetings held either in Steinbach or Niverville, Manitoba. My first conference was in Steinbach, where the meetings were held in one of the large Mennonite churches. My first impression of rural Mennonite kids was that they were quiet, subdued, and almost boring. I still recall the first Friday evening meeting wondering how I was going to stay interested for the whole weekend, when suddenly we were asked to sing. The richness and harmony of Mennonite singing, which hitherto I had not known, lifted my spirits and aroused my interest. I attended three more conferences like this during my high school years and made several acquaintances with Mennonite students.

Through ISCF I came to know one of my high school teachers, Hardy Enns, who is now a very close friend. He became a sponsor for our ISCF group and in the process he befriended me and often took me to his home where I first learned to appreciate Mennonite cooking. In that sense I owe much to his wife for introducing me to Mennonite traditions and food. To this day I still enjoy dropping in, sometimes unexpectedly, to enjoy a tasty lunch with borscht, perishky, and *zwieback*.

During my university years I came to meet several Mennonite students through Varsity Christian Fellowship and later on in medical school our Christian Medical Society brought many of us together for Bible studies and discussions. At United College in 1966 I met Norm Fehr and James Nikkel—two faithful "plodders for the Lord"—who through VCF promoted the triennial Urbana missionary Conference in Illinois. It was on the train ride home from this weeklong meeting that I met my wife-to-be somewhere near Chicago.

For a while in my ignorance I assumed Mennonites were more or less all the same, that is of one church background. It wasn't until I worked up north one summer at the hydroelectric power project near Gillam, Manitoba, that I learned that differences existed. I became good friends there with Ron Braun, now associate pastor at North Kildonan Mennonite Brethren Church, who was serving as a summer assistant to the chaplain in the camp. I also chummed with two fellows from a General Conference background and it was through these relationships that I learned about Low German, the different Mennonite conferences, and even Mennonite humor. I quickly learned to adapt to a phenomenon known as "spotting"—a unique way of dealing with life's woes!

As one might expect, the strongest influence in my life (Mennonite culture notwithstanding) was my wife, a vivacious energetic farm girl from a Mennonite Brethren background. When she first took me home to her parents I couldn't help but think that they probably thought I was an "outsider": I didn't speak German, I knew only a fragment of Mennonite traditions, and I was from a different religious denomination. But I loved the Lord and I loved their daughter so we had a lot in common. I can truly say to this day that I have never once felt uneasy or unaccepted by my wife's family. There was a very warm relationship which was paramount in my association with the Mennonite church. For years whenever we visited our parents in the country we would attend their church and this too created a greater appreciation for the Mennonite faith and way of life.

It was back then I suppose that I first entertained the question of what constituted being a Mennonite. I recognized the extensive missionary work undertaken by the various conferences and the diligence of evangelization by Mennonites. What happens when an outsider like myself is so attracted to their faith that he joins the church? Does he or she then become a Mennonite?

In preparation for this paper I mentioned to several Mennonite people that I was writing an essay on "Why I am a Mennonite." In several cases the first reaction was a quizzical look and the statement "But you're not a Mennonite!" These observations were made by people who supported missions and the concept of proselytizing others to the faith. It is ironic that so much time, prayer, and effort can be made by a church body in bringing others into the fold only to recognize them as not really belonging on the basis of culture, language, and tradition. I'm sure similar problems were faced by the early church when Gentiles were first added to the body of Christ. Perhaps it is time for Mennonites to take a second look at what it means to be a Mennonite.

Another aspect of the Mennonite church to which I was attracted was the doctrine of pacifism. Although as a child I was somewhat of a "scrapper" in the schoolyard, I have learned that peaceful means are often more effective in settling an issue. My grandfather had a profound influence on my life and thinking. He was an itinerant preacher with the Brethren Assemblies, a religious denomination often referred to as "Plymouth Brethren" because it originated in Plymouth, England, in the early 1800s. One of the distinctives of the Brethren Assemblies is pacifism. In fact, many members of this group were confined in detention camps during World War II for their nonresistant stance. Although this point of view was ridiculed on a large scale then, it is interesting to observe how widespread the peace movement has grown today in the secular world. Mennonites may someday have to face this issue again as they have in the past. It is easy to let this tenet of our faith fade away in times of peace and prosperity only to face it unexpectedly in time of war or oppression.

I realize that in war one supports the cause by paying one's taxes, but I would not go out of my way to kill someone. Fortunately, at my age and as a medical doctor, I would not likely face this difficult situation.

While cultural aspects have attracted me to Mennonites, I consider myself to be a Mennonite more for doctrinal reasons than anything else. Culture will no doubt change but biblical truths are eternal. It disturbs me to see that for many Mennonites "Mennonitism" is a cultural phenomenon only; they stress music, language, and traditions, whereas pacifism, adult baptism, sin-consciousness, and other elements of Anabaptist tradition seem to have fallen by the wayside. I feel, however, that the Mennonite Brethren Church today adheres more closely to the original Anabaptist and biblical distinctives than most other churches.

One confusing aspect of Mennonite tradition for me is the apparent contradiction between the well-known history of Mennonites to support, comfort, and help one another with a strong spiritual community-mindedness and the lack of expression of love and affection in the family. I grew up feeling quite comfortable kissing my mother and aunts whenever I met them or said good-bye to them. My father often puts his arm around me and touching as an expression of affection does not bother me.

I feel it is important for children to have this reassuring expression of our love for them. I see this more in ethnic groups from Latin countries and Jews but sadly lacking among Scottish, German, and

Mennonite people. Many Mennonite patients I have counseled over the years have admitted that they do not feel loved by their parents because of this reluctance to express love by a gesture as simple as a hug or a kiss. On the positive side perhaps this lack of physical expression of parental love may contribute to a behavior pattern later in life that seeks acceptance by achieving and excelling.

Over the years I have been involved in various activities associated with the MB Church. For two years in the sixties I worked with the Christian Service Brigade at the Portage Avenue MB Church, the church in which we were married. I have served twice on the board of Camp Arnes, a Mennonite Brethren supported camp which is the largest camp in western Canada. Currently I am on the board of the Winnipeg Mennonite Elementary School, where two of my children attend, and I enjoy reading the *Mennonite Brethren Herald*. Both my wife and I were enrolled in Mennonite Studies courses at the University of Winnipeg and for the past few years I have greatly enjoyed taking theological courses at the Mennonite Brethren Bible College. We were privileged to support several Mennonite missionaries over the past decade. I should emphasize once again that the motivation behind these activities for me is spiritual rather than cultural or ethnic. I am still aware of my English roots and was delighted to visit Britain two years ago to visit relatives and learn more about my English ancestry and heritage.

In summary I should state that it has not been easy for me to write this paper. It is not always apparent what attracts a person to something. It would have been equally difficult for me to answer why I love my wife. Sometimes there is no clear-cut answer when it comes to our motives. I feel the Lord has led me and guided me throughout my life as I have put my trust in him. For some reasons known to him, he has seen fit to minister to my needs by bringing me to the Mennonite people and for the present at least I feel called to serve and worship him in the Mennonite Brethren Church.

24

A Place
to Stand On

John Schroeder

*John Schroeder comes from a conservative Mennonite background
in southern Manitoba. While education and travel have expanded
his worldview, John has remained most appreciative of the ordinary things in life. During the week he manages a successful
travel agency in Winnipeg and on weekends he turns into a
gentleman farmer near Carman, Manitoba. John is married and
has two children.*

One of Canada's major authors, Margaret Laurence, describes her attempt to come to terms with her background as the gradual process of "freeing oneself from the stultifying aspect of the past, while at the same time beginning to see its true value." Included in one's past, she reminds us, lies a more distant past which one has not personally experienced. This past was forged for us by those of whom a Canadian poet wrote: "They had their being once/and left a place to stand on."

Our historians have helped us sort out our more distant past, and I, like so many of our Mennonite people, am in the continuing process of reevaluating this heritage, and determining what it is in my past that has a lasting claim on me. Here, in part, I have outlined my own pilgrimage, with its beginning in a Mennonite context, its continuation "elsewhere," and a gradual returning "home" where, for better and for worse, we were given by our forebears a place on which to stand.

I was born into a poor southern Manitoba farm family. My childhood environment was predominantly set in the Sommerfelder Church and its community. What was required of us by our ministers, with whom to this day I enjoy a continuing dialogue in the Low German language, was to attend church regularly on Sunday mornings, help a neighbor in need, and to work hard physically. ("Schaffet und wirket dass ihr selig werdet," was taken literally.) There was virtually no contact with a non-Mennonite world, and life remained simple.

With the closing of the Sommerfelder Church in 1949, my family attended the only remaining church in the area, the Mennonite

Brethren. In the Mennonite Brethren Church, as in the Sommerfelder Church, we were given our answers in terms of black and white. We now had midweek services in addition to the Sunday morning service, and so we were given more "answers," as well as a long list of "noes."

During the 1940s, with the coming of the American evangelists, I was at a very low point in my experience with my people. There were two or three, sometimes four, campaigns in one summer. It was not unusual for a number of the local Mennonite people to be "saved" several times in one summer. At that time the prime thrust of the church in my area was to "convert" people, and that on the basis of rewards and punishments. (Hence the frequent conversions—one would have considered oneself a fool not to make every effort to "save one's hide from the heat.")

In the 1950s I was first exposed to the historic peace position of the Mennonite people through an article written by J. A. Toews. It made me aware of the fact that, historically, our people concerned themselves not only with personal salvation, but with seeking to change and improve the world. For me this was a shaft of light in the darkness.

A few years later I left home to attend the Mennonite Brethren Collegiate Institute and the Mennonite Brethren Bible College in Winnipeg. To this day I appreciate the many meaningful associations that had their origins in these two schools.

In the 1960s, while spending several years in Europe traveling and working, I was for the first time in my life in a totally non-Mennonite setting. It was a very interesting and enlightening experience for me. I confess I did not yet have the courage to take my shaky identity out of the closet, because the prevailing attitude in Europe toward sects was a negative one. The Mennonites were among the sects generally regarded as the lunatic fringe of Protestantism.

My contacts within my new environment provided stimulating debates on topics such as the faith, the church and its relevance, and the church and politics. I greatly enjoyed my new friends in their church setting, but I was troubled by their lack of a peace position. I found myself deeply revolted when I was proudly shown medals and awards received for having destroyed the lives of human beings. I felt privileged, I discovered, to have had forefathers who were a people who strove for peace comparatively consistently throughout difficult periods of war and war hero worship, and this at a time when a pacifism ideal was not popular, nor the grim necessity it is today.

When I returned home and attempted to reconnect with my old church, I was disappointed to see the influence that the American TV evangelists had had on the content and form of our church services. My absence had given me an opportunity to reevaluate my church, my people, and my faith. It seemed to me that the mouthpiece of our church was out of tune and unaware of contemporary issues and the modern mind. We were speaking an "evangelical language," which could be understood only by those engaged in it. Discussions of the faith seemed to be always in line with the experience an individual had with Jesus on a personal level. (C. S. Lewis speaks to this where his senior devil, Screwtape, advises Wormwood not to waste his time with those who are totally preoccupied with a personal relationship with Jesus Christ, but rather concern himself with the real enemies, the ones who pattern their lives on the teachings of Jesus.)

Though I now was convinced that the Anabaptist position on peace and service was the one I wanted to adopt for my life, I was at the same time at the lowest point of being interested in the local Mennonite church and community. I was at this time working hard in business, associating with a large variety of people to develop a clientele. I saw people moving from one class to another, supposedly wealthier and more sophisticated, for a better clientele. Many of my Mennonite acquaintances seemed to try to pass as either English or German. Even my wife remarked, in jest, that she must have lived her former life arrogantly in a privileged class in order to have been sentenced to endure this one as an ethnic. Then several experiences came my way that helped me see things in a clearer perspective.

It was about this time that my wife and I were invited into the home of a Jewish friend, Judge Manley Rusen. During the course of the evening he remarked, regarding a Jew who had converted to the Christian faith, "You people haven't gained much, and we Jews haven't lost much." He went on to say, "John, I wouldn't respect you if you didn't remain a Mennonite. I must be a good Jew; you must be a good Mennonite."

In conversation with another friend, Father Paradis, I became more generally aware that we Mennonites are not unique in having to work through the problems that we inherit through being born into a particular faith. A truly sensitive and genuine human being, he shared with me the frustration he sometimes felt with the legalism within the Roman Catholic Church. He mentioned he sometimes envied us Mennonites, for instance, for the way in which the issue of birth control resolved itself naturally among our people without the church taking a dogmatic position on it.

It was also at this time that I had a moving experience with one of my clients, an interesting, elderly lady who identified herself as Mrs. Taylor. Because she appeared to be one of "our own," I wasn't surprised to learn, when I checked her passport, that her name had been Wiebe, changed to Kehler by marriage, then to Taylor by request. With infinite sadness she told me her story. Her father, who had immigrated to Canada with the 1874 Mennonites, had always felt that he had been denied a much desired job with the civil service because of his ethnic origin. This lady was so affected by her father's lifelong disappointment that she with her husband decided to change their name from a recognizable Mennonite one to an Anglo-Saxon one, move from the farm to the city, and join the United Church in order to resolve the problem once and for all. The legal name change presented no problem, and joining the United Church was technically possible too.

Becoming an active, accepted part of the church and its social life was another story. They worked at this. By extending dinner invitations to church members, by cleaning their houses and yards and offering other menial services, they pleaded for acceptance, only to be regarded always as outsiders. Their children too were subtly rejected, even when they excelled at university. Pained, the children finally moved to another province, changed their name back to Kehler, and joined a local Mennonite church. When "Mr. Taylor" died several years later he was still janitor of the United Church. "Mrs. Taylor" was now alone and lonely. She had left one people and not found another. She felt she had wasted her life and given her children wrong direction in their early years. At the time I met her, she was planning a trip to South America to visit her childhood friends and relatives.

On another occasion I became increasingly aware how through true appreciation for one's own peoplehood it is possible to develop a profound respect and caring for the peoplehood of one's neighbors throughout the world. My wife and I attended a fund-raising banquet for "Friends of the Hebrew University (in Jerusalem)." The speaker outlined a peace plan for the Arab-Jewish conflict in the Middle East that would have distressed us greatly, so "Zionist" was it in spirit and substance, were it not for the fact that the speaker was none other than Philip Habib, United States Ambassador to the United Nations, and an Arab.

> But there is neither east nor west, border
> nor breed nor birth,
> When two strong men stand face-to-face,
> though they come from the ends of the earth.

On a smaller scale, experiences with a family in our immediate neighborhood have reinforced for me the value of extending one's appreciation of community beyond one's own cultural boundaries. Boris and Oxanna Shulakewych with their children Markian and Zdan nurture their Ukrainian Catholic roots with great care. We were deeply moved each Christmas when the four of them dropped in to sing Ukrainian Christmas carols for us and our children Mark and Patricia. This is a tradition they have carried over from their own childhood. They come in the generous spirit of appreciation for what we are and a genuine offer to share with us what they are.

Finally, I would like to give tribute to a family from within our own Mennonite community. We had lived next door to Neil and Elly Fast for sixteen years and watched them raise their children in the "Mennonite" tradition, which they in turn now continue with their own children. When in August of 1984 Elly was given only a short time to live, the Fast family freely opened their doors to the caring community that was "theirs" to join them in their suffering. We experienced how one of "our own" died with quiet dignity, her faith strong, her familiar wit uncurtailed, and that special love given and received to the end. We were privileged to have been able to partake of this enriching and moving experience with one of "our own." Through suffering and in death, we have seen the caring community say to her, "We will be there for you." But more than that, we were there to receive the dying person's "I will be there for you."

And so, when all is said and done, why have I chosen to remain—

for better or for worse—with my own people?

There is a renewed interest for all people everywhere in one's roots. Not only is it "safe" to be ourselves, with our roots in Mennonitism, but it is also expected of us by other people in the modern world who are similarly engaged in their own search. (I say this, confessing to my shame, as a result of having heard the cock crow more than once up to this point in my life.) It is in mutual acceptance of who we are that we enrich each other, through our various artistic expressions, as well as our ideas and ideals, and return each to his own "tribe" with a renewed sense of identity, and the hope: "That the great light be clearer for our light,/And the great soul the stronger for our soul."

Like Malcolm Muggeridge, I feel I can "believe no creed wholly." I feel comfortable with the Mennonite emphasis on action and fellowship in place of a clearly laid out theology.

I take pride in those of our people in our schools, in Mennonite Central Committee, and other areas of service, who are showing us that we can survive as a people if we meet new challenges with relevant responses. (Dr. Gordon Harland of the University of Manitoba put it this way in an address to our Mennonite people: "To repeat what our fathers and mothers in the faith said in the same way in which they said it, is to fail to say what they said.")

If we disconnect ourselves from our people, the living and the dead—even if it were possible—what do we get in exchange? And very importantly, what do we offer our children in their place? Cut off from our heritage, how do we find our own personal identity? Where do we go for the nurturing and healing community which is our center and from where we see all people everywhere as the children of God, as brothers and sisters in one human family?

25

Mennonite Identity: Primary and Secondary Concerns

George Shillington

George Shillington comes from an Irish Baptist background. He joined the Mennonite Brethren Church in Kitchener, Ontario, and was ordained there to the ministry. He holds three graduate degrees and has written articles and reviews on New Testament and ethical themes and issues. At present he teaches Biblical Studies at Mennonite Brethren Bible College in Winnipeg, Manitoba. He is married and has one son and one daughter.

The Canadian Mennonite Brethren community, the context out of which I write this chapter, is currently pondering the question of identity. Few leaders in the Mennonite Brethren Conference are prepared to articulate the precise form of the question; many would reject the notion that a question of identity is in the air at all. That there should be some concern about identity among Mennonite Brethren, however, has been sufficiently documented in a recent issue of the Mennonite Brethren journal, *Direction*, under the general title "Mennonite Brethren Church Membership Profile 1972-1982" (Vol. 14, No. 2, 1985), and in the recent publication by John Redekop, *A People Apart* (Winnipeg: Kindred Press, 1987).

The ensuing discussion represents one perspective on the issue of Mennonite Brethren self-understanding on the Canadian scene, a *Sitz im Leben* which I would even dare to call "identity crisis." Since the perspective is strictly my own, not that of the conference, it would be well to etch in some relevant pieces of landscape from my own personal journey.

I was born in North Ireland and nurtured in a Presbyterian form of Christian experience and life, beginning with infant baptism. At fourteen, after participating in membership classes, I was incorporated into full membership in the Armagh Presbyterian Church upon confession of faith in Christ, admitted to the Lord's table, and eligible for service within the community of faith.

My Christian horizon expanded when my oldest brother, whose example to the rest of us became unsuspectingly powerful, married a Baptist and joined her congregation. He began to advocate the merits of Baptist theology, especially believer's baptism by immersion, failing all the while to convince my aging father, but making a lasting impression on my thinking, one that I carried with me to Canada.

Convinced of the "truth" that baptism should be a conscious act on the basis of personal faith, I was rebaptized in a Baptist church in Toronto in 1966 along with my wife, Grace. The new status afforded me the privilege of congenial studies at Central Baptist Seminary and pastoral leadership in a Baptist church.

At some point in my program at seminary (1966-1970) I was introduced to Dr. F. C. Peters, and thus encountered a "living" Mennonite for the first time. All other Mennonites of my acquaintance were mirrored in church history courses and textbooks. Fascinated already with the Mennonite heritage of faith found in history, literature, and art, my interest intensified significantly upon hearing F. C. Peters, then president of Waterloo Lutheran University, an educated Mennonite, lecture on psychology and theology. Later on in 1971 when my educational pursuits took me to Kitchener-Waterloo, Ontario, I made a point one Sunday morning of finding the church of which Dr. Peters was pastor.

He preached an impressive sermon to an attentive congregation. The people were friendly, sincere, eager to take my family to their homes for Sunday dinner. Welcomed warmly by pastor and people, we continued to attend the Kitchener Mennonite Brethren Church for one year. Then in 1972 Grace and I approached Pastor Peters about becoming full members of the congregation. His response was open and encouraging: "We ask only that you are willing to study the Word with us," he said.

Increased involvement in church and conference ministry, coupled with my full-time teaching in biblical studies at Emmanuel Bible College, prompted the Kitchener Mennonite Brethren Church to extend ordination to me in 1976. Shortly thereafter, Dr. Henry Krahn, president of Mennonite Brethren Bible College at the time, invited me to a teaching position at the college in the area of New Testament. I accepted, joined the faculty in 1981, and continue to enjoy the assignment and relationships within the academic community of MBBC.

I write this article after an enriching fifteen-year sojourn within the Mennonite Brethren Conference, having made meaningful contact with other Mennonites in various settings along the way. Moreover, he thoughts expressed here are no longer those of an outsider, but of one in continuous search of identity within the particular people of God called Mennonites. What I have to say springs from personal observations, conversations, business meetings, board meetings, visits to churches, involvement in the lives of Mennonite students at college, and reading accounts of the stages of Mennonite tradition to the present day.

1. *Appeal of the Anabaptist Heritage*

A question frequently put to me at Mennonite gatherings is, "How did you, an Irishman, become *involved with* the Mennonites?" Despite the temptation to query the inquirer about the semantics of the question, I usually take the opportunity to highlight aspects of Anabaptist faith that captured my interest and led to my *becoming* a Mennonite.

One of the distinctive features of the sixteenth-century Anabaptists that caught my attention was the emphasis on peace and peacemaking. Prior to my association with Mennonite Brethren in Kitchener in 1971, I had not given serious thought to the peace position. Obliged by sheer association with a Mennonite community to think about my conviction (or lack thereof) regarding nonresistance, I reflected repeatedly on the viability of the historic Anabaptist vision of peacekeeping and peacemaking. The more I reflected, the more inclined I was toward the Anabaptist understanding.

But I noted that the so-called peace position of Anabaptists was not held in isolation from other aspects of faith and life. All of life revolved around the center of faith in Jesus Christ expressed in a community context. Discipleship meant active thinking about how to live as a redeemed community in an unredeemed culture. Community life, so I discovered in my reading, while given a high priority, did not lead to negative sectarianism. On the contrary, the community was to consider itself to be a redemptive principal in the social order, not conforming aimlessly to the social patterns, but relating nonetheless to persons in need outside the community of faith. And every member joined the faith community voluntarily.

The voluntarism of the Anabaptists was not mere individualism. Although the commitment to Christ and to the community of faith was to be voluntary and personal, faith thus expressed in community was not permitted to degenerate into psychic introspection or private interpretations of Scripture (cf. 2 Peter 1:20). I had earlier witnessed various forms of mystical pietism in Christian groups and had been quite disenchanted with what I perceived to be a disconnection between religious experience and the rigors of everyday living. Moreover, my inclination toward the Mennonte faith followed upon an understanding of the Anabaptist emphases. They appealed to my sense of God's activity in history: redeeming people, capturing the whole realm of life, creating a new community out of the old, reconciling the world to Christ, relieving the oppressed, loving persons out of limitless grace. This was how I read the record of the early Anabaptist covenanters.

But I knew also that modern Mennonites valued other aspects of their heritage as well. They seemed to treasure genetic relations in a way I had not encountered before, using such relational designations as "cousin-uncle." They spoke of Mennonite names, Mennonite food, Low German, Russian immigration. Clearly, I could not identify in depth with these aspects as most Canadian Mennonites could: True, I have learned to appreciate verenike and summer sausage when it is served at banquets, but I scarcely get emotionally involved with it. And I do not intend to change my name, not even from Shillington to Schillington.

After fourteen years of involvement in a Mennonite conference, I still ask myself, What constitutes a person Mennonite? Am I a Mennonite? Initially I was convinced that Mennonite identity centered primarily on theological and practical implications of Christian faith, and only secondarily on language, food, heredity and ethnicity. In a secondary position these latter factors of Mennonite self-consciousness are not threatening to those of us whose ethnic and sociological ancestry resides elsewhere. Regrettably, however, the parameters of Mennonite self-definition seem to have been shifting in recent years in the Mennonite Brethren setting with which I am more familiar. Perhaps the same is happening in other settings as well.

2. *More Than Inversion*

The shift is not simply that primary and secondary features of Mennonite self-awareness are being inverted. That would be serious enough. But the situation as I see it happening in my own Mennonite conference is even more disconcerting. The primary elements of historic Mennonite faith are being replaced with a modern and conspicuously popular form of Christianity that poses as "the truth" for all. This mode of Christian self-understanding, promoted aggressively in the United States but found widely in Canada as well, tends to define Christian faith in terms of a number of fundamental formulations to be *professed*, resulting in a good feeling and material well-being. Adoption of this way of thinking is certain to break down authentic piety characteristic of historic Anabaptist Christian self-understanding. And the recent profile on Mennonite Brethren tends to confirm this assessment. Reflecting on the results of the collected data for the profile of Mennonite Brethren, 1972-1982, John E. Toews says:

> Mennonite piety looks more popularly evangelical—"save me Lord and make me feel good, but ask little of me"—and less Anabaptist-Mennonite—"empower me Lord to be a disciple-missionary for the Kingdom of God" ("Theological Reflections," *Direction*, 14, 2, 1985, pp. 61 f.).

I can see how this move would occur. The Mennonite Brethren Church is no longer an isolated community as it was in its early history in North America. With its increased involvement in North American urban society—in economics, professionalism, politics, etc.—the church's theological and religious parameters have adjusted in keeping with the acculturation process. To cite John Toews again:

> The forces of religious group acculturation progressively pulled Mennonite Brethren into popular American evangelicalism. Mennonite Brethren acculturation has meant a shift from a discipleship centered understanding of the faith to a belief centered understanding of Christian faith ("Theological Reflections," p. 62).

Although the process of religious acculturation is less advanced in Canada according to the recent study, its signal can still be clearly cited in some of the significant activities of the Canadian Mennonite Brethren Church. In 1985 the Canadian Conference of Mennonite Brethren sponsored a convention on evangelism entitled "Disciple Making '85" held in Winnipeg. All but one of the keynote speakers (besides Canadian Conference leaders) represented modern American evangelicalism. The other single voice was that of the well-known Myron Augsburger, also from the United States but committed still to the Anabaptist way of thinking and living.

It was encouraging to me to know that our Canadian Conference leaders thought it appropriate to include an Anabaptist-Mennonite in such a convention. But it was noticeable at the same time that the preponderance of lectures focused on modern evangelical methodology of church growth, popularized by the Fuller School of World Missions.

Moreover, the shift that has been taking place in the Canadian Mennonite Brethren Church is more than inversion of the primary and secondary aspects of Anabaptist-Mennonite faith and life. It is a shift away from the center of the Anabaptist heritage of faith, leaving the other aspects, the secondary culture ones, as the *only* marks of Mennonite identity. This condition concerns me, because I am not and cannot be personally committed to this vestige of Mennnonite identity by virtue of another cultural heritage and heredity from which I am not prepared to extricate myself.

Coming back to the question frequently put to me, "How does it feel to be among the Mennonites?" I have come to understand, I think, the reason for the structure of the question. To be a Mennonite, to actually be one, a person has to be born of Mennonite parents and enculturated in Mennonite customs. The fact is, I feel just fine among the Mennonites. I feel accepted, respected, loved. And yet I still have the feeling of not being a Mennonite. What saddens me about that "feeling" is the fact that while I treasure the Anabaptist-Mennonite heritage of faith I am not completely free to call myself "Mennonite."

Even more disturbing is the situation in which a so-called ethnic Mennonite leaves a Mennonite conference for a non-Mennonite church and is still considered a Mennonite. I encountered such a situation once. In conversation with an administrator of a Mennonite institution I learned that he was seeking someone to fill a position in the institution. A "Mennonite name" was mentioned. But that person had joined a non-Mennonite church, had been a member there for years, drove past a Mennonite church to attend the non-Mennonite one. I asked if the position in the Mennonite institution was open to a non-Mennonite, to which the administrator replied: "But he *is* Mennonite; I have known his parents for years." Immediately I wondered if I had the right to think of myself as Mennonite, coming as I did from a non-Mennonite home, not having a Mennonite name, etc.

Yet here I am, an active member in the Mennonite Brethren conference, teaching in a Mennonite Brethren school, and writing a chapter in a book entitled *Why I Am a Mennonite*. On what basis was I incorporated in the Mennonite fold? And on what condition am I allowed to remain in the fold? These two questions have come very much to the surface of my mind over the last number of years. Obviously the Mennonite Brethren Church did not admit me to membership on the basis of my heredity. Neither was I attracted to the Mennonites on the strength of their heredity. The transfer into the church must have been effected in terms of my Anabaptist-Mennonite faith convictions, or so I thought. Upon further reflection on the experience of incorporation into the congregation in Kitchener in 1972, I can not recall being asked any questions about my understanding of the Anabaptist heritage of faith. I believe I was accepted on the strength of a very basic statement of faith experience, and by the fact that I had been baptized by immersion. If I had been asked concerning my Anabaptist convictions my voice would doubtless have faltered, since my commitment to Anabaptist-Mennonite thought was still in the formative stage.

Since joining the Mennonite Brethren Church I have had many occasions to hear testimonials from candidates in preparation for their membership in a Mennonite Brethren congregation. And I have listened attentively in each case to hear something that represents the distinctives of the Anabaptist-Mennonite heritage, only to find that in many instances—not all—the central convictions that welded the early Mennonites into a community witness for Christ are muted behind the more popular, American evangelical formulations. Where will the new member thus instructed and incorporated, even the one from a so-called Mennonite family, find authentic Mennonite identity in the community? Will it be with reference to the rich heritage of faith or to heredity? In my own case, it cannot be with reference to heredity. And as long as the name "Mennonite" is associated strongly with culture and heredity it will tend to exclude those whose genetic and cultural background is otherwise.

But Mennonites today have no desire to exclude. On the contrary, they are increasingly evangelistic, and in that mode are inclined to think of the name "Mennonite" as an obstacle to the evangelistic program insofar as it signals exclusiveness. And that is a tension in the Mennonite Brethren Church at present. The solution, as I see it, is not to drop the name "Mennonite," as some are suggesting. That move would almost certainly accelerate the acculturation process in the direction of the popular American notion of Christian faith experience.

The answer, I believe, should be sought more appropriately in the area of theology and ethics. Church leaders should begin to call for a radical reorientation to the historic Anabaptist vision of discipleship to Jesus in the context of a community witness within the surrounding world. This reorientation should not be construed as a static transplanting of sixteenth-century Anabaptist experience into our twentieth-century Mennonite church and world. But it would involve serious reflection on the central tenets that governed the Christian thought and life of the Anabaptists in that period, leading many of them to persecution and death. To interpret the vision so that it becomes an authentic witness in our own time will take a very conscious effort on the part of church leaders and Mennonite educational institutions. But the outcome, I believe, will be well worth the effort. Young people from our churches, who find it difficult to identify any longer with cultural and ethnic Mennonitism, some of whom leave the Mennonite church altogether, are looking for a way to live out their faith in the rigors of everyday situations of life. The secondary aspects of Mennonitism, even heredity, will not save the day for them. And I submit also that a private kind of mystical faith will not be sufficient to sustain them in church-and-world. Young people, I find, are drawn to the Anabaptist understanding of Christian faith when the heritage is opened up to them in a meaningful way.

3. Peoplehood

One of the greatest challenges facing Mennonites in our time is that of maintaining a vibrant awareness of the peoplehood against the prevailing mood of individualism. When Anabaptists read the Bible they found there a people united around a common faith commitment, seeking meaningful existence in a hostile environment. The faith community that the Anabaptists found in the Bible did not simply coexist with the surrounding society, nor did its members infiltrate the society unnoticed. If any member should succumb to social, cultural, political, or religious pressures, they were called to task by the prophetic leaders and encouraged to endure. Solitary faith was unthinkable; people of faith in the Bible were the people of God and of Christ (cf. 1 Peter 2:9-10). The Anabaptists saw themselves in that light. They linked their story with the biblical story of deliverance, distinctiveness, promise, inheritance, witness, in a salvation-historical continuum.

Our question now concerns the way we connect with the faith community present and past. What constitutes Mennonite peoplehood? Is it a salvation-historical connection or an ethno-cultural connection? Mennonites need to face up to this question squarely and repeatedly. How it is answered will largely determine the course that Mennonite churches will take over the next decade of religious ferment in North America.

In conclusion, I want to say from the depths of my heart: "I am a Mennonite!" I want to say that, because I have adopted the faith and worldview of the Anabaptist forebears. My story connects with their story; my faith with their faith. To be sure, their language is not mine; their culture is not mine. But their God is my God, and that makes them then and now my people.

26

Mennonite: A Way of Following Christ

Walter Unger

Walter Unger describes himself as an evangelical Mennonite Christian. His specialty is Anabaptist history. He is the president of Columbia Bible College in Clearbrook, British Columbia. He is a frequent contributor of popular and scholarly articles to magazines and journals. As head of a college which is sponsored by both Mennonite Brethren and General Conference Mennonites, he seeks to demonstrate how the spirit of Mennonite ecumenism can find practical expression.

*I*n light of my early faith pilgrimage, it is a wonder that I ever aligned myself with any one church tradition. Until I was in my early twenties my exposure to various expressions of the Christian faith was very broad. Perhaps this is what led me to take up church history as my main field of interest in graduate studies.

My parents were not established in the Mennonite Brethren Church until later in their life and this meant that as a child and young person I had a great deal of liberty to explore different denominations. I remember as a child going to a Baptist Sunday school—which brand of Baptist I do not know. I attended the Salvation Army for a short period of time. My parents took me to a United Mennonite Church in the late 1940s. Later we attended an Associated Gospel Church, where at a series of evangelistic meetings I was converted. Finally, my parents cast their lot with the Mennonite Brethren Church and after attending this church for a number of years I was baptized and accepted into membership. I was about sixteen years old.

Before and after my baptism a strong spiritual influence in my life was Youth for Christ and the whole train of evangelical superstars of the fifties, led by Billy Graham and Bob Pierce. Graham inspired me in the direction of forthright evangelistic preaching. Pierce taught me compassion, moving my heart to be touched by the things that break the heart of God.

A final strong influence in my teen spiritual pilgrimage was Theodore Epp and the Back to the Bible Broadcast. I listened regularly to Epp in the fifties and to other radio speakers like him.

Mix all these ingredients, shake them well, and then add three years of Bible college at Mennonite Brethren Bible College, further studies at Teacher's College and at three universities, seminary train-ing at an Evangelical Free Divinity School (really interdenomina-tional) and what do you get? Well, unless there was a great deal of sifting and sorting out, you would *not* get a person with Anabaptist/ Mennonite convictions. However, significant evaluation did occur and I have come to freely and joyously affirm my faith position within the Mennonite branch of the church of Christ.

The Contribution of Other Faith Traditions
Most of the experiences along the way of my spiritual pilgrimage contributed to the affirmation of my faith commitment as a Men-nonite Christian. My firsthand exposure to a variety of churches— Baptist, Associated Gospel, Evangelical Free—taught me to be more understanding and appreciative of these denominations. I saw many similarities in faith and practice between these groups and my own Mennonite church.

My Youth for Christ, Billy Graham, and Bob Pierce experiences were helpful in kindling a zeal within me for evangelism and a concern for homeless orphans and victims of war. I consider evange-lism and social concern to be at the very heart of my Anabaptist faith.

The evangelical spirit I found in some of the conservative denomi-nations and parachurch organizations had something very authentic about it which was rooted in the New Testament. I discovered later that same spirit was very strong in the early days of both Swiss and Dutch Anabaptism. My experiences in non-Mennonite circles helped me to identify what ought to be some of the biblical characteristics of a New Testament church. I found these characteristics in the Men-nonite church.

My graduate studies taught me to view my Mennonite faith within the perspective of the broader stream of church history. Mennonites are only a tiny segment of the church universal. God has done his mighty acts through others besides my forebears and to the immense benefit of the present-day Mennonite church. In many ways, my Anabaptist/Mennonite forefathers built on the foundation stones others uncovered, while uniquely uncovering some truths themselves.

Before he became a Christian, Menno Simons read the writings of Luther and the other mainline Reformers. Conrad Grebel and Felix Manz were disciples of the Swiss Reformer Ulrich Zwingli before they started the Anabaptist movement. Grebel said of his reforming zeal: "Zwingli brought me into this thing!"

I know that it is popular in some Mennonite circles to do a fair bit of "Luther bashing," with extra barbs thrown in for the intolerant Calvin. We find it difficult to forgive Zwingli for his part in the exiling of Anabaptists from Zurich and later their martyrdom.

There is no way such actions can be condoned, even by sixteenth-century standards, let alone twentieth-century norms. Yet I have come to see the Magisterical Reformers as persons of enormous conviction. They lived in a violent, intolerant age in which their rediscovery of cardinal Christian truths was seen as threatened by any group which suggested that certain aspects of these truths were not being followed through to their logical ends. This was precisely the complaint of the Swiss Brethren against Zwingli regarding his inconsistent application of the strict biblicism he had taught them.

On the positive side, I learned to be deeply grateful that the Reformers did clear away much of the rubble heaped up by medieval Catholicism so that the foundation stones of true Christianity could once again be seen. Salvation by grace alone, in Christ alone, through faith alone, revealed in Scripture alone (the four *solas*)—this is the basis of evangelical faith.

I discovered that Luther's understanding of faith as going beyond mere mental assent to trust, commitment, and a throwing of oneself on God was the key to Menno Simons' conversion. Marks of Luther's definition of faith as given in his *Preface to the Epistle to the Romans* are clearly evident in Menno, who wrote that faith was "the gift of God. All who receive it from God receive a tree loaded with all manner of good and delicious fruit. . . . He that receives it receives Christ Jesus, forgiveness of sins, a new mind, and eternal life [and] true faith makes one active, confident, and joyful in Christ Jesus!"

I have learned that one cannot ignore God's work in the history of the church and leap from the New Testament to the present. The substance of Christian teaching is found in the New Testament, but one cannot overlook the interpretation and application of that truth by a multitude of witnesses. These witnesses include Church Fathers, Christlike monks, medieval mystics, and sixteenth-century reformers, as well as Arminian, Pietist, revivalist, and present-day charismatic representations of important facets of Christianity.

Affirming My Faith as a Mennonite

With so much good evident in other faith traditions, what did I see in the Anabaptist/Mennonite understanding of Christianity which led me to fully identify with this faith community? I was drawn by a number of basic biblical convictions I saw fleshed-out in the early Anabaptists of South German, Swiss, and Dutch origin as represented by men such as Michael Sattler, Conrad Grebel, and Menno Simons. Although there were many Anabaptist groups with differing emphases in the sixteenth century, it is this stream which most impressed and influenced me.

Although these early Swiss and Dutch Anabaptists agreed with the Reformers in breaking with Rome and with evangelical doctrine as expressed in the four *solas*, they went beyond the Reformers in a number of fundamental ways. By rejecting infant baptism, which had been an essential ingredient in the church/state synthesis for more than a thousand years, the Swiss and Dutch Anabaptists pointed out that the monolith of Christendom, yes even the Reformed version, was not biblical. The church was to be a *believing* community called out from the world.

What really drew me was the Anabaptist view of the church which, in my opinion, is the chief distinctive of the movement. Baptism was a corollary. The church was for believers who voluntarily obeyed Christ in baptism and in a life of discipleship. The new birth had to be demonstrated by a new way of life. High priority was placed on discipleship, both individual and corporate.

Baptism was the door to the visible church. In baptism, the Anabaptists saw a visible means of expressing corporate discipleship. Membership in the body of believers meant taking on responsibility to admonish and be admonished, to care for one's brother and sister and be cared for—in other words, to provide mutual aid. Salvation and membership in the church was not the highly individualistic matter it has become for many today.

The basic commitment of the Anabaptists who were my inspiration was to the kingdom of God and not to the state or earthly kingdoms, although some Anabaptists did try to set up an earthly kingdom. The church was to be a visible representation of the invisible kingdom, which had already begun in the believing community. This meant the practice of limitless love, the modus operandi of kingdom citizens.

The early Anabaptist brothers and sisters chose to die for their faith rather than become involved in the use of violence or give up their "heretical" convictions. At the same time, they urged religious liberty for all and became the founders of the free church movement.

I also discovered that the Anabaptist zeal for spreading the gospel was unique among sixteenth-century Christians. Menno Simons expressed the evangelistic concern of the early Mennonites thus: "We wish that we might save all mankind from the jaws of hell, free them from the chains of their sins, and by the gracious help of God add them to Christ by the Gospel of His peace. For this is the true nature of the love which is of God." Sebastian Franck, a contemporary friend and critic of the early Anabaptists was impressed by their sense of mission, although he was skeptical. He wrote: "They wish to imitate apostolic life . . . move about from one place to another preaching, and claiming a great calling and mission." Some were so sure of their calling, Franck added, that they felt themselves responsible for the whole world.

A Way of Following Christ

For me, being a Mennonite is a way of following Christ and being Christian which has much in common with other Christians, *yet has a special vision.* I am captivated by that vision of a believers' church of reborn people living reordered lives based on kingdom principles; a vision of corporate discipleship, peacemaking, and a sense of mission which is holistic—melding word and deed. This vision I believe to be based on the New Testament, and the Anabaptist forebears I have described tried to recapture it and live it. This vision has drawn me to the Mennonite way of being a Christian.

For me, being a Mennonite is *not* an ethnic matter, nor is culture the glue which bonds me to this body of believers. Living faith, not ethnicity or culture, defines a Mennonite Christian. Paul in Galatians 3:26-28 and 6:14-15 rejected social, ethnic, sexual, and ritualistic considerations in defining the essence of being Christian. Faith in Christ, lifting high the cross of Christ, and living out the "new creation" was what constituted being Christian. It was the desire to be this "new creation," a holy people of God, which called the Anabaptist/Mennonite movement into being.

Three quarter of a million people around the world call themselves

Mennonite Christians. They live in fifty-seven countries and represent more than forty nationalities. Each of these Mennonite groups have their own culture rooted in their own environment and history but this culture has nothing to do with the *essence* of being a Mennonite follower of Jesus Christ. There *are* cultural expressions of that following of Christ, to be sure, but these are not to be so intermingled with the faith that one cannot distinguish between the two. When cultural expressions become the essence, biblical Christianity has been abandoned. If a specific ethnicity and culture were essential to being a Mennonite, then I by my own definition of Mennonite would have to drop out of the Mennonite fold.

Many years of study, thoughtful consideration of numerous church traditions and careful reevaluation of the Anabaptist/Mennonite heritage has brought me to an appreciation of other Christian groups, but to even a deeper appreciation of what it means to know and follow Christ as a Mennonite Christian. I cannot follow Christ alone—I need the church to help sustain my faith. I am glad I can identify with a host of fellow Christians in the Mennonite church—a faith tradition which I believe sincerely seeks to recapture what Christ called me to be and do as a member of this particular portion of His church.

27

Staying On

Roy Vogt

Roy Vogt, the president of the Mennonite Literary Society in Winnipeg, Manitoba, teaches economics at the University of Manitoba. He is an ordained minister in the First Mennonite Church in Winnipeg. He has published articles on corporations, property rights, and employee decision-making, and he is a coauthor of a first-year text in economics which is widely used in Canadian universities. He is the chairman of the Soviet-East European Studies Programme at the University of Manitoba. He is married and has three children.

Mennonites have no confessional, but that doesn't mean that they have no need or desire to confess. On the contrary, by virtue of a strong ethical emphasis in their religion and because they imagine that in the distant past their forefathers had a near-perfect life and vision, Mennonites seem doomed to confess again and again. They must tell and retell their story, to measure it against the biblical story and the story of their ancestors. This book may be considered a small proof of that.

At the core of the Mennonite imagination is the persistent, deep awareness of the wide gulf which separates Christian ideals from daily human reality. The Anabaptist vision of the sixteenth century was a heroic attempt to close this gap. The problem of the twentieth-century Mennonite is to appropriate and mobilize basic elements of that vision while doing justice both to its highest aims and to the complex needs and structures of a world in which the best is sometimes the enemy of the good.

But is the Mennonite faith worth appropriating at all? Are there good reasons for being a Mennonite today? I find this question problematic on two counts. First, how can it be a *real* question for me when I *am* a Mennonite? How sincerely can one question a choice that has already been made? I will try to face this problem in a moment as honestly as possible. Prior to this, however, I would like to deal briefly with a second problem: How *free* have most of us been in choosing to become Mennonites in the first place? This question too must be treated as frankly as possible.

Choosing to Become a Mennonite: A Real Choice?
It occurred to me a long time ago that if I had been born in India I

would likely be a Hindu today, or perhaps an atheist. The chances are very small that I would be what in fact I have become. Growing up in Canada, in a Mennonite community, there was a very good chance that I would become a Christian with a Mennonite "bent" or an atheist. So I am largely a child of the chances that were given to me. Largely, but perhaps not entirely, or so at least I choose to think.

The initial decision to join the Mennonite church was made in my case after several years of university study during which time I deliberately avoided going to church. However, on occasion, at the invitation of friends or relatives, I ventured to First Mennonite Church in Winnipeg, where the preaching of the late Rev. J. H. Enns and the singing of a good choir made their impact. A solitary summer reading and hiking in the Caribou Mountains of British Columbia persuaded me that among the·many different ways that one might choose to live life, the Christian way was the most appealing. In retrospect I realize that despite the considerable reading of that summer there weren't all that many alternatives that I considered. The choice was essentially between Christianity and atheism, or between affirmation and negation of meaning in life—which really seemed to be the question that I was trying to resolve. The decision made quietly and privately that summer led the following year to membership and participation in the Mennonite church.

What did I affirm at that time? Nothing very complicated. I don't recall the exact words of my baptismal vows, but I believe that what I was trying to affirm was something as follows: I recognized myself as the child of a personal God who had implanted in me a desire to do good and the freedom to do otherwise. Through the person and the teachings of Jesus of Nazareth (and undoubtedly under the influence of such genuinely good people as my parents) I had come to think of this God as a loving and forgiving Father, who cares equally for all human beings and desires our cooperation in overcoming both our own weaknesses and the failings and suffering of others. To be a Christian meant to accept this responsibility with all the joy and sorrow that might come with it. I felt that this was the most glorious adventure that a person could undertake.

There was much in the Christian tradition that I was not prepared to affirm. Some ideas, such as the notion that God will damn sinners to hell and save Christians from hell, I found repulsive and completely at odds with my understanding of the gospel (the "good news"). Other ideas, such as particular interpretations of the atonement, I found too mysterious to reduce to a proposition that one can affirm. However, what I did affirm seemed revolutionary enough to me—and enough to form a base for the rest of my life. These beliefs obviously do not encompass the range or the types of beliefs that I might have come to hold if I had broadened my search for alternatives or if I had had different teachers. However, as these beliefs have been tested over the years with the accumulation of new knowledge and experiences I feel that they have become *mine* as much as anything will ever be identified as mine. They have been shaken on numerous occasions, but though I have not tried desperately to hang on to them they have always emerged stronger than the doubts and problems that momentarily shook them. I must confess that I have looked into the abyss of meaninglessness more than once, but it was faith more than fear that pulled me back.

So much for the initial impulse to accept the Christian faith as over against atheism and my decision to join the Mennonite church. I have now been a member of the Mennonite church for more than thirty years. Is there any point in asking whether I still consider it to be a good decision? Isn't the question merely rhetorical? Actually I think I have found it more difficult to remain a Mennonite than to become one. This may mean nothing more than the fact that it is within a particular Christian denomination that most of us test the real power of the Christian faith to change people, and the failures that one observes are attributed not only to the Christian faith itself but to one's particular church. Whatever the reason, *staying on* as a Mennonite has not always been easy, and in asking the question now whether one should continue to stay on, I would like to respond as sincerely as possible by reexamining those areas of Mennonite teaching and practice that appear to me to be most problematic. Only after such an examination will an answer seem justifiable.

Staying On: A Reasonable Choice?

When I joined the Mennonite church I didn't reflect much on what made it different from other churches. I had heard virtually nothing about the Anabaptist Reformation of the sixteenth century and certainly wasn't prepared to assess the issues raised by that

Reformation. In subsequent years I was privileged to examine the Anabaptist "vision" at our seminary in the United States, and to test it in further study at the Lutheran theological faculty at the University of Hamburg and in numerous formal and informal seminars with Christians and non-Christians of many different backgrounds. I believe I have learned most from members of the Mennonite community in Winnipeg among whom I count my dearest friends, and from colleagues at St. Paul's College in Winnipeg, where Catholic-non-Catholic dialogue is maintained daily.

What has all this meant to my understanding of the Mennonite faith today? I would like to restrict my observations largely to the unique Anabaptist roots of that faith. Over the years I have come to the conclusion that in some quite significant ways the Anabaptist vision is badly flawed. The flaws that I wish to point out must be understood against the background of what the Anabaptists tried to do. As was asserted earlier, the Anabaptists sought above all to close the gap that exists between the highest Christian ideals and daily human reality. In their formulation of a "correct" Christian approach to this problem they were aware of approaches used by other Christians and they deliberately rejected such alternative solutions as inferior to their own. It may be useful to recall briefly what some of these alternatives were and what was unique about the proposed Anabaptist solution.

All Christians, to the extent that they take their ideals seriously, are haunted by the gulf between Christian dreams of perfection and human reality. Some Christian groups have tried to solve this problem by creating an elite vanguard of believers who in their cloisters and academies attempt to exercise the "perfection" of the Christian faith. Simultaneously, somewhat lesser demands are made on rank-and-file members. This may be called the "class" solution to the dilemma of ideal vs reality. Other groups distinguish between a private, personal world, in which all Christians are assumed capable of attaining perfection or something close to it, and the sociopolitical world where perfectionistic counsel is deemed inappropriate. This division of degrees of responsibility into "spheres" is the essence of what might be called the "pietist" solution.

The Anabaptists saw problems in both of these approaches and rejected both. The division of Christians into classes was replaced in the Anabaptist vision by the "priesthood of all believers," while the division into spheres was rejected on the grounds that Christian ethical principles are to be applied to all areas of life, social as well as private. The Anabaptist vision was consistent and strong: *all* Christians are to apply the highest Christian ideals to *all* spheres of life.

Can there be anything wrong with such a strong, consistent vision? There are, I believe, a number of serious problems with it. First, I will try to show that the Anabaptist vision *misdirects* Christians to a pursuit of perfection. Second, in the course of this pursuit it produces simplified standards of perfection which result in turn in destructive behavior within the Christian community. Third, its perfectionist zeal tends to produce, paradoxically, the type of "class" and "sphere" solutions to the ideal vs reality dilemma that Anabaptism originally condemned.

The Anabaptists wanted Christians to be perfect. Is there something wrong with that? There is, I think, if personal or community perfection becomes the *object* rather than the *fruit* of Christian behavior. The pursuit of perfection is a self-centered one. The person who undertakes it will, in the course of it, engage constantly in self-evaluation. Have I achieved it? Am I getting closer to it or falling further away? The same problems will emerge in a community that aims for perfection. Much of the energy of that community will be consumed in keeping score of its own progress (or lack of it). Mennonite history is replete with such self-centered, overly critical behavior. Instead of losing oneself in service to others, the Christian becomes preoccupied with self in a never-ending round of critical self-examination.

To be fair to the Anabaptists, theirs was not a search for self-perfection as such, or for what might be called personal saintliness. Their mission *was* service-directed; they wanted to learn to love their neighbor perfectly. However, their zeal to do this *perfectly* inevitably caused them to focus more and more attention on themselves. This inevitably produced schisms in the church, and in general resulted in an inner-directed type of behavior which, in my opinion, is quite at odds with the other-directed nature of Christian love. Near-perfection may ultimately be a gift to those who lose themselves in service to others, but it will invariably be missed by those who deliberately pursue it.

The pursuit of perfectionist goals creates another problem. Communities concerned with perfection will find it necessary to establish clear-cut standards by which perfection can be measured. Unfortunately, such standards, because they must be clearly defined for purposes of scorekeeping, will almost invariably do violence to the essence of the ideals which they seek to represent.

Within Mennonite communities at least two types of perfectionist standards have been established, and both, I think, fail to accomplish their real aims. The first has to do with the search for a "true" Christian faith. The Anabaptists hoped to produce Christian communities that would be perfect in their faith. But how does one define and measure such faith? The task may seem relatively easy because there is something concrete about the Christian faith: it focuses on an historical person and describes God in some quite specific ways.

Nevertheless, I would maintain that the degree of faith that people actually have in such a God is virtually impossible to ascertain. It may be connected only very tenuously to the number and type of propositions they are willing to affirm about God. And yet, in their diligent pursuit of the "true" faith, some descendants of the Anabaptists have produced communities in which a very high premium is placed on doctrinal orthodoxy and in which members are constantly being tested and judged by the standards of such orthodoxy. Such communities will sometimes stress the need for a *simple* faith in God, but I am often amazed at the number and complexity of the things they feel one must believe in order to demonstrate such faith. There are many people around us who believe in a Christian God but they would undoubtedly be barred from membership in many Mennonite congregations because they would fail to meet the standards of faith set by such congregations.

Another type of perfectionist standard has to do with behavior. Anabaptists identified love as the keystone of Christian ethics. To be a disciple of Christ is to love one's neighbor. So far, so good. But can one define the form this love will take in tough, real-world situations? The Anabaptists thought they could. A basic standard which they adopted and which has been "recovered" among segments of the Mennonite church in the twentieth century was that of nonresistance or nonviolence. (Nonviolence is not the same as nonresistance but it seems increasingly acceptable as a substitute.)

In some Mennonite circles today a commitment to nonviolence has been made virtually synonymous with a commitment to the ethic of Christian love. Though love seems to be linked most naturally to nonviolent forms of expression, are nonviolent means adequate to express love under all conditions and is an ethic which limits itself to such means an adequate ethic for Christians? In my opinion the answer is no. I assume that to love one's neighbor means to take some responsibility for the welfare of that neighbor. When problems arise which will likely harm the neighbor the Christian's primary question should not be, "How can I now act so as to be true to my previous definition of correct morality?" but rather, "What must I do to help my neighbor?"

There are, unfortunately, numerous situations in the world today where "neighbors" are being oppressed and killed through actions which will not be stopped by nonviolence. Will the Mafia cease their activities in the presence of an unarmed police force? Would Idi Amin, to name just one of dozens of such leaders, have relinquished power without the use of force? To pretend that they would, is to betray a shallow grasp of the depth and tenacity of human evil. To argue that being true to our moral standards, even to the point of martyrdom, is an adequate response to the needs of our oppressed neighbors, might be a good way of dealing with our conscience but not an adequate way of helping our neighbor.

The world presents us freqently with the following dilemma: to act "rightly" (i.e., nonviolently) toward neighbors such as Idi Amin and Al Capone is to act wrongly toward those neighbors who are harmed by them. No one can define in advance what the best response will be in all such situations. The simple standards of love developed by the Anabaptists and promoted by some twentieth-century Mennonite followers may be profoundly helpful in many situations, but in a world of complex human relationships and incredible evil they may often be quite inadequate.

This leads me to a third problem with the Anabaptist vision. If the world *as it is* is not always fit for Anabaptist ideas, retreat from the world becomes a necessity. This has in fact occurred frequently in Mennonite history, though some retreats are more obvious than others. The creation of separate colonies by Mennonites in various parts of the world is well known. It was hoped that in such separated communities the highest ideals of the Christian faith, including nonresistance, might be realized. In twentieth-century North America more subtle forms of retreat and separation are being attempted. Mennonite professionals, for example, generally support theories of cultural interaction and take a lively interest in world affairs, but they remain largely aloof from the conflicts and power struggles that occur in the world arena. Like the priests of old they have effectively retreated into a class which dispenses highly idealistic theoretical advice but which remains unsullied by social and political struggle. The art of politics, for example, is widely disdained by those in the forefront of Mennonite thought.

It is true that a strong desire to help the oppressed around the world in nonviolent ways (of which more will be said below) often places Mennonites in the midst of world conflicts. Their courage in such situations can only be commended. But even when this happens Mennonites remain on the periphery of the actual decision-making processes.

In practice, if not in theory, Mennonites have reverted to the kind of "class" and "sphere" solution to the ideal-vs-reality dilemma which their Anabaptist forefathers tried to reject. From relatively safe positions they promote ethical guidelines which may have considerable relevance for small, highly dedicated communities, but which contribute little to the solution of racial, economic, and military oppression in the world.

To summarize, through its insistence on perfection the Anabaptist-Mennonite tradition has produced Christian communities which are extremely judgmental and inner-directed, legalistic in enforcing doctrinal orthodoxy, and escapist. These things are not said lightly, and though there are outstanding exceptions to one or even all of these critical assessments, most of them accurately describe Mennonite church life, past and present.

If this is so, why would anyone want to remain a member of the Mennonite church? The fact is that the conditions just described have led many very good people to give up and leave. In the city of Winnipeg alone there are hundreds of ex-Mennonites worshiping in other churches and an even larger number who have stopped worshiping altogether.

Despite this and not, I trust, because of a hopeless case of masochism or inertia, I believe there are reasons for staying on. The reasons may not always seem compelling, but neither are they based on a kind of spiritual bravado which declares, "My church right or wrong!" Let me begin a brief catalog of reasons by observing that the Christian faith is for all people an extremely daring and complex undertaking. As I have mentioned, I consider my faith in God to be a simple one, but what is not simple is the appropriate application of that faith to the conditions that we encounter in the world. Evil is tenacious, its gradations, both in myself and in others, are myriad. In developing strategies for coping with it, Christians are bound to come up with different solutions. None of these will prove adequate for all situations, and very often, it seems, the unique strengths of a certain position will be inextricably bound up with unique weaknesses. If you reach hard for perfection you may develop disciplines which make you into an extremely reliable and useful person, but also, alas, into a harsh and judgmental person whose life is not infused with grace and compassion. If, on the other hand, you focus on qualities like grace and forgiveness, your ethical seriousness may be blunted. It is surely one of the great tragedies of the Christian church that cheap grace has sometimes been accompanied by cheap ethics. Augustine says somewhere, "Love God and do what you like," and some people merely do what they like.

All this is simply to say that while I find the Christian faith itself meaningful, I do not find much to choose between the different institutional expressions of that faith. It may seem too easy to say it, but the fact is that they all have partial vision and their visions probably contain an equal mixture of truth and error, both in teaching and in practice. I complain to a United Church friend that our annual congregational meetings are often marred by angry confrontations over small issues, and he responds, "If people in my church would only get mad about something! So many don't seem to care at all." As I have tried to show, we descendants of the Anabaptist vision must contend with a theology that is inadequate and even destructive at times. But then my Catholic friends may be worse off than I. They have to come to terms with such incredible teachings as the infallibility of the pope and the possible damnation of unbaptized children.

There is, however, a more positive interpretation of our differences. Each tradition has unique strengths. From the Lutheran tradition I have learned what I consider to be the greatest gift in the Christian church, namely the meaning and experience of grace. Virtually no Mennonite could have written what Dietrich Bonhoeffer, a Lutheran, wrote in 1944, shortly before his death: "God goes to all people in their distress,/ satisfying body and soul with his bread,/ dies for Christians and heathen on the cross/ and forgives them all." From Catholic colleagues I am hopefully learning what I would call a "holy patience." This rests in the knowledge that God patiently accepts and works with our weaknesses, and even the most terrible sinner is capable of housing his indwelling Spirit.

Similarly, there are, I believe, unique strengths in the Mennonite tradition and in current Mennonite community life. In the midst of the judgmentalism, escapism, and often just the sheer boredom of an inward-looking religion, there are, incredibly, thousands of persons who care very deeply about their faith. Not only that, they are willing to work hard and even suffer for it. It is possible to be inspired by the spectacle of hundreds of Mennonite young people around the world expressing their love to others in practical, nonviolent ways. Although their ethic of nonviolence is not, as I have tried to suggest, as complete an answer to world problems as they may think, it is in very many instances a powerful healing force. In our local congregations, too, there is often a caring and brotherhood spirit. Just as some people are worse than their theology, so others are better than what they ostensibly believe. A person's faith may be judgmental at the roots, but the person may sometimes catch the spirit of a more compassionate and forgiving Lord and express it in daily acts of kindness to others.

When I sit in our church on Sunday morning I am moved to say more than anywhere else, "These are my people." Despite all the normal human weaknesses which I naturally share as much as anyone else, there is faith there and a lot of strength. Those who turn their back on that may, I suspect, be rejecting the most precious gift that life has to give them: a caring community of faith. I say "may" because I know there are congregations in which this gift may not be present.

While I believe that all this can be affirmed about the Mennonite church, there is a great deal that we can and should learn from others: both from other Christians and from non-Christians. We must learn how to be more forgiving and patient and how to respond more responsibly to the needs of the world. We must particularly develop a new approach to the challenge of peacemaking, listening carefully to the insights and experience of those whose involvement in world problems has been much deeper than ours. We know that God can bless our little efforts, but we must stop pretending that we have a superior or complete answer to human conflict. We remain at the periphery of society not only because we are few in number and meek as doves but because we don't love our neighbor enough to shape our theology according to his need.

There are many Christians in other traditions with whom I feel a strong kinship and there are non-Christians with whom I feel bound in spirit, but I believe I'll stay on as a Mennonite, not because Mennonites are further along the road of faith than others but simply because they are on that road, and *that* road, I believe, takes us in the right direction.

28

By Chance and by God's Grace

Bernie Wiebe

Bernie Wiebe has been a longtime editor of The Mennonite, *a General Conference Mennonite magazine. At present he is a teaching and research associate at the Mennonite Studies Centre at the University of Winnipeg. Like many other conservative Mennonites in southern Manitoba the young Bernie found his life dramatically changed when he "went forward" during an evangelistic campaign in the mid-1940s. Arriving at the altar he found to his surprise his parents and three of his sisters there as well. "That night's public commitment," he writes, "imploded upon our home and family. For me it was an awakening to 'being.'"*

A *small German smorgasbord.* Growing up in the small, monolithic Alt-Bergthal school district southwest of Altona, Manitoba, I did not know of or hear about Mennonites. There were Sommerfelder, Old Colony, Rudnerweider, and Bergthaler churches. In Alt-Bergthal we were mostly Sommerfelder. There were two Rudnerweider families, and two Jehovah's Witness families. A big Bergthaler church existed in Altona.

Of course, we had it figured out. We Sommerfelder were "in"; Rudnerweiders were on the "fringe"; the Bergthalers were the "educated rich" and "suspect"; JWs were "out."

High German was what God preferred on his day in his place. Low German was our daily "mother" tongue at home and with friends.

Our world was small. A trip from Altona to Winnipeg (about 110 kilometers) was a major exposure. My mother began taking me in my turn after about age eight to help her with that strange language—English—they spoke there.

Our choices at the smorgasbord were small or less. It was assumed we would become Sommerfelder members as part of marriage preparation. Reciting catechism, being baptized, taking communion, were sure signs of a pending marriage.

God spoke German; English was a language of the "world"—best to be avoided whenever possible. It was a way to "wall" God in and to "wall" the devil out.

So we lived in the wall-to-wall West Reserve (tract of land west of the Red River acquired by the first Mennonite immigrants from Russia). The Bible (a huge well-bound volume) and the hymnbook (*Gesangbuch ohne Noten*—also well bound and with gold-stamped letters) sat on a little mantelpiece in the living room. Till I was eleven, I can recall seeing the Bible removed from that shelf only to insert precious photos; I'd never heard it read from, nor had I read in it.

Being number ten of twelve siblings (six of both varieties) meant having to fend for myself. I never was a good athlete or a devoted farmer; it wasn't easy. There on our half-section of land was little room for a dreamer who preferred the world of books and learning over the tilling of the soil.

There was religion at home, but it was mainly expressed in table grace, bedtime prayers, and the occasional turn to accompany our parents to church. With eleven sisters and brothers, I can recall being in church about a half-dozen times in my first eleven years. Church seemed "out there"; we had no church building in our district.

Education was compulsory to age fourteen. Many kids attended in the morning when they turned fourteen; they were graduates in the afternoon. Some of my older siblings might have gone on, but the Great Depression ("Dirty Thirties") and the stigma (Why would you want to go to school? Are you too lazy to work? Besides, if you learn too much English, those English people will make soldiers of you!) kept them out of school. Of the twelve I was the only one to complete a high school education. Several of the younger and older siblings did go beyond age fourteen and later also did special studies for their vocations. One sister studied a year at Bible school and then studied through to become a Licensed Practical Nurse.

A spiritual implosion. In the mid-1940s a series of "revival" meetings generated considerable attention in southern Manitoba. Some Rudnerweider evangelists were conducting a three-week campaign (*Erweckung*) in the district (Eigenhof) south of ours. It caught the interest also of my parents.

In addition, a new schoolteacher—Peter B. Krahn, a recent, more educated immigrant from Russia—had started a choir, Sunday school, and Bible study (Bibelstunde) in our district. And my oldest brother, who had by now been living in the "world" for some years, came home carrying an English Bible in his hand. The 1929 Model A Ford was loaded each evening to go and hear the two "Friesen" preachers. My turn came the second night, March 11, 1946. I was eleven years of age.

When the evangelistic altar call was made, I felt something moving inside of me. There was a force that wanted to push the church from outside to inside. My emotions and my thinking felt totally disrupted; my spirit was troubled. An older man, the Eigenhof schoolteacher (Mr. Enns), nudged me to stand up and go to the altar. When I went, I met there my parents and three of my sisters!

That night's public commitment imploded upon our home and family. Next morning father brought the Bible from the mantelpiece to the kitchen table. As best I recall, it stayed on or near the table from that day until both my father (1963) and my mother (1968) died.

For me it was an awakening to "being." I cannot recall ever having even the slightest temptation to go back on that commitment. That does not mean I found it easy to become a faithful disciple. But, life became to me so much more than eating, working, sleeping, and playing. I became convinced that within each of us exists a vast spiritual dimension waiting to be explored. The adventure of discovery beckons "whosoever will."

We were now people who had been "converted" *(bekehrt)* and became subject to all kinds of ridicule. My first return to school after that night was greeted by my classmates throwing me off my bicycle and taunting me to fight them or cuss at them.

The new religion promoted by those evangelists was narrowly defined. No smoking, no dancing, no drinking, no swearing, no fighting, or other "loose" living. I inhaled heartily at that fountain and traded my former retreats into the world of novels (I'd read every book in our little school library by the time I was ten) for retreats into an imaginary, angelic world. The latter could only be maintained by a set of strict rules. It was not truly freeing, but it was an island of security.

Mennonite by chance. In 1951, after completing two years of high school by correspondence and showing little natural inclination for farming, my father gave permission for me to attend the Mennonite Collegiate Institute. The Gretna (Man.) MCI is the oldest Mennonite Institution of higher education in Manitoba. Here I got my first significant impressions about Mennonites. P. J. Schaefer, principal, had written several study volumes about the origins and future of Mennonites *(Woher? Wohin? Mennoniten)* and used them as texts for compulsory classes.

I discovered that my history was included in these stories. We talked about "ethnic" Mennonites and "spiritual" Mennonites. It seemed I had little choice. Being born "Wiebe" in a wall-to-wall Mennonite community made me a Mennonite too. Besides, I had never been to any other churches, nor had I heard good things about them.

I took my turn at catechism, offered to us in grade 12. That was already revolutionary, since no pre-marriage plans were in sight. Oh yes, "But where will you be baptized?" My first choice would have been the security of that Rudnerweider group next to our home district. But my parents had started to attend the Bergthaler church in Altona, because my father was hard of hearing and they had a loud-speaker system. So the choice was again simple—go with the family! Now I became a Bergthaler Mennonite. This process was mostly evolutionary and my Mennonite consciousness was in its infancy. It felt like I was a Mennonite by chance—strictly destiny.

Some of the realities I discovered upon being at a Christian "Mennonite" high school were most disconcerting to my inner spiritual idealism. There came times when I felt that if this is the essence of being Mennonite, then if I'd never see one again it would probably be too soon.

A taste of new wine. Upon MCI graduation in 1953, I had accepted Mr. Schaefer's counsel and my dream—since seeing the impact of Mr. P. B. Krahn—to be a teacher. My father approved because teachers obviously are necessary; he had served his turn on the local school board.

My teacher studies in Winnipeg opened a new world to me. I participated in youth groups that summer session at Grant Memorial Baptist, Central Alliance, and Calvary Temple. Their magnetic brand of effervescent spirituality increased my inner restlessness. It was like a taste of new wine (Mark 2:22) that had to collide with the old wine. My teaching two years back in the wall-to-wall Mennonite reserve confirmed my interest to work with people. It was deeply rewarding. And my Mennonite world had now grown to include Mennonite Brethren. While my relatives warned me about the "over-zealousness" of MBs, I married one. It exploded some more myths.

Marge (nee Letkeman) was also a teacher and she had been raised in town (Winkler, Man.). We were both ready to try some more new wine and went to teach in northwestern Ontario. Our community there had never had Sunday school or Bible study at school. Both were initiated and accepted. We worshiped with Baptists at Kenora, Ontario. Soon we were youth sponsors and, partly through our request for Bibles from the local Gideons Camp, I began to "supply" pulpits for the Gideons. It was their policy to offer pulpit speakers for pastors on vacation or away for other reasons. Soon I was preaching almost weekly in a variety of churches.

It became clear to me that I needed more formal biblical studies to continue this direction. The Baptists offered a scholarship to their Bethel College (Minnesota). Upon reflection, I realized I had never gone beyond the surface of studying the Mennonite heritage. There were roots I needed to deal with. We made an agreement. I'd go to Canadian Mennonite Bible College (Winnipeg) for one year. We'd keep in touch with the Baptists all year. If, by the end of a year of studies, I did not find myself a "Mennonite," I'd transfer to the Baptist college.

At CMBC I got my first voluntary look at the Anabaptist story. Within about a month, my choice was made. What had felt like *chance* until 1958, now became *choice*. My heart, soul, and mind resonated with Blaurock, Grebel, Manz, Marpeck, Sattler, Menno Simons, et al.

In retrospect, I recall the following conscious affirmations and "aha" experiences: 1. *The concept of confrontation.* My past experiences on the West Reserve and with the Baptists suggested that Christians too readily accommodated to environments we find ourselves in. To live peacefully and well, much of contemporary Christianity has become radically accommodational. Christian beliefs become tied even to an almost extreme nationalism ("civil religion").

The Anabaptist beginnings reflect a radical confrontation style. Their commitment to biblical living led to radical qualities of covenant and community. It startled the other Reformers, the dominant Catholic Church, and the world of their day.

Our having become the Quiet in the Land (Stillen im Lande) was a détente response to the ensuing persecution and other pressures. The isolated and insulated conclaves we had developed on the Manitoba reserves had not necessarily been consciously deliberate responses to our beginnings and beliefs. That our radical confrontation in Manitoba was now being used against fellow Mennonites and, ironically, generated 23 flavors of Mennonite groups, we probably did not understand. It was part of a radical accommodation style that had come among us over a period of several centuries.

2. *The concept of tabernacle.* The "stories" told about Mennonites were of a people en route. I read E. K. Francis' *In Search of Utopia.* Cornelius Krahn spoke of a people with a "built-in motor."

The early Anabaptists were like the people of God in the Old Testament—a people of promise (Hebrews 11) who followed God to the unrealized ("not having seen what was promised"—v. 13). But the glory of God—the Shekinah—"tabernacled" with them as they followed in faith.

Amazing responses were generated by the biblical faith followers and by the early Anabaptist faith followers. Just as God permitted Israel to build a temple and choose a king to become more stable, so he allowed Mennonites to choose abiding places and governments.

In the beginning we were a people of "tabernacle"—God with us as we moved—and without fancy temples. Anabaptists were "becomers." Salvation was a certain and sure experience and discipleship was its natural consequence. The latter was never an option; there was no "discount" on salvation.

3. *Shepherds, servants, and lambs.* The first Anabaptists *reluctantly* used any leadership titles referring to hierarchical positions, e.g., priest, bishop. They felt more comfortable with "Servants of the Word" *(Diener am Wort)* and other more egalitarian terms. The biblical images of the lamb having "power" to open the Book of Life (Revelation 5) and shepherds caring deeply for sheep (Luke 15:3-7) were to them in keeping with our calling ("But you are . . . a royal priesthood . . . that you may declare the wonderful deeds of him who called you out of darkness into his marvelous light"—1 Peter 2:9).

Temple people love priestly leaders who speak with judgment on their behalf. Tabernacle people need shepherd/servant leaders who identify as one of us and lead out in self-giving ways. Like Jesus did. It calls for the courage to be weak so that Jesus by the Holy Spirit can be strong in us (2 Corinthians 12:7-10).

Such salt and light and leaven captured me totally. From CMBC on to Goshen College to Mennonite Biblical Seminary. I came back to the Manitoba West Reserve to join the staff at my first Mennonite alma mater—the MCI. Then to serve the Bergthaler churches and the Conference of Mennonites in Manitoba (in family counseling and in radio and gradually television broadcasting). Along the way I had been ordained in 1960 and have preached twice weekly, on the average, ever since.

My father was at first disillusioned that I would leave the necessary vocation of teacher for preparation to ministry. ("How will you as a minister ever be able to support a family?") He forgave me along the way and, by train, together with my mother, came to my college graduation (1961). We became fast friends for his remaining few years.

I went back to graduate school for an M.A. and a Ph.D. Now a chance came to translate my Mennonite zeal into the president's office at Freeman (South Dakota) Junior College and Freeman Academy. I had never been happier as a Mennonite. This was never seen by me as meaning that other Christians and other denominations were invalid. They too have their places and their "people." For me it simply meant that Mennonites are "my people."

Then came the fire. From the mountaintop, my life was suddenly rudely tested by outrageous tragedy. As is so often the case, immediate overwhelming closeness to God is followed by life-shattering frustration (even as Jesus' disciples went from the Mount of Transfiguration to have to face Jesus' prophecy of suffering and death—Mark 9).

Our firstborn son, Glen, a specially gifted person (interviewed by the press for his creative ingenuity before he started school), in his adolescent years began to struggle deeply with life and death. From age fifteen he expressed his struggles openly to my wife and to myself. Frustrated at his physical condition (insomniac, back trouble), relating to change (we moved to South Dakota when he was fifteen), coping with spiritual inconsistencies and contradictions (within self, with us, and with other believers), and somehow coming to terms with a world of injustice and waste, he despaired of living.

Glen was no quitter. He fought valiantly for eight years. Changed schools, took time out to work, lived independently, and then returned home and enrolled in engineering at the University of Manitoba.

As part of our family anxiety, we had moved back to Manitoba for him to be close to former friends and the extended family. I had now become editor of *The Mennonite* (General Conference Mennonite Church denominational magazine) and thoroughly enjoyed this continuing pilgrimage with my people.

Glen attempted suicide already in South Dakota. At first, back in Manitoba, he was extremely happy and grateful. But then the struggles came again. There were times we feared daily to lose him. He agreed to psychiatric care and even volunteered for institutional care. I suspect he was more intelligent than most of the health care professionals he went to see. To my best perception, they dealt with him poorly.

His fight and the support of family seemed to pay off. At age twenty-one he told Marge and myself we need not worry about suicide anymore. It was not the answer. At age twenty-three he had completed two years of engineering (with near perfect grades) and told us, "This is going to be my summer." He got the exact summer job he wanted. He rented a nice apartment within five minutes' walking to work. We were thrilled with him and deeply grateful to God.

A few weeks later, June 9, 1981, he was found dead in his car (carbon monoxide). He had given up his life. No clues could be verified to discover the crisis(es) that precipitated this sudden climactic tragedy. We buried Glen's ashes June 13 at Winkler.

It was "Apocalypse Now!" Matthew 24 suddenly leaped out at me: ". . . tribulation, such as has not been from the beginning . . . until now" (v. 21) came upon our family (we have a daughter and two other sons). Our sun seemed darkened, the moon gave no light, the stars looked pale, and our heavens were shaken (v. 29). Torrents of questions, remorseful tears, buckets of guilt feelings, and multiplied protestations went out to God. Some were also directed at Glen.

My personal grief was devastating. Feeling like the worst failure ever, my being was numb. I asked God: Why? Why did Glen have to feel so hopeless that he gave up?

The silence of God was almost more than I could take. I wrote, about it in *The Mennonite* (editorials, June 30 and August 25, 1981). The valley seemed too deep and too long. There was no exit.

Then the avalanche began. Over a thousand letters, over a thousand calls, and probably about a thousand visits. They came from all over—overseas letters, long-distance calls, visits from believers and unbelievers—and from many walks of life. Hundreds came to weep with us—many as part of their own cathartic needs from similar family tragedies.

Everything positive that I had ever heard and learned about the Mennonite sense of self-giving, sharing, servant and covenant community, became incarnate to me—and more. People who had severely criticized my editor's work joined the caring community. Some simply spoke or came to sit with us. Others wrote a few lines and sent letters unfinished. There was sharing of how others had found God's grace. We often read God's Word together and prayed in tears. Nobody came with easy answers.

Gradually I found strength to go on. It came largely through God's "Mennonite" people. This family called Mennonite is my family.

Finding God's grace. The wounds are more profound than most people can ever imagine. Doubt, fear, irrational behavior, depression, stress, guilt, anger, resistance—are still part of my life, now well over six years later. The "stages" of grief so neatly fixed by Kuebler-Ross and others, simply are inadequate. Time flows differently than the clock or the calendar. Scars become most vivid in situations where other people—unintentionally, to be sure—are not sensitive to such experience.

I connect with Jeremiah. He cursed the day he was born (20:14, 18). I feel with Jesus. He cried about being forsaken by God (Mark 15). I believe with Paul, "... we were so utterly, unbearably crushed that we despaired of life itself. Why, we felt that we had received the sentence of death; but ... he will deliver us; on him we have set our hope ..." (2 Corinthians 1:8b-10). And I agree with David J. Bosch that "a god who provides all the answers becomes an explicable and comprehensible god, but also ceases to be God" (*A Spirituality of the Road*, p. 33).

Hope is to be found in God's grace. Upon seeking release—in triplicate—from his "thorn in the flesh" (2 Corinthians 12:8), Paul receives the answer, "My grace is sufficient for you, for my power is made perfect in weakness" (v. 9a). The supreme sign of power Jesus gives to our world is to lay down his life to save us from our sins. Human temptation is to reject weakness. In God's eternity vision, our weakness becomes a channel for his amazing grace.

Jacques Ellul in *The Politics of God and the Politics of Man* writes a "Meditation on Inutility" as an appendix to his book. Ellul points out how easily even Christians become preoccupied with all that we must "do" to bring in the kingdom. But, says Ellul, we begin to discover God's grace only when we come to understand that all our doing does not bring the kingdom. The kingdom is God's all the time. Our calling is to be faith-full (Matthew 25:21). God is the one who is entitled to pronounce things "good." When we begin to accept that, we begin to respond more freely and openly to what we don't understand. That is God's grace. It helps us feel his presence. It corresponds with the basic Anabaptist understanding of true power—in the cross instead of in nuclear bombs.

Being a Mennonite is helping me, as a wounded person, to discover God's amazing and-sufficient grace. I am eager to see it shared as widely as possible. That is one reason I made another career shift in the summer of 1986. Through my work with the Mennonite Studies Centre at the University of Winnipeg, I join others in the pursuit of some fresh visions in Mennonite education.

As Paul did, so do we "have this treasure in earthen vessels (literally 'clay pots'), to show that the transcendent power belongs to God and not to us. We are afflicted in every way, but not crushed; perplexed, but not driven to despair; persecuted, but not forsaken; struck down, but not destroyed; always carrying in the body the death of Jesus, so that the life of Jesus may also be manifested in our bodies" (2 Corinthians 4:7-10).

The journey is not over; God is not finished with me yet. To be pilgrims, strangers, refugees in this world of fixed and insured assets, is to be an anomaly. It means to live the adventure of dangerous living—dying to self and being born again and again to new dimensions of life in God's Spirit. We are "becomers" as long as we live. There is a certain legitimacy to being a people with a "built-in motor."

My hope is in finding God's grace by his Spirit as I journey on. To date I am finding truth in his assurance of "sufficient" grace.

29

A Tale of Seduction

Katie Funk Wiebe

Katie Funk Wiebe is a frequent and popular speaker at conventions, symposia, and workshops throughout the Mennonite communities in the United States and Canada. She has written numerous articles, curriculum materials, and other writings, primarily for the Mennonite press. She teaches English at Tabor College in Hillsboro, Kansas. She seeks to foster a greater awareness of and appreciation for the role of women in the Mennonite churches.

I blame it all on my father. And on my mother, who usually set him up to tell stories about life in the shadow of the windmill on whose powerful blades they depended for their livelihood. It sat high on the hill at the edge of the village, as windmills always did in Mennonite villages in South Russia. I am not a Mennonite primarily because I discovered the refinements of theology I had been searching for among Mennonite doctrines. I wish I could say that was the case. Then this telling would be simple.

I am a Mennonite because I was irrevocably drawn by the Mennonite mystique, that peculiar mixture of stubborn believing, patient suffering, and glad sharing as Christ-followers inherent in my ancestors, which drove them from one country to another in search of a true home.

My becoming a Mennonite happened slowly, subconsciously, over a long period of time, like water seeping from a barely-turned-on hose, not quite wetting the soil yet slowly and surely nurturing the deep roots. With me there was no memorizing of a catechism. No formal application for membership. Yet one day I could gratefully say, "I am a Mennonite" and knew I was welcome.

The happenings of that life in Russia were still very recent in my parents' memory when our family established a home in a small Russian community in northern Saskatchewan after their migration in 1923 with about twenty thousand other Mennonites in that period until 1929 when Russia closed its doors to outward-bound citizens. The painful wounds of war, revolution, and of being lost and found, geographically and spiritually, were still not fully healed when they told us children their stories, again and again, often with humor, other times with poignant longing or even with an aching bitterness.

The healing was in the telling, as I see it now; but the telling gave me a usable past that I had to learn to deal with and that eventually established my identity.

As I grew up I had always known that my family was Mennonite, but I never felt like a true Mennonite until years later. But the conception took place there, around the red-and-white oilcloth-covered dining-room table, as my father joked about dodging cannon balls while crossing no-man's land to visit Mother before they were married and of working in a mental hospital as a volunteer, but reminisced more seriously about serving in the Red army as a stretcher-bearer, of nearly dying of typhus, of becoming a Christ-believer while in the army (and he already a conscientious objector), of burying money, boots, and cabbage in the back yard as protection against anarchist plundering. The ethnic and spiritual aspects of the mystique were interwoven in this verbal portrait of Mennonite faith and life experienced in that distant country where neighbors greeted one another in Low German and walked the streets in *Schlorren* and sometimes found the idea of a religious conversion a strange concept.

In my essay, "You Never Gave Me a Name" (*Good Times with Old Times*, Herald Press), I write that one day when I was about nine or ten, "some snot-nosed English child informed me I was a Mennonite. To us children, anyone who was not born of immigrant parents was English, even if the person was anything else, like Irish or French. It had to have been an English kid, for they thought of themselves as being on top of the heap." I rushed home to ask Mother if this were true. I knew her answer. "But to be told this by an outsider seemed so final—almost as final as the eternal hellfire the preacher shouted about at the revival meetings in summer. Final and fatal. Now I was a Mennonite, whatever that meant."

But I wasn't one, really. I knew I had been born into a family that had a Mennonite name, a Mennonite past, and Mennonite customs like *Zwieback* and Low German. But a person is never a Mennonite until he or she chooses to identify with, not the culture accretions, as joy-bringing as they may be, but with that group's spiritual realities. This true identification happens only when one walks the paths of history together with leaders and adherents and sees and hears and feels what they experienced. And for me this process took a long time.

At important junctures in Israelite history, the leaders reviewed their history with their people, a history which began with Abraham, Isaac, Jacob, and Moses, to give them an identity. Likewise, the New Testament apostles, when preaching to the crowds, frequently showed their listeners how they, too, were part of history. They were assured they belonged to the story of Abraham, Isaac and Jacob, and of David, and finally to that of Christ, the fulfillment of prophecy. The Jews had a strong sense of history; they knew they were part of a tradition—of being the people of God. They were part of the flow—if they chose to become part of the movement. Black poet Langston Hughes writes, "I've known rivers ancient as the world, and older than the flow of human blood in human veins. My soul has grown deep like rivers." The Israelite soul grew deep in their rivers of being God's people. Without knowing it, my parents, in reviewing their history and with it the history of the Mennonites again and again, let me feel the tug of current moving swiftly forward.

For me, choosing to be a Mennonite was choosing to be part of the stream of one branch of human history, which included Conrad Grebel, Menno Simons, and other Anabaptists; my ancestors Franz and Maria Funck, who with four children, forty head of livestock, five pieces of farm equipment, and two spinning wheels, traveled from Prussia to the Ukraine in 1798; Lutheran minister Eduard Wuest, Mennonite Brethren trailblazers Johann and Katharine Klaassen, who made spiritual beginnings for a segment of the Mennonites in Russia; and statesmen B. B. Janz and David Toews, leaders who helped my grandmothers, my parents, and hundreds more to become part of an America-headed procession of pilgrims in search of a new life.

On my way to becoming Mennonite, I personally did not make a long land pilgrimage, but I found the spiritual and psychological journey culminating in my choosing to stay with the Mennonite church arduous for other reasons. My barriers were not rivers, oceans, plains and mountains, or even political bodies, but spiritual barriers apparently erected on all sides of me by some august body to prevent my crossing over to whatever could nurture my faith in the wide-open spaces beyond them. And their essence seemed to be Mennonite. And therefore these barriers had to be eradicated like an obnoxious thistle in a lawn or I couldn't find a home among this body. At the time being a Mennonite seemed to make growth into a whole person impossible.

Admittedly, like many other young people of the late forties who were fascinated by the newly discovered vigor and glamor of the mainstream evangelical movement, I thought for a time I had outgrown the Mennonite church like one does an overwashed sweater. As young Bible college students, we argued the case repeatedly: Mennonitism approached the gospel narrowly and rigidly. To identify with Mennonites hindered the spread of the gospel, and therefore the name and the peculiar ethnic customs should be discarded for a more viable approach to evangelism and missions. Joining the Alliance Tabernacle or other progressive modern denominations seemed an attractive prospect.

I was ready to shed all aspects of Mennonitism, for I didn't like the new backward label I received at college—*Russlaender*. I felt ashamed to be a member of an immigrant minority at a time when immigrants were being encouraged to forget their ignominious past and join the glorious present in becoming New Canadians. The spirit of the times told us to disregard our parents' past with their memories, pleasant and terrifying, along with the *Evangeliums-Lieder* and head-coverings for women. The future would look brighter without such shackles. I, who knew only my parents' history, a history which had come to me in disconnected sections, accepted the invitation to become historyless.

History looks like a tiresome burden rather than a plenteous resource to some people. Like other church groups which have sprung from an immigrant background, and who necessarily bring along much ethnic baggage with their memories and religious beliefs, but few artifacts other than stories to share with their children, Mennonite Brethren, which group my parents adhered to (formerly having been Allianz), came to America without a blueprint for society, without many social concerns. They wanted the privilege to earn their living honestly, to worship peacefully, and to continue to pursue denominational objectives begun in Russia to evangelize and spread the gospel in overseas countries. They had not come to Canada to lead either the general religious, political, or social community.

Having originated in 1860 out of the compulsion to know purity of doctrine and moral living—admirable traits—Mennonite Brethren loyalists thought of the past as an account of a fiercely won battle for those goals, making it difficult for them to shift to other fronts. The refusal of the church in later decades to raise questions for which its history and early theological positioning offered no solutions or precedents, such as the role of women in the church and social justice, was part of that barrier over which I could find no way and which tempted me to look elsewhere for spiritual nurture. What I didn't know at the time was that I was sorting through not only whether I wanted to be a Mennonite Brethren, but more basically a Mennonite, that larger family group spread across the continents of the earth. The two were connected, yet different. Becoming Mennonite Brethren did not necessarily mean being Mennonite, for MBs had a double-shafted theology, being at one time both Anabaptist and Baptist. Eventually I found that I could decide both issues with one ballot. But first there were other issues to deal with.

As a young girl I secretly wanted to write. Write? The word was foreign to my parents. Young girls married, or typed, taught or nursed until they died. Mennonites were agrarian, poking the ground, making green things grow, not producing words on paper. I could not envision writing as a possibility for me, for I was conditioned to accept the image of the ideal Mennonite woman in Russia and the early years in Canada: silent, modest, and obedient. As I wrote in "The Barriers Are Not Real" (*The Ethnic American Woman: Problems, Protest, Lifestyle,* ed. by Edith Blicksilver), women's place

> was not with men. Not with thinking. Not with dreaming, declaring, determining sin, disciplining, deciding to stay or leave Russia. Her place was at home kneading the soft dough with strong hands, stripping milk from soft warm udders, serving *Prips* and *Schinkefleisch* to tired men when they came home from the fields, cradling children into quietness, loving deeply without open words, praying silently with head covered. The poetry of living had no real attachment to the poetry of words, as Mennonites in their search for a pure God-life isolated themselves from society through language, customs and geography.

As a young married woman I indulged in what fiction writer Tillie Olsen refers to as "trespass vision," the daring to hope for the kind of comprehension, in my case of spiritual realities, which come only from situations beyond the private, most often reserved for men. On a few occasions I ventured cautiously into the "men's sphere," only to find myself turned back by Mennonite Brethren male leaders—but also by myself.

I felt guilty questioning the Scriptures about what seemed right and pure: that a woman's fulfillment lay in her God-ordained role as a wife and mother. I longed for, yet resisted, the craving inside me to write for God, for the Mennonite church, for the secular press, for anyone. However, men in black suits with large thumb-indexed open Bibles said these longings shouldn't be in me, and I did want to please them.

> I was looking for an identity that satisfied God's Word and fit the times in which we lived. Magazines were full of articles about the growing pains of women my age, but the church was silent. When I talked to men about the matter, some were immediately threatened and defensive, unready to yield position and make room for women in the church other than in traditional roles. If they did budge, it was frequently with an attitude of dispensing favors to the peons. Few women I spoke to at that time had the liberty to consider what seemed heresy. The Bible had sufficient texts that I should know my role, they said. ("The Barriers Are Not Real")

Could I find such an identity within the Mennonite Brethren Church? Within the Mennonite community? I stayed with a denomination that examined the present only through its own past and relegated women to lesser citizenship because to leave would have been a greater personal loss than to stay. It took me a while to realize I would only be free of the past, including its determination of present women's roles, if I returned to it and embraced it as my own. Until I did that I was not actually leaving anything. I turned the corner toward the Mennonite Brethren very slowly, not making any big attempts to signal to others changes in my thinking.

In the early sixties in an effort to improve my facility with the German language, I began reading German books. I came upon *Tiefenwege: Erfahrungen und Erlebnisse von Russland-Mennoniten in zwei Jahrzehnten bis 1949* by Jacob A. Neufeld. Neufeld kept a journal on the trek of the German-speaking citizens of Russia who returned to Poland and Germany with Hitler's army. The book moved me greatly. As I plowed through that book I became aware that some of my own relatives might have been part of this dreadful suffering.

I read more Mennonite history and biography, sorting events and fitting what I had heard as a child into its proper sequence. The stories my parents had told us as children now had a real connection with my reading. Suddenly a pattern took shape. The essence of the Mennonite mystique was showing through and providing me with a usable past. I felt myself being drawn into the Mennonite fold and being willing to identify myself as one openly. I recognized that I could find many aspects of Mennonite Brethren doctrine in other denominations, but the Mennonites had something additional I would never find there.

I found in these stories a legacy of suffering for faith which had begun with believers mentioned in the New Testament. It was replicated in the stories of believers in the early church, in Anabaptists, and then in stories of other Mennonite martyrs, from 1525 through many migrations, fleeings, schisms, wars, revolutions, and famine to the present. Sometimes my forebears suffered openly and readily. Other times it occurred because they were hooked into violent political forces outside their control. But their response was that of biblical believers. Trust in God was the first priority.

Abraham went forth not knowing where he was going—but he knew God was with him. Joseph lay in prison, separated from his family for many years, but he could acknowledge God's leading to his brothers later on when they were reconciled. The apostle Paul was persecuted for his faith. Hebrews 11 is replete with many stories of heroes of the faith. Though my reading of the Great Trek included stories about close and distant relatives and their journeyings, their stories and others, whether from New Testament times to the present, were additional spans of a bridge to a land of faith, freedom, courage, and joy. The Christian faith helped people to endure.

My forebears had suffered that I might enjoy freedom and truth. Their stories showed me that the conflict and tensions of the biblical writers were often the same as those of my parents and of my own—conflict between knowing God's promise to his people to never leave or forsake them and the reality of the moment: "Lord, why have you forsaken me? Why must I endure this?" I learned that in spite of the dark horror of the moment large numbers of Mennonites chose not to forsake Christ and his Word but be true to him. And their faithfulness paid off in spiritual rewards. Other denominations also had their accounts of suffering and faith, but why go elsewhere for them, when my own denomination had a large legacy readily available. I sensed my personal identity was traveling a new direction as I acknowledged this God-trust apparent in my past.

I also remained a Mennonite because I saw the Mennonites willing to hear the hard sayings of Christ and then to move with Christ into the answers. They took these tough statements at face value. For example, my parents' stories told me that being a Mennonite meant making sure the whole human family had enough to eat, particularly members of one's own faith-family.

The famine of 1920-21 in Russia drove some families to eat mice, dogs, dead livestock, crows, or even to boil leather. Bread was baked with anything that might yield some nourishment, such as roots, leaves, hay, corncobs, bones, weeds, bark, and sawdust. If help had not arrived by the spring of 1922 from the American Mennonites, hundreds might have died. Often we children heard how mother, who had spent many years cooking in large institutions prior to her marriage to my father, was hired as a cook, with dad as her assistant at one of the first relief kitchens set up by the forerunner of Mennonite Central Committee, the *American-Mennonite Relief Administration* during the famine years in the Ukraine. This long title was a familiar word in our home when I was a youngster. At the age of 90 mother wrote, "Now when I read how the MCC is working worldwide, I thank God that we were able to be part of that vision." Could I turn my back on that vision, a vision that shared in keeping my parents and their neighbors alive? Hardly.

That vision also expressed itself in other ways, also part of my early life, but which I had never connected with Mennonites. I assumed all people behaved similarly. For years my parents, as the only Mennonites in our community, had often provided overnight lodging to Mennonites who were complete strangers on their way from the northern Mennonite settlements in Saskatchewan to those across the river where relatives lived. In winter, when farm work slackened, they traveled by horse and cutter the two-day journey, stopping overnight in Blaine Lake, where we lived. Without money for hotel accommodations, some spent the night in the livery barn with the horses. But if my father saw a mother with children preparing to bed down with the animals, he brought them home to our small house. Why?

Though strangers to one another, my parents and their guests shared a common past of suffering neither had to explain. They both knew intimately the nature of humanity—the depth of human degradation when evil takes over but also the height of love possible in the Spirit of Christ. It wasn't always convenient to have overnight guests, but hospitality to strangers came with the Mennonite territory.

I grew to understand that Mennonite meant sharing even if the house was already full, because "family" members, even if total strangers, are never expected to sleep in the cold. The Russia experiences had done something to the Mennonites' sense of community. When I shake a jar of loosely packed raisins vigorously, each raisin moves closer to the next one because of the tremors I have caused. War, revolution, and famine had done the same for these people. Community, drawing together, seemed to me a strong Mennonite trait, one I wanted. It was followed by others: the recognition that a Mennonite's word could always be trusted, and the individual relied upon to give an honest day's work for whatever he or she received. I watched them reaching for excellence in all aspects of life, of having a concern for their own children's education, of the need for Bible training.

My acceptance that nonviolence could be a powerful witness to Christ's love came fairly late in life, possibly because I, a woman, never had to decide its relevance to me. For many years it seemed to me that nonresistant love, never a strong Mennonite Brethren doctrine, was a folk teaching, like milking a cow from the left side, only intended for one segment of the population—men. My father had been a nonresistant medic in the army for nearly four years before he became a believer because that was the way Mennonites in Russia did it at the time. Young men automatically accepted the nonresistant position when they became of military age. Fathers with many sons growing up into military age, and sensing the threat of war in the near future, sometimes packed up their belongings for another country. A father with a family of girls wasn't as bothered by threats of military conflict.

We are always heirs to the climate of opinion in which we grow up, and unless we spot weaknesses in it and face them head on, these weaknesses become a part of us. I had accepted that nonresistance was only for men. My church had excused me from rigorous thinking about nonresistant love during wartime—but also during peace. I had not had the models of Abigail, wife of Nathan, who made peace with David's soldiers, or models of more contemporary peacemakers before me, because the whole matter was not considered pertinent to young women. Only as I accepted myself as a person responsible to Christ in this area, did I study the matter and slowly edge into its issues.

But somewhere during that time I became a Mennonite Brethren, although I was already a church member. Openly. Surely. I was willing to stake my future with them—at least for the time, despite my love-hate affair with them. I couldn't see many visible strong connections between them and the Mennonite world to which I was leaning, but I saw in the Mennonite Brethren a spunky and cohesive church conference, not easily daunted by scriptural mandates to teach, preach, and witness—mandates that had scared off much larger denominations. Some call this faith, others audacity, but it seemed to be working for the Mennonite Brethren. I also recognized strong emphases on biblicalism, evangelism and missions, conversion, and so forth that gave them vitality.

At the turn of this century Mennonite Brethren historian P. M. Friesen wrote, "What does God expect of us as a group? Should we who call ourselves Mennonites become a conglomerate of Lutheran, Baptist, Plymouth Brethren . . . traits? What is the particular heritage of faith, our history, and our present situation?" Mennonite Brethren still have not satisfactorily answered this question for themselves as they sidle toward both mainstream evangelicalism and historic Anabaptism. Some Mennonite Brethren feel too strong an identification with historical roots will cut them off from fellowship with evangelicals and the power to do their task of evangelizing; others think that to bed down with fundamentalists will lose them the rich benefits of their distinctive heritage. Yet as I learned more about Anabaptist-Mennonites, I found myself crawling into bed with them without guilt. I was identifying with the stream in my past that had first attracted me to fuller identification with the Mennonite Brethren.

Clearly, unless I openly identified with both the Mennonite Brethren and the Mennonites, I had no right to test their "doctrine and teachings against the Scriptures in the interests of personal growth and of the whole body" (*Who Are the Mennonite Brethren?*). I needed an arena in which to write. And I had to love those for whom I wrote.

I see my identity as a Mennonite coming from my spiritual heritage, and particularly those aspects of it where positive change has taken place within the church. It has not derived from the ethnic practices such as food, clothing, social customs, though always part of any culture. I achieved a major victory when I understood that the barriers which I saw as preventing me from crossing over to clearer air were not divine interdicts. Those barriers were man-made, erected over the years by leaders desirous of being Christ's servants and interpreting the teachings of the New Testament as best they could. But because these barriers were also in me, I had to move them first. "Bumping, blundering, blustering, battering, bluffing, and blessing, I crossed over" ("The Barriers Are Not Real") to my Mennonite Brethren home, where I could praise, criticize, and comment upon its life and work because it was mine.

To have a history means change has taken place. A stone has no history unless someone has pried it from the ground, ground it, shaped it, and used it to build a foundation, or to make it into a piece of jewelry. A church that doesn't change is like a stone left in the ground. Any change that takes place in a congregation or denomination contributes to that group's spiritual identity—or lack of it. Likewise, individuals either grow or stagnate as they discard their spiritual legacy or allow it to change their lives.

So, as a more mature woman, I went back to my father's stories and listened to them again, but this time I acknowledged, not the shame but the glory. I could hear my father saying in his own mixture of English and Mennonite German, "When we were young, we had dreams and visions, and sometimes we failed; sometimes we moved ahead. You younger ones must also dream and hope, risk and trust— not be satisfied with the status quo." He offered me the stories and said, "Katie, now it's your turn. Find meaning in life and pass it on."

Father was telling stories to make sense of the atrocities and absurdities he had experienced in Russia. Most of us aren't immigrants or refugees, yet in an era of fast change we are all immigrants—political, technological, social, economic, and even religious. We move about, change professions, change spouses, change allegiances to value systems. To survive as immigrants in this brave new world, we have to find the patterns of living that work. I found these patterns for myself in his stories, in the stories of the Mennonite Brethren, of the Mennonites, of the Anabaptists, and of God's people in Scripture.

> I embraced my roots—the Mennonite ones and those grafted in by this variegated community in which I had lived almost eighteen years. My chains fell loose at my feet. My ancestors had not been complacent, accepting blindly what others told them to believe about God, life and themselves. They had chosen. Mother and Dad had chosen a new way of living in a new country. That was their gift to me. I too could choose. (*Good Times with Old Times*)

I am a Mennonite because someone told me a story and told me that it was also my story. And if I tell this story often enough to others, they can also accept it as theirs whether or not they are biologically part of it, for it is part of a much larger, grander pattern of those who are "looking unto Jesus, the author and finisher of us all."

30

The Anabaptist Shape of Liberation

John H. Yoder

John Howard Yoder is one of the very few Mennonite creative thinkers whose influence extends to the wider Christian communities. In his numerous articles and books he seeks to dialogue concerning important theological and ethical issues with Catholics, Protestants, and other faiths. He teaches theology at the University of Notre Dame in South Bend, Indiana. Previously he served the Mennonite Board of Missions and Goshen Biblical Seminary as professor and president. His book The Politics of Jesus *has become a classic in its field.*

To define the specificity of a community's identity many paths can be taken. One can lift commonalities and distinctives inductively from the historical record, once one has chosen which of one's ancestors to avow. One can be guided by some key theme, or by some key contrast separating a given movement from the contemporary real alternatives. Here the attempt shall be made to reach past the empirical analysis of history, to grasp the "salvation" vision intrinsic to the "Anabaptist" movement's sense of its mission.

1

We are called to proclaim *liberation from the dominion of Mars*. If you follow the risen Jesus, *you don't have to* hate or kill. *You don't have to* defend yourself.

What is usually called "peace witness" or "pacifism" or "nonresistance" is more than that. It is not simply a matter of doing or not doing certain deeds related to war-making. It will always involve that: any Mennonite community should and will question military service and the use of war for or against the authorities. Nonresistance is one of the most clearly attested and widely recognized elements of what Mennonites affirm they accept from their Anabaptist antecedents. Yet liberation from Mars means far more than this. It means recognizing that we live in a world under the domination of powers which dictate human relations, which distort truth and goodness, which leave us not really free to be ourselves or to love our neighbors. War is not simply one social institution among others, not simply one instrument of political activity besides others, or even just one more social evil besides others. War is a cult, a form of worship: Mars is a god, functionally defined as one by the fact that he demands human sacrifices. The early Christians and the Radical Reformers saw this. This proclamation should be heard as liberating good news, not solely as costly moral rigor.

The appropriateness of "idol" language to describe how the claims of Mars, or of his modern incarnation, militant nationalism, work, does not mean that nationalism can be mocked or underrated as irrational. Powerful and apparently reasonable claims are made regarding the "necessity" of war for the defense of evidently worthwhile values, the practicality of the means being used, and the careful calculation of the effects of one's weapons or the losses that threaten if they are not used. Thus the denunciation of the idol must not be an empty diatribe; it must imply and include a reasoned rejection of those rationality claims.

2

We are called to proclaim *liberation from the dominion of Mammon*. If you follow the risen Jesus, *you won't have to* have more.

Mammon is the only divinity identified in the Gospels by name as being a power which makes people its slaves. As with regard to war, we must set aside the idea that money is a "neutral" power equally available to be used for good or for bad purposes. That can become true, but only under special circumstances, whereby its usability for good is won by hard work or conflict.

In the normal state of fallen mankind, money is one of the powers which have risen above the neutrality or servanthood of simple instruments, and have become autonomous, i.e., a law unto themselves, giving their own orders. One example of this is the great place occupied in any modern economy by the nonproductive institutions of investment and banking. Another example is the way in which people who otherwise would not justify social and racial discrimination feel quite free to do it on the basis of the appeal to "property values," or to "security." People who would not otherwise be selfish still assume that it is proper that they should limit their responsibility for others by an obligation which they believe they are under to save or maintain their capital. These are but superficial specimens of the way in which mankind is in the services of money rather than the other way around.

The prophets, Jesus, the early Christians, and many Radical

Reformers have incarnated this challenge in various ways. Sometimes it has been done by prescribing a lifestyle of honesty, simplicity, and work, sometimes by creating alternative, sometimes communal, structures for production, property-holding, or consumption. Sometimes it has been done by defining the duties one has to give to others or to care for the poor, sometimes by affirming the gratuitous virtue of giving money away or not being careful with it.

This is one face of gospel liberty which is not easy to define in the culture of occidental ease. It is easier to describe the shape of liberation from Mammon in the first generation of the life of the church than the third, easier in a poor world than in a prosperous one, easier in a rural or primitive society than in a developed one. It is rendered yet more difficult by the fact that in recent generations the interpreters of "Anabaptism" or "discipleship" have attended more to eschewing Mars than to denouncing Mammon. Facing this call, the argument "of course you don't have to join a commune" has too often been thought to dispense us from the discipline of defining a real alternative. Yet "you don't have to" is as legalistic as whatever demand it sets aside.

3

We are called to proclaim *liberation from the dominion of myself.* If you follow the risen Jesus, *you don't have to* do your own thing.

This third idolatry of our time needs a harder look. It is not present, or at least not named with the same clarity, in the ancient world, where Mars and Mammon were known by name. There did exist the mythical image of Narcissus back in classic culture, but not in Christian usage. The modern usage of the concept of the "self" says (1) that the substance of my personal dignity is knowable, so that I can identify wherein my "self" consists; (2) that it is doable—i.e., that what it takes to live out my selfhood is not difficult, is within my own reach; and (3) that it is morally imperative: "to thine own self be true."

There is *some* truth behind the search for one's "real self." There can be difference between what I really am and the mask I wear. I can be unfair to others by "hypocrisy" (i.e., role-playing). Others can be unfair to me by seeing in me what I really am not. But to spin out from these legitimate concerns a whole new gospel of "authenticity" is false. There is no one univocal "real me" down in there which it is my right to demand recognition for, or which it is my duty to uncover and live out.

There has long been a tension in Christian thought about the sense in which the Christian should seek his or her own interests. Are there duties to the self intrinsically, or only the duty to maintain oneself so as to serve others? The conversation has been complicated by the development of arguments about the duty of self-affirmation or self-esteem which had been called forth as correctives over against unwholesome styles of self-abnegation or self-doubt. Wrong notions of parental or pedagogical moral guidance or of church discipline have provoked as backlash equally wrong insistence that each individual must "do his or her own thing," that the road to wholeness is self-expression, that one must first "find oneself" or "accept oneself" before loving others, so that the only ultimate sin is inauthenticity.

Some of the correctives were needed. Some of the kinds of self-denial, self-doubt, or self-hatred which they denounced as unhealthy were that. I am not advocating what they oppose. Yet the affirmation of the "self" as a cure is no cure. It is at best a restatement of the problem. What is that "self" which I should "find" or "realize"? How can I tell it apart from the self which I should deny? To this, Jesus' answer is that I am to seek first the rule of God and his righteousness and that in so doing I shall find "everything else," i.e., also my true selfhood. The way to make operational that commitment to God's rule and righteousness is the structure of the Christian community which Jesus called "binding and loosing," which Paul called "restoring one another in a spirit of meekness," what James called "bringing back a sinner," and what the Reformers (not only the Anabaptists, though they followed it through more thoroughly) called "the Rule of Christ." It moves forgiveness from the pulpit to the body of the church. It disciplines self-affirmation not by condemnation but by invitation to covenant.

Such communal pastoral concern for the freedom and welfare of each individual seeks wholeness in the unity of the body. It thereby frees the disciple of Jesus Christ from the temptation to make his or her own perspective, feelings, and impulses the criteria of God's purposes.

In other ages and cultures it was possible for an extended family or a rural neighborhood to exercise this kind of caring responsibility, for admonishing and forgiving the individual without being formal or self-conscious about it. In our world such "binding and loosing" will not happen unless we take time for it, discuss why it is imperative, and define the ways of doing it for one another.

It could be argued that by naming and denouncing the unholy trinity of "Mars, Mammon, me," we have said enough to describe why and how an "Anabaptist" commitment should be identifiable. No other major denominational heritage is marked by these three specifics. They are not representative of the Catholic, Lutheran, Anglican, or modern liberal visions of Christianity. They could suffice to identify the specificity of the "Radical Reformation" heritage. Nevertheless, it will be fruitful to add to these three a further set of perhaps less evident idols, a second circle of freedoms, to make yet more concrete our picture of what it means to be *redeemed*. These further dimensions of liberation will not necessarily correspond point by point with classical "distinctives" as comparative ecclesiology lists them; they do essay in a global way to sketch an alternative *Gestalt*.

4

We are called to proclaim *liberation from the dominion of the mass*. If you follow the risen Jesus, *you don't have to* follow the crowd.

We already observed that the thrust toward absolutizing individual self-fulfillment, although unhealthy in itself, is an understandable reaction to something else which is also unwholesome: namely to the person being subjected involuntarily to the totality of the society in which he or she is hidden or denied personhood. Ever since Marduk, most "religion" seeks to or tends to further such subjugation of the individual by glorifying the human mass as a whole, by assuring the society, especially its ruling elite, of God's blessing, celebrating the legitimacy of its borders and its rulers, by affirming it as the framework of all meaning. Hegel in one way and Marx in another deny meaning to the person or the small group by attributing it to the totality of the course of events as they finally add up in the end. I am only someone, we are only significant, they say, as we find our place in that mainstream.

The gospel frees us from the mass: not by making every individual an absolute unto himself or herself (which would be a contradiction in terms), but rather by identifying within the mass a particular people, by selecting or electing within history at large a particular strand, and by calling the individual to decision in favor of that alternative—by discerning within the wider profusion and confusion a specific pattern and call.

The Christian community is not Christendom. It is not the total course of world history, or even of the Western world. It is the visible congregation of those who knowingly gather around the name, the teachings, and the memories of Jesus. Yet that name and those teachings are so knowable, so meaningful that they provide the leverage, the identity, or the motive to stand out from the mass and move against the stream.

In our individualistic age, baptists have developed an individualistic understanding of the reason for not baptizing infants. Only an adult, the argument says, can be born again, can testify to a life-changing conversion experience. That is true as far as it goes; it is the baptist, pentecostal, and disciples' version of rejecting infant baptism. The critique of Anabaptists and Friends was just as clearly anti-pedobaptist, but not on individualistic grounds. Believer's baptism makes the baptized (in the Quaker version, without water) a part of a new people, incorporated into the body of Christ. The body is prior to each of its members. It is made up of its members, each of whom must freely adhere to it, thereby being liberated from the crowd, but it is not constituted only by their freely associating themselves.

The sociological name for this liberation is "nonconformity." The term has sometimes been given a bad taste by unworthy usage, but its proper meaning remains. There is no liberation from the empire of Mars, Mammon, or me, there is no liberation from this or that temptation or pressure, which does not at the same time both presuppose and enable liberation from conformity.

5

We are called to proclaim *liberation from the dominion of the milieu*. If you follow the risen Jesus, *you don't have to* be one of the gang.

Liberation from the mass can all too easily be deformed into conformity to the smaller mass, domination by the ghetto or the enclave.

In an earlier age, the clan or the village was automatically the small world in which one became a person. In our more pluralistic societies it is still quite possible to constitute small circles of acquaintances (the gang, the clique, the subculture), with like values who defend one another against the threat but also against the promise of encounter with more divergent positions and personalities. In fact the greater mobility of modern culture can enable more separate milieux to live tolerantly but ignorantly beside one another without either stifling or challenging one another's peculiarities. The sociologist will call this the dominion of the milieu. The psychologist might call it the control of mama.

From such insularity the gospel frees us. It brings into one new body, Jews and Gentiles, rich and poor, breaking across divisions within any one society. It enjoins and enables love for the enemy and service to the stranger, undercutting provincial loyalties and sending people away in mission. John Wesley said the world was his parish: the "Anabaptist" can say "the world church is my home church." What we call "peace witness" is not merely the rejection of the nation as an unworthy object of loyalty; it is also the affirmation of that wider belief world. It is for this reason that the redefinition of "Anabaptist" theological commitment in the context of self-conserving Mennonite ethnic identity is not merely a dilution but a betrayal. It denies the cross-ethnic and cross-provincial vision of the body of Christ in favor of the more securely defensible values—sometimes good ones—enshrined in the privileged experiences of Germanic migrants. (See my article "Mennonite Political Conservatism: Paradox or Contradiction," in Harry Loewen, ed., *Mennonite Images*, 1980.)

A subset of the "milieu" temptation is the fixation of one's values and obligations in the form of one particular "movement." "The movement" in the early 1960s meant the civil rights struggle of American blacks, seen as promising to lead the entire nation forward in line with God's purposes. Toward the end of the same decade "the movement" meant the same kind of saving meaning was being attached to criticism of the Vietnam War. This is the youthful form which much "movement" definition of "where it's at" can take. Older or more conservative observers can do the same thing with a longer stretch of time or a wider slice of society, but retain the same readiness to get their signals from "the way things are going," to state a truth claim in forms like "now it has become clear that . . ." or "historians a generation from now will see that. . . ."

Part of our liberation from the dominion of the movement comes from historical sobriety about whether we can be sure what is really happening that really matters, and where it is really leading. Some of it comes from trust that God knows better than we which of the things that are happening will last and which are good. We are made aware of other perspectives, other populations, other elites, other places. We do not replace "the movement" with no movement, or with nothing, but rather with a deeper perception of the real movement within history, which tradition calls "the church militant." This critical perspective on the movements of the moment is one of the ways Scriptures work. The salvation narrative provides a point of leverage enabling moral independence from the close-in pressures of the context.

6

We are called to proclaim the good news of *liberation from the mold*. If we follow the risen Jesus *we don't have to* stay the way we have been.

We are what we have been made by where we come from. The analysts of culture will call it "tradition" or "the past." The classicist will speak of the *matrix*, which may mean either the womb where the fetus grew to personhood or the form into which molten metal was cast. The matrix precedes one and makes one what one is.

From the perspective of what makes the individual what he or she is, a hot and ultimately insoluble philosophical debate has long been raging about the components of "nature" and "nurture" in making us what we are, but both factors are our past. The gospel frees us from the tyranny of the past by offering us space and power for change so fundamental that it can be spoken of as a new birth. That change is not merely a new vision of things: it is incarnated and offered to us by the alternative community into which we are invited, by the alternative history and the alternative hope the people of God celebrate. Whether the burden of my past be that of guilt, of ignorance, of oppressive cultural patterns, of racism or xenophobia, or of Christendom's unfaithfulness, the good news of liberation offers us (as Paul said it) "a whole new world."

7

We are called to proclaim the good news of *liberation from the dominion of the moment*. If you follow the risen Jesus *you don't have to be* "with it."

We have observed the need (and the power) to be freed both from an illegitimate universalism (the "mass") and from a small particularism (the "milieu"). What we saw there in terms of space or of society is comparable to what needs to be said as well in terms of time. It is our normal tendency to be more aware of the present than of past or future. Our culture has exacerbated this tendency by the growth of instantaneous communications media. A similar thrust has been fostered by cultural movements which have denounced tradition and dogma in the name of the priority of "where it is at" just now. That the contemporary is better is an assumption which in our culture is as pervasive as it is illogical. Sometimes the label under which "now" is absolutized is "relevance," as if the present moment itself somehow contained the criteria from which it could be criticized. Sometimes the claim of such a perspective is strengthened by appeal to the tastes, the limited background and the judgment of the so-called "youth culture."

However we explain it, the sovereignty of the moment is a genuine threat to human value. It implies the claim that one's present condition, which in other connections used to be called "lostness," can be the criterion of authenticity or well-being.

We are freed from the dominion of the moment by the biblical proclamation of a *story*. We are given a past which stretches from Abraham through Jesus to Sattler to ourselves, which can become contemporary in any culture, but is protected by its anchorage in the past, from selling out to the mood of the majority of the market or of the moment.

This past is also our future. The crucified Lord is also the Lord who is to come. The obedience of the disciple is not merely reported from the past; it is a key to where God is taking us. We do not simply remember what distinguishes us from the tyranny of the moment; the same story also gives us more hope than the moment can. The past divine faithfulness we celebrate is the earnest of the coming victory which we likewise celebrate.

One dimension of the moment's tyranny is the claim that we

"must" behave in some way; that the situation gives us no choice. For Freud it is an inner psychodynamic "must"; for Marx the necessity is economic. In the superpowers' arms race, it is the enemy who gives us no choice. "No choice" is the general justification for any evil deed. Control is in someone else's hands.

The answer to this denial of choice is not to argue about freedom as a theory of human nature or as alternative psychological theory. To confess the lordship of Christ is a statement not about the person but about the cosmos. Its validation is not an alternative set of ideas about how free our choices are, but an alternative group of people living another story.

One of the simplest forms of the tyranny of the moment is what recently was called "situation ethics"—the claim that in the given time and place what one ought to do is self-evident, being dictated by the context. This attitude is certainly right in the question with which it begins. The only place we can be is where we are. There is no right answer which does not take up the question which is put to us by the moment. *But* our story enables us to see more than one answer to that question. In the face of our story, the situation is no longer self-interpreting; its "demands" are no longer self-evident. We come into the situation not blank but with momentum. The memories of Moses and Miriam, of the saints Martin and Maximilian, of Martin King and Mohandas Gandhi, and their sisters and mothers arm our minds and provoke a creativity which is both genuinely faithful and genuinely situational.

Remembered models are not the only way our past frees us from and for the moment. The past alternative story provides us also with promises, commands, legend and poetry, and with substantially different definitions of the nature of people and things. The story of the faith community demonstrates how confessing Christ's lordship has sparked resistance, given meaning to suffering, invented alternatives, changed worlds, enabled hope, and extended the process of making all things new.

The Editor

Harry Loewen was born in the Ukraine and immigrated to Canada after World War II. After attending Mennonite theological institutions, he studied at several Canadian universities, earning B.A., M.A., and Ph.D. degrees. His areas of specialty were Reformation history, German literature, and Russian-Mennonite history and culture.

For several years he taught history and German at a Mennonite high school and at Mennonite Brethren Bible College, Winnipeg, Manitoba. Between 1968 and 1978 he taught German language and literature at Wilfrid Laurier University, Ontario, and was chairperson of the German department there.

When in 1978 the University of Winnipeg established its Chair in Mennonite Studies, Loewen was invited to fill this position. He developed an academic program of Mennonite studies at the University of Winnipeg, taught classes in Mennonite history, culture, and literature, and established the *Journal of Mennonite Studies* of which he became the founding editor.

Loewen has authored and edited several books and published numerous articles and reviews on Mennonite history and culture and German literature. Among his seven books are *Goethe's Response to Protestantism* (1972), *Luther and the Radicals* (1974), and *Mennonite Images* (1980).

An ordained minister in the Mennonite Brethren Church, Loewen takes out time to preach and teach in churches and schools. Especially his lectures on Mennonite history and peace issues are popular and in demand.

Married to Gertrude Penner (also from the Ukraine), he is the father of three grown and married sons, Helmut-Harry, Charles, and Jeffrey and the proud grandfather of several grandchildren.